Dave Dusseau • Douglas Wilson

D0506676

An Introduction to Business

Seventh Edition

Cover Art: Courtesy of Digital Vision/Getty Images.

This material was developed by:
David Dusseau, Ph.D.
Doug Wilson, MBA
Lundquist College of Business
University of Oregon
Eugene, Oregon 97403-1208

Foundation ™ is a trademark of Management, Simulations, Inc. ™ and was developed by:
Management Simulations, Inc.
540 Frontage Road, Suite 3270
Northfield, Illinois 60039
847-501-2888
www.capsim.com

Screen shots courtesy of Courtesy of Management Simulations, Inc.

Pearson Learning Solutions, 501 Boylston Street, Suite 900, Boston, MA 02116
A Pearson Education Company
www.pearsoned.com

Printed in the United States of America

1 2 3 4 5 6 7 8 9 10 V031 17 16 15 14 13 12

000200010271697219

JL/TY

ISBN 10: 1-256-84830-1
ISBN 13: 978-1-256-84830-1

Table of Contents

Prologue

Most people's jobs relate to business. No matter what their major in college or what career they choose, most people will find themselves working in some type of business setting. Artists sell their work, physicians oversee their practices, architects manage their firms, and even nonprofit organizations must generate income and pay expenses—it all relates back to business.

This information provides a framework for understanding the essential aspects of business. The material will demonstrate how the private enterprise system and businesses that participate in that system provide value for customers, clients, and society through the products and services they offer.

This overview of business concepts accompanies an online simulation called Foundation™. This simulation places *you* in the position of making business decisions for *your* company. A series of decisions you will make will enable you to see the outcome of your business choices in a competitive marketplace. The simulation requires you to establish your strategy, position your product, determine how you will promote your product, create a sales forecast, set inventory levels, and make a variety of other decisions regarding issues that most businesses need to consider.

The objective is to offer an interesting, interactive experience and to teach you about business, its terminology, and its concepts. The combination of the material you will be exploring along with the simulation will help you to better understand and appreciate the role business plays in our economic system, our society, and our lives.

Private Enterprise: An Economic System

The private enterprise system seeks to find and create opportunity through individuals acting in their own self-interest as they direct resources and compete to create and keep their profits.

Key terms to look for:

- Demand

- Economic costs

- Economics

- Innovation

- Markets

- Opportunity costs

- Specialization

- Supply

Resources are required to produce the goods and services that we need to survive and thrive in our environment. In the most basic sense, there are three kinds of resources required to produce these goods and services. These are called the factors of production and include three essential elements:

1. Raw materials *or natural resources;*
2. Tools and machinery, and;
3. Labor *or human resources.*

Our desire for goods and services is based on our wants. In many cases, those wants are greater than the resources available to satisfy them. This scarcity of resources requires that we make choices as to how these resources are to be used.

Dictionary.com defines the term **economics** as:

> "A social science that deals with the production, distribution, and consumption of goods and services and with the theory and management of economies or economic systems."

Therefore, economics is a study of distributing resources for the production of goods and services within a social system. All economic systems address the same basic set of questions:

- What goods and services and how much of each will be produced?
- How will the goods and services be produced?
- Who will produce them and with what resources?
- How will the goods and services be distributed?

One view of economics is to categorize jobs into four sectors: agriculture (primary sector), manufacturing (secondary), service (tertiary), and the fourth sector (quaternary). This fourth section distinguishes intellectual and information services, such as education, research and other knowledge-based activities. Before the Industrial Revolution began in the late 18th century, more than 60% of the world's workforce was employed in the agricultural sector. During the Industrial Revolution, machines replaced humans and the primary job sector became manufacturing. Computers began to replace humans in manufacturing (like in the auto industry), so jobs moved to the service sector. Since 1950, both agriculture and manufacturing have been in steady decline and machines are rapidly replacing jobs in the service industry.

The Clark-Fisher sector model, shown below, illustrates these job transitions over time.

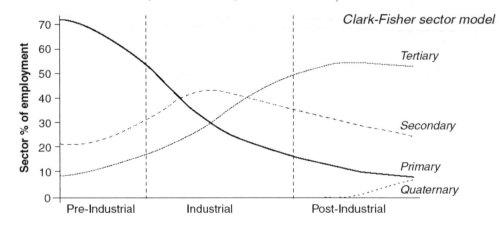

Communism, socialism, and capitalism are different ways in which the economic system can be structured and organized. In a capitalist, or **private enterprise system**, individual citizens own and operate the majority of businesses and the market determines the distribution of resources. Individuals act in their own self-interest and compete to participate in transactions in the markets available to them.

The terms of the transaction, or the quantity traded and the trading price is determined by the supply of and demand for any particular good.

> **Demand** is the quantity of goods and services that consumers are willing to buy at different prices.

> **Supply** is the quantity of goods and services that businesses are willing to provide at those prices.

Self-interest and competition will produce an efficient allocation of resources. Goods and services are desired and used where they produce the greatest benefit or are most productively used. Throughout this process, pressure is exerted from several areas. For example, there is pressure to lower prices and pressure to innovate through technological and procedural improvements.

The private enterprise system requires the existence of four conditions:

1. Private property;

2. Freedom of choice;

3. The right to keep profits, and;

4. An environment where fair competition can occur.

There are times when this system requires boundaries. Therefore, governments establish the economic system through the rule of law and acts to correct failures of the system.

Back in the U.S.S.R.

"We want a *voluntary* union of nations—a union which precludes any coercion of one nation by another—a union founded on complete confidence, on a clear recognition of brotherly unity, on absolutely voluntary consent." V.I. Lenin's words expressed the concept behind what became known as the Union of Soviet Socialist Republics (U.S.S.R). The economic implications of this system evolved into a government that would determine what, how, and at what volume most goods and services would be produced and distributed. After surviving for more than 70 years, this communist totalitarian state collapsed in December of 1991.

Markets

The historical creation of markets involved actual market places where potential buyers and sellers came to exchange goods and services. Today, we consider markets as any mechanism that facilitates the exchange of goods and services between buyers and sellers. The grocery store is a market where food is purchased, NASDAQ is an electronic market where buyers and sellers of stock come in contact, and the Internet enables online stores and trading sites to function. From a village square to eBay, markets have come a long way.

Markets are both specialized and complex. Consider all of the separate activities that have to be precisely coordinated in order for you to buy breakfast at a local café. Farmers, truck drivers, grocery workers, warehouses, distribution centers, cooks, and waiters represent just a few of the functions and people whose efforts contributed to the production, processing, transportation, and distribution of your meal.

In an economic context, **specialization** is a measure of how broadly or narrowly defined the range of included activities are. A bicycle shop is a more specialized retail store than Wal-Mart because the bicycle shop focuses on a narrow and deep range of products. Specialization creates an opportunity for greater efficiency and increased productivity. The division of tasks that comes with specialization introduces a need for coordination of those specialized tasks. These different levels of specialization and different kinds of coordinating mechanisms create a complex economic environment.

Markets are also characterized by **uncertainty** and **risk**. Uncertainty is having a lack of knowledge of what will happen—the unpredictability about the consequences of your choice—in a decision situation. The greater the uncertainty, the less you know about the results of a particular choice. Decision makers work to reduce uncertainty by compiling as much relevant information as possible about a decision situation. Risk is also associated with the consequences of choice and, therefore, risk is a measure of the significance of those decisions.

For example:

> Consider flipping a coin. You cannot consistently predict when you flip a nickel whether it will land with the "head" or the "tail" side up. Not knowing which side will land facing up is a form of uncertainty. If you place a bet with a friend about which side will land facing up, the amount of the bet would be a measure of the risk. If you are of average wealth in the United States and bet a nickel, then the risk associated with the bet would be small. If you are in the same economic position and bet $100,000, the risk associated with the bet becomes larger.

Decision Making

The process of defining problems and opportunities that merit attention, generating and evaluating alternative courses of action, and committing to the action that is most likely to produce the optimal result is one way to describe decision making. Decision making involves comparing the economic and opportunity rewards (benefits) and sacrifices (costs) involved in a course of action and committing to the one that best meets your goals. The objective is to make the parties involved "better off" than they were before the transaction took place. Typically, good decisions are commitments that help you accomplish your goals in whatever way you define those goals. Business decisions primarily focus on gaining economic rewards. This refers back to the assumption that we only engage in transactions that offer the potential to improve our "position." When we choose a course of action, it requires a sacrifice to obtain the reward.

In economic terms, this sacrifice is a "cost." A decision maker considers two kinds of costs, the economic cost and the opportunity cost, when evaluating alternative choices available:

The ***economic cost*** is the money spent implementing the decision.

The ***opportunity cost*** is the cost of what you gave up doing when you committed to the course of action you chose.

Opportunity Cost

Assessing opportunity costs is important to determine the *true cost* of any decision. Opportunity cost can measure *anything* that is of value. The opportunity cost is not the *sum* of the available alternatives, but rather the benefit of the best *single* alternative. If there is no explicit accounting or monetary cost attached to a course of action, ignoring opportunity costs may create an illusion that the benefits cost nothing at all and, therefore, becomes a ***hidden cost*** associated with that action. The opportunity cost of a business decision to build a new plant facility on a business's vacant land, for example, is the loss of the land for another purpose, such as using it to build a facility to be leased to another business, or to have access to the cash that could have been generated from selling the land. Only one choice is possible. Only one benefit is attainable.

For example:

Consider the decision you made after graduating from high school. You had two choices:

1. You could have begun working immediately after high school and taken a job that pays $28,000 a year

2. You could attend a college or university with the goal of earning a degree.

The *economic cost* of the college alternative is the cost of tuition, books, fees, and living expenses while you attend school. The *opportunity cost* of the college alternative is the income that you gave up when you did *not* take the job. Once you complete your degree, your options to generate additional income in the future increase. In the long run, opportunity costs are often more important than economic costs.

Business decisions consider economic and opportunity costs and provide a structure to make those decisions. Business has its own vocabulary and there are terms that will be helpful to know. A few of these terms include the following:

- A ***business*** is an organization or individual that seeks a profit by providing products that satisfy people's needs (or wants).

- A ***product*** is a good, service, or idea that has both tangible and intangible characteristics that provide the satisfaction or benefits.

- ***Profit*** is the basic goal of business and is the difference between what it costs to make and sell a product and what the customer pays for it.

- ***Stakeholders*** are groups of people who have a vested interest ("stake") in the actions a business takes (decisions a business makes). There are four major groups of stakeholders: (1) owners, (2) employees, (3) customers, and (4) citizens. The specific interests of each of these stakeholder groups may conflict with each other.

Activities of Business

The most basic way to categorize the activities of business is to place them into the one of the following areas: marketing, production, finance, or accounting.

- *Marketing:* The activities designed to provide goods and services that satisfy customers. These activities include market research, development of products, pricing, promotion, and distribution.

- *Accounting:* The process that tracks, summarizes, and analyzes a firm's financial position.

- *Production:* The activities and processes used in making products. These activities involve designing the production process (investments in facilities and equipment) and the efficient management and operation of those processes.

- *Finance :* The activities concerned with funding a business and using resources effectively.

PrepMe   *A business profile*

Receiving a perfect score on the SAT may have given Joseph Jewell additional confidence to pursue his business idea. At the age of 24, Jewell not only wrote a business plan and won $20,000 in the University of Chicago business plan competition, but also launched the online SAT-preparation service PrepMe. With intense competition from larger companies, PrepMe is experiencing impressive growth by offering students a customized approach to study for the SAT exam. In addition to the online experience, PrepMe also offers live coaching for writing essays via email, instant messaging, and telephone communication.[1]

Managing a Business

Decisions that shape the marketing, production, and financial functions of a business are often made in market environments that are specialized, complex, uncertain, and risky. Managing these functions requires planning, organizing, operating, and controlling the various aspects of the business.

- *Planning:* Determining what the organization needs to do and how to get it done.

- *Organizing:* Arranging the organization's resources and activities in such a way as to make it possible to accomplish the plan.

- *Operating:* Enacting the plan, including guiding and motivating employees to work toward accomplishing the necessary tasks.

- *Controlling:* Measuring and comparing performance to expectations established in the planning process, and adjusting either the performance or the plan.

---

[1] Maggie Overfelt, "Start-ups on fire: PrepMe," *FSB*, November 2005, pp. 34-36.

Achieving Organizational Goals

Managers need to be both ***effective*** and ***efficient*** to achieve the goals and objectives of an organization.

Effective *means doing the right thing.*

Efficient *means doing things right.*

Being effective involves committing to a course of action that will allow you to accomplish your goals. It is a measure of the "goodness" of the outcomes of your actions. Being efficient refers to employing an appropriate process to achieve your goals. Measures of efficiency involve comparing the resources invested to the outcomes achieved.

Foundation™

The Web-based simulation that you will experience called "Foundation" will require you to apply these important business concepts. You will address marketing, production, accounting and finance issues and manage your company's production and sale of goods. You will need to plan, organize, operate, and control the direction of your company as you compete for market share with other firms in this free enterprise environment. With less than perfect information, you must decide what volume of product to produce, how to promote your products, how much to invest in your sales activities, how to finance your expenses, and how to assess your financial performance. After each set of decisions, you will then receive your results based upon your ongoing performance in the market, the profitability of your firm, and the value you have provided to your stockholders.

Foundation™ *is a registered trademark of Management Simulations, Inc.*

When businesses compete in a private enterprise environment, value is created for consumers. Customers are offered additional choices as businesses are motivated to innovate often through technological advancements to improve their offerings and make them more attractive. ***Innovation*** also motivates businesses to price their products and services attractively to position themselves for future success.

Chapter Summary Questions

Be able to answer these types of questions in these areas:

Economic Systems

1. What set of questions do all economic systems address?

2. What are the four conditions that must exist for the free enterprise system to exist?

3. How would you define supply?

4. How would you define demand?

5. What are some examples of economic costs?

6. How would you describe the concept of scarcity?

The Private Enterprise System

7. What are the implications of the relationship between supply and demand?

8. The private enterprise system requires the existence of four conditions. What are those conditions?

9. What best describes the concept of "scarcity?"

10. What does it mean to describe markets as "specialized"?

11. What roles does innovation play in the private enterprise system? What is the incentive to innovate, and why might that incentive not exist in other economic systems?

Decision Making and Opportunity Costs

12. Give an example of "uncertainty" and how it relates to risk and decision making.

13. How would you illustrate the concept of "uncertainty"?

14. How would you illustrate the concept of "risk"?

15. Provide an example of an opportunity costs that is relevant to taking this course.

16. What process allows managers to manage in an uncertain and risky environment?

Managing a Business

13. What are the general activities of business and what roles do they play?

14. Which business activity requires funding the business and using its resources effectively?

Build Your Understanding

Foundation Exercise 1 - *You Are In Charge*

When Sensor, Inc., a monopoly, was broken up, six companies were formed: Andrews, Baldwin, Chester, Digby, Erie, and Ferris. The board of directors of the Andrews Corporation hired you to be the President and Chief Executive Officer.

Andrews is a corporation. The Board of Directors who hired you represents the owners' interests. You are now responsible for managing the company. When they hired you, they gave you five goals (or performance targets) to meet each year:

Your primary responsibility each year is to:
- Increase the company's stock price
- Generate Net Income greater than $0
- Have a Contribution Margin greater than 30%
- Do not stock out but also do not have more than 60 days of inventory at year end

Do not run out of cash at any time throughout the year'""""
Even though you will be compensated based on your ability to meet these goals each year, you won't directly focus on these goals until the very end of your orientation process.

Your Product

The first thing you would like to know is what does one of your sensors look like. You are currently offering one product called Able, so you pull up a picture from the website. You can see the basic design ... there is a plastic housing with mounting brackets that contains the sophisticated processors and there are connectors that allow the sensor to be integrated into your customers products.

Over time, the size of the product will have to get smaller and the processor will have to get faster to meet the ongoing demands of the market.

Courtesy of violetkaipa/Shutterstock

The next thing that bothers you is you don't have a real sense of how the product is incorporated into your customers' products. When you were preparing for your interview, you read that NASA was using solar radiation sensors that incorporated your sensor. You look that up in your company's information system and it is as you expected. Your sensor is the centerpiece of the product … pretty cool.

Product Photo and Diagram

Courtesy of Mikhail/Shutterstock

Courtesy of fet/Shutterstock

Your Management Team

When you were hired, the Board of Directors recommended several people for your management team. They are all seasoned managers with excellent experience. Several came from Sensors Inc., so they know the customers, the industry, the business processes, and many of the managers who are now running the competing companies.

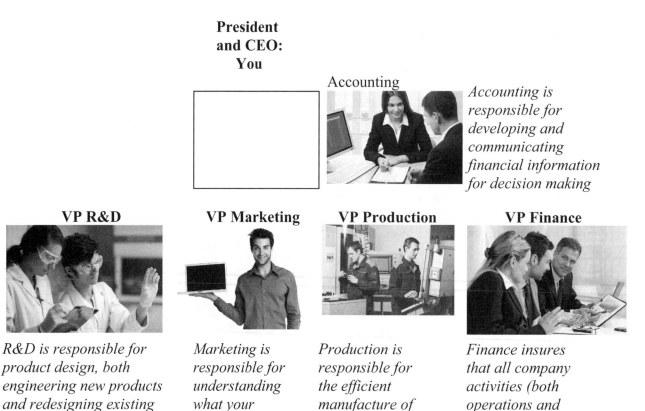

President and CEO: You

Accounting

Accounting is responsible for developing and communicating financial information for decision making

VP R&D

R&D is responsible for product design, both engineering new products and redesigning existing products

VP Marketing

Marketing is responsible for understanding what your customers want and creating value for them

VP Production

Production is responsible for the efficient manufacture of your products

VP Finance

Finance insures that all company activities (both operations and investments) are funded

Courtesy of Konstantin Chagin/Shutterstock; Courtesy of wavebreakmedia ltd/Shutterstock; Courtesy of Yuri Arcurs/Shutterstock; Courtesy of Dmitry Kalinovsky/Shutterstock; Courtesy of Rido/Shutterstock

Your Facilities

A tour of your physical plant leaves you quite impressed. Everything is located on one campus. You have been assured that you could add as many as four new production lines so there is plenty of room to grow without relocating.

Courtesy of Photoroller/Shutterstock

Andrew's Company Headquarters

Your office along with your executive team and their staff
You see where you want your parking place to be.
The factory, the location where you produce your products, and the warehouse, where you store the finished goods, are located at the same site.

Courtesy of B.A.E. Inc./Alamy

Factory

The factory currently has capacity to make 800,000 units a year per shift. Last year the factory employed 154 production workers in the first shift (7:00am – 3:00pm) and another 94 working the 2nd shift (3:00pm – 11:00pm). There is no possibility of working a 3rd shift. You are a little surprised because the production machinery is not as technologically sophisticated as you thought it would be.

Courtesy of Matusciac Alexandru/Shutterstock

Warehouse

This facility stores the:
- *Component parts inventory (the pieces that are combined to produce your product)*
- *Finished goods inventory (the number of units of your product Able that are available for sale)*

Your Orientation

You have asked your management team to put together a plan. You will review the basic principles then invest time in learning how they apply in this company. You asked your management team to formulate questions that test your understanding and set up a basic structure for the orientation:

1. An overview of the industry: Size, growth, and customer decision processes
2. Marketing Management: Decisions, trade-offs, tools, and strategies
3. Forecasting Sales
4. Accounting Information
5. Production and Inventory Management: Decisions, trade-offs, tools
6. Production Investments in Capacity and Automation
7. Finance: Decisions, trade-offs, tools, and strategies

Resources

There are these resources available to help you get up to speed:

- **Team Member Guide:** A printed guide, called the "Team Member Guide" or TMG, is a briefing book given to the management team of all of six companies formed when the monopoly was broken up.
  The first step in your orientation is to read TMG 1. Introduction

- **A website - www.capsim.com:** This includes tutorials, information and reports. It also provides a system to help you track what you are doing and how you are doing along with access to the model of your company.
  The next step in your orientation is to log onto www.capsim.com and complete the Introductory Lesson and Quiz.

- **Foundation Spreadsheet:** This file, in either form, provides a model of your company and enables you to:

  1. Make decisions in the areas of Research and Development, Marketing, Production, Human Resources, Finance and Total Quality Management

  2. Access to proforma accounting documents including the Balance Sheet, Income Statement, and Statement of Cash Flows. These proforma statements are projections of what may occur for the coming year based upon the decisions you have made.

  3. View reports such as the FastTrack and Annual Reports. These report the actual results of last year's decisions and establish the starting conditions for the year in which you are making decisions.

     The Foundation Spreadsheet is used in three ways:

     1. Rehearsal Simulation - *A tutorial that coaches you through the process*

     2. Practice Round - *Experiencing the interface, potentials decisions and outcomes*

     3. Competition Rounds - *Actually running the company where your results matter!*

Build Your Understanding: Foundation Exercise 1 Questions

You are responsible for understanding

1. The basic information about the company and your role in managing it.

2. The sources of information and the differences between this information. (This includes the FastTrack Report, Proforma Statements, and the Annual Reports.)

3. The decisions made by Research and Development, Marketing, Production and Finance.

4. The difference between the Rehearsal Simulation, the Practice Rounds and the Competition rounds.

Chapter 2

Marketing: Creating Customer Value

Marketing is the process of planning and executing the conception, pricing, promotion and distribution of ideas, goods and services to create exchanges that satisfy individual and organizational objectives.

— American Marketing Association

Key terms to look for:

- Accessibility

- Market research

- Marketing mix

- Marketing strategy

- Promotion

- Sales

- Sales forecasting

- Segmentation

- Target marketing

A business must entice people to trade to be successful in a private enterprise system. Individuals will only trade goods and services *if* they are going to be "better off" as a result of the transaction. The essential questions become who are those people and how can you create value for them? Marketing addresses these questions.

Marketing defines your strategy for competing in the marketplace. Marketing is a group of activities designed to expedite transactions by creating, distributing, pricing and promoting goods services and ideas. Managers need to understand and develop marketing programs to promote their products and services. Business success is based on the ability to build a growing body of satisfied customers. Marketing programs are built around the "marketing concept" and performance that directs managers to focus their efforts on identifying, satisfying, and following up on the customer's needs—all at a profit.

The Marketing Concept

The marketing concept focuses on the importance of providing customers value. Ideally, all company policies and activities should satisfy customer needs. Realizing a profitable sales volume is better than maximizing sales volume at the cost of profitability. To apply the marketing concept, a business must understand how to accomplish the following:

- *Market Research:* To determine the needs of its customers

- *Market Mix:* To determine how to satisfy those needs through addressing product, price, place, promotion, and service

- *Market Strategy:* To analyze its competitive advantages, plans, and actions

- *Target Marketing:* To select specific markets to serve

Managing the Market Mix

The marketing mix is used to describe how owners and managers combine these five areas into an overall marketing program.

1. *Products and Services*

   Effective product strategies for a small business may include concentrating on a narrow product line, developing a highly specialized product or service or providing a product-service package containing an unusual amount of service.

2. *Price*

   Price and pricing policies are a major factor affecting total revenue. This includes determining the credit policy: Will you allow your customer to pay for the product *after* they receive it, or do they need to pay for it *when* they receive it? In the most general sense, higher prices mean lower volume and lower prices mean higher volume. However, small businesses can often command higher prices because of the personalized service they offer. In addition, there have been situations where higher prices are associated with higher quality, and increasing the price to a certain point, results in increased volume. Hair care products are one category where this has occurred.

3. *Promotion*

This set of marketing decisions includes leveraging the Internet, various forms of advertising, salesmanship, and other promotional activities. Offering special financing or extended terms is another form of promotion. In general, effective promotional strategies are a must for businesses because of the cost of extensive advertising campaigns and the limitations such cost imposes.

4. *Place or Distribution Channel*

The manufacturer and wholesaler must decide how to distribute their products. Working through established distributors or manufacturers' agents generally is most feasible for small manufacturers. Small retailers should consider cost and traffic flow as two major factors in location site selection, especially since advertising and rent can be reciprocal. In other words, low-cost, low-traffic location means you must spend more on advertising to build traffic. Investing efforts to increase accessibility are key factors in product distribution.

5. *Service*

This area is a relatively recent addition to the traditional four Ps —product, price, place and promotion—of the marketing mix. Customer service is another way that an organization can provide value and differentiate itself from others that offer similar or identical products. Organizations like Nordstrom, Lexus, North Face, and the Pacific Northwest's Les Schwab Tires have created highly successful businesses based on offering exceptional customer service.

Nordstrom   *A business profile*

Luxury retailer Nordstrom thrives on providing exceptional customer service resulting in customer folklore and powerful word-of-mouth marketing. Every register at Nordstrom stores has pen and paper for customers to share their stories. Before each store opens, Nordstrom employees gather in the main lobby for the store manager to share stories from the previous day and reward the employees. Legends of Nordstrom pampering are widespread. These stories include the customer who received a refund for returning pants that had clearly been worn for an extended amount of time, the employee who made a house call to exchange a pair of shoes, and splitting two pairs of shoes in order to fit the man with different sized feet. A Portland, Oregon story tells about a father who needed an Armani tuxedo for his daughter's wedding. As a last-ditch effort, he went to Nordstrom. His personal shopper took his measurements and the next day, the suit was available. It fit perfectly. The personal shopper had found a New York distributor who put the Armani tux on a truck, shipped it to Chicago where a Chicago Nordstrom met the truck at a rest stop and retrieved the tux. Once in the Chicago Nordstrom store, the tux was over-nighted to Portland and altered at no cost. Unbelievable service? Nordstrom doesn't sell Armani tuxedos.[2]

---

[2] ToddAnd, Advertising, Marketing, Public Relations, Web blog retrieved July 14, 2012, http://toddand.com/2007/02/18/legends-of-unbelievable-nordstrom-service.

Market Research

To be successful, a business must know and understand its market. Market research is the systematic gathering, recording, and analyzing of data about problems relating to marketing goods and services. Market research is simply an orderly and objective way of learning about people; specifically, the group of people who buy from you or have the highest propensity to do so.

Market research is not a perfect science. It deals with people and their constantly changing likes, dislikes, and behaviors, all potentially affected by hundreds of influences. Market research attempts to learn about markets scientifically and to gather facts and opinions in an orderly and objective way. Market research seeks to find out how things are, not how you think they are or would like them to be. Market research attempts to find out what specific products or services people want to buy, rather than focusing on what you want to sell them.

Market research is an organized way of finding objective answers to questions every business must answer to succeed. Every business owner-manager must ask:

- Who are my customers and potential customers?
- What kind of people are they?
- Where do they live?
- Can and will they buy from my business?
- Am I offering the kinds of goods or services they want at the best place, at the best time, and in the right amounts?
- Are my prices consistent with what buyers view as the product's value?
- Are my promotional programs working by creating awareness in the market place?
- Are my sales programs working to create accessibility for my product through the distribution channel?
- What do customers think of my business?
- How does the value my business offers compare with that of my competitors'?
- Are there specific reasons customers would make the decision to purchase from my business rather than from my competitors?

Reasons for Market Research

It is difficult—maybe even impossible—to sell people things that they do not want. Business managers have to view their businesses from a customer's perspective. They combine this perspective with their sense of the market that comes from experience. However, experience is not always a good thing. This experience may include information acquired over a number of years, and some of that information may no longer be timely or relevant to making decisions today. Some facts may be vague or create misleading impressions that may lead an organization in the wrong direction.

Market research focuses and systematically organizes marketing information. It ensures that such information is timely and meaningful. Sound market research provides what you need to:

- Reduce business risks.
- Identify problems and potential problems in your current market that you can solve in a unique manner.
- Discover and profit from sales opportunities.
- Acquire facts about your market to develop a marketing strategy and implement action plans.
- Assist you in making better decisions and make corrections as needed.

Conducting Market Research

Many managers are unaware that they conduct some form of market research every day. In their daily managerial duties, they check returned items to see if there is a pattern of dissatisfaction. They run into one of your former customers and ask them why they have not been in lately. They look at a competitor's ad to see what that store is charging for the same products you are selling. These activities provide a framework that enable managers to objectively evaluate the meaning of the information they gather about their market.

A more formal market research process may include the following eight steps:

1. Defining the problem or opportunity
2. Assessing available information
3. Gathering additional information, if required
4. Reviewing internal records and files; interviewing employees
5. Collecting outside data (secondary and primary)
6. Organizing and interpreting data
7. Making a decision and taking action
8. Assessing the results of the action

Defining the Problem or Opportunity

Defining the problem or assessing the opportunity is the first step of the research process. This process is often overlooked, yet it is the most important step. You must be able to see beyond the symptoms of a problem to get at its cause. Seeing the problem as a sales decline is not defining a cause, it is merely listing a symptom.

You must establish an idea of the problem that includes causes that can be objectively measured and tested. Look at your list of possible causes frequently while you are gathering your facts, but do not let it get in the way of the facts. To define your problem, list every possible influence that may have caused it.

- Have your customers changed?
- Have customer tastes changed?
- Have customer buying habits changed?
- Do our services still meet our customer's need?
- Is our product still relevant?

List the possible causes of the problem. If there are areas that cannot be tracked, realize that you may not be able to objectively measure your progress toward that goal.

Assessing Available Information

Once you have formally defined your problem, assess the information that is immediately available. You may already have all the information you need to determine if your hypothesis is correct, and solutions to the problem may have become obvious in the process of defining it. Stop there. You have reached a point of diminishing returns. You will be wasting time and money if you do further marketing research and do not gain additional insight.

If you are uncertain if you need additional information, you must weigh the cost of more information against its usefulness. You are up against a dilemma similar to guessing in advance of what return you will receive on your advertising dollar. You do not know what return you will get, or even if you will get a return. The best you can do is to balance that against the cost of gathering more data to make a more informed decision.

Gathering Additional Information

Begin by "thinking cheap and staying as close to home as possible." Before considering anything elaborate, such as market surveys or field experiments, explore your own records and files. Look at sales records, complaints, receipts, and any other records that can help you better understand where your customers live, work, what they buy, and how they buy it.

Credit records are an excellent source of information about your markets. Credit records provide information about your customers' addresses, employment, income levels, and marital status. Offering credit is a multifaceted marketing tool, although one with well-known costs and risks.

For example:

> Your customers' addresses can tell you a lot about who they are. You may be able to gain insight about their life-styles by knowing detail about their neighborhoods. Knowing how they live can give you hints about what the might to buy. Gaining this knowledge may allow you to better understand, communicate and sell to this group more efficiently.

When you have finished reviewing the available information in your records, turn to that other valuable internal source of customer information: your employees. Employees may be the best source of information about customer likes and dislikes. They hear customers' complaints about the store or service—often the ones the customers do not think are important enough to take to you as the owner-manager. Employees are aware of the items customers request that you may not have in inventory. They can probably supply good customer profiles from their day-to-day contacts.

External Data and Secondary Research

Once you have exhausted your internal sources for information about your market, the next steps in the process are to do primary and secondary research outside. Secondary research involves collecting published information. This information may come from surveys, books, magazines, and other resources and then applying or rearranging the information to apply to a particular problem or potential opportunity.

For example:

> Imagine that you sell tires. You might guess that sales of new cars three years ago would have a strong effect on present retail sales of tires. To test this idea, you might compare new car sales of six years ago with replacement tire sales from three years ago. Suppose you found that new tire sales three years ago were 10 percent of the new car sales three years before that. Repeating this exercise for previous years reveals that in each case tire sales were about 10 percent of new car sales made three years before. You could then logically conclude that the total market for replacement tire sales in your area this year should be about 10 percent of new car sales in your locality three years ago.

Naturally, the more localized the figures you can find from secondary research, the better. For instance, there may be a national decline in new housing starts, but if you sell new appliances in an area in which new housing is booming, you obviously would want to base your estimate of market potential on local conditions. Newspapers and local radio and television stations may be able to help you find this information.

There are many sources of secondary research material. Much of it is free. You can find it online, in libraries, newspapers, magazines, and in trade and general business publications. Trade associations and government agencies are also rich sources of information. Other organizations, such as market research companies, sell secondary research.

Primary Research

Primary research is the collection of original data. Primary research can be as simple as asking customers or suppliers how they feel about your store or service firm or as complex as the surveys conducted by sophisticated professional marketing research firms. Primary research includes among its tools direct mail questionnaires, telephone or on-the-street surveys, experiments, panel studies, test marketing, behavior observation, and so on.

Primary research is often divided into reactive and non-reactive research. Non-reactive primary research is a way to see how real people behave in a real market situation without influencing that behavior. Reactive research, such as surveys, interviews, and questionnaires, is what most people think of when they hear the words marketing research. Reactive market research is a complex field. It is critical to ask the right questions and to avoid creating a bias in the responses. People may answer questions the way they think they are expected to answer, rather than telling you how they really feel about your product, service, or business.

Organizing and Interpreting Data

After collecting the data you must organize it into meaningful information. Go back to your definition of the problem, compare it with your findings, and prioritize and rank the data.

- What strategies are suggested?
- How can they be accomplished?
- How are they different from what I am doing now?
- What current activities should be increased?
- What current activities must I drop or decrease in order to devote adequate resources to new strategies?

Making Decisions and Taking Action

Prioritize each possible strategy from the standpoint of determining the:

- Immediate goal to be achieved;
- Cost to implement;
- Time to accomplish, and;
- Measurement of success.

If your market research, for example, suggests ten possible strategies, select two or three that appear to have the greatest impact potential or are most easily achievable and begin there. For each strategy, develop tactics, which may include:

- Staff responsibilities
- Necessary steps
- Budget allocations
- Timelines with deadlines for accomplishing strategic steps
- Progress measurements

Based on this information, make a final decision on the strategies and go to work on the tactics.

Assessing the Results of the Action

Analyze your progress measures. If adjustments are appropriate, make them. At the conclusion of the time you have allotted for accomplishing your goal, take a hard look at the results.

- Did you achieve your goal?
- Should the decision be renewed on a larger scale?

If you are disappointed in the results, determine why the plan went awry.

The Possibilities

Market research is limited only by your imagination. You can conduct a significant amount of market research at very little cost except your time and mental effort. While large companies generally have and use a wealth of available data on many business problems, smaller companies often ignore such data because they are unaware of its existence, although it may be as close as next door. Here are a few examples of techniques business owners and managers use to gather information about their customers.

> The local public, trade school, college or university library is a prime source of inexpensive, targeted information about business topics such as competition, the law, government, society, culture, economics, and technology. Although the resources of public libraries vary widely, the library's four walls and the size of its collection do not limit its service. New information technologies have changed libraries dramatically. Many academic libraries are open to the public. A typical library includes reference and general books, periodicals, and

possibly specialized collections. Several tools and services are available to help find material.

Indexes help find information in leading magazines, journals or newspapers. Among these are the Business Index, the Business Periodical Index, the Public Affairs Information Service Bulletins (PAIS), the Statistical Reference Index, the Wall Street Journal Index, and the American Statistics Index. These indexes list articles according to subject headings; they supply the title and author as well as the publication title, date and page number. Indexes are available in several formats including printed versions, optical disks, film, CD-ROMs, and on-line databases.

The Index to U.S. Government Periodicals is another source, and much of this information is accessible online. One example is information provided by the U.S. Census Bureau found at www.census.gov.

Information about industries and individual companies can also be found under Standard Industrial Classification Code (SIC) headings. SIC is a uniform coding system developed by the federal government to classify establishments according to their type of economic activity. Codes for specific industries are listed in the Standard Industrial Classification Code Manual. Four-digit codes define specific industries, such as SIC 2653 for corrugated and solid fiber box manufacturers, or SIC 5812 for eating establishments. Most federal government economic data and many business and industrial directories use SIC codes.

In order to manage the marketing functions successfully, good information about the market is necessary. Frequently, a market research program can disclose problems and areas of dissatisfaction that can be easily remedied, or new products or services that could be offered successfully.

Market research should also encompass identifying trends that may affect sales and profitability levels. Population shifts, legal developments, and the local economic situation should be monitored to enable early identification of problems and opportunities. Competitor activity should also be monitored. Competitors may be entering or leaving the market, for example. It is also very useful to know what your competitors' strategies are, as such knowledge may provide competitive insight.

Marketing Strategy
Marketing strategy encompasses identifying customer groups, or target markets, that a small business can serve better than its competitors, and tailoring its product offerings, prices, distribution, promotional efforts, and services toward that particular market segment. This may be referred to as "managing the market mix."

Ideally, the marketing strategy should address unmet customer needs that represent adequate potential size and profitability. A good marketing strategy implies that a small business cannot be all things to all people and must analyze its market and its own capabilities. This provides a focus on a target market it can serve best, increases the effectiveness of marketing activities, and provides a better return based on the use of the marketing budget.

Marketing strategy is most successful when it has a marketing orientation. A marketing orientation is an approach that requires an organization to gather information about their customers' needs through research, share that information throughout the firm, and use that information to help build long-term relationships between the organization and their customers.

Target Marketing

Owners of small businesses have limited resources to spend on marketing activities. Concentrating their marketing efforts on one or a few key market segments is the basis of target marketing. The major ways to segment a market are:

Geographic segmentation: Focusing on understanding the needs of customers in a particular geographical area; for example, a neighborhood convenience store may send advertisements only to people living within one-half mile of the store.

Demographic segmentation: Focusing on the attributes of the market based upon gender, age, income, education, or other measurable factors.

Psychographic segmentation: Identifying and promoting to groups of people based on lifestyle and behaviors that are most likely to buy the product. This may be based on interests, fears, behaviors, or actions that can be categorized into groups.

Target marketing enables you to identify, access, communicate with, and sell to those that are most likely to purchase your products.

Nissan GTR   *A business profile*

Nissan promotes its high-performance Skyline GTR through a highly targeted approach. Nissan markets GTR to relatively upper class on the income distribution as well as to customers who has an interest in high performance vehicles. One way Nissan accomplishes this by creating a different website for GTR itself. The GTR website differentiates itself from rest of the Nissan cars and adds prestige to the product. The website discusses things such as stories of GTR, making of the car, and heritage. These information may not be relevant to ordinary customers but effectively attracts the niche market in high performance cars.[3]

The nature of the product or service also is important in location decisions. If purchases are made largely on an impulse basis, such as flavored popcorn, high traffic and visibility are critical. On the other hand, location is less a concern for more specialized products or services that customers are willing to go out of their way to find. The ability afforded by the Internet to reach highly segmented customers online has enabled many businesses to operate anywhere and serve local, national, and international markets.

The Sales Forecast

Another aspect of marketing is to create a sales forecast to attempt to predict your unit sales and revenue performance. The sales forecast process often begins by assessing how the total market will perform. From there, you may attempt to assess your performance and what market share it will realize from that total forecast. To do this requires that you speculate on how your competitors will perform as well.

---

[3] Target Marketing, *Marketing Examples*, January 16. 2010, Web blog
http://uwmktg301.blogspot.com/2010/01/target-marketing.html

Forecasting sales is often a challenging task due to the multiple variables involved in the process:

- What will the overall economic climate be like?

- Will consumers make decisions on the same basis they have in the past?

- At what level will our competitors perform?

- Will existing competitors introduce new products, and if so, when?

- Will there be new competitors, or will existing competitors drop out of the market?

These are challenging questions. Considering their potential outcomes may provide insight into making better sales forecasting decisions.

In Foundation™

You will have the opportunity to determine how much you spend on marketing and to observe its impact on your business. You will learn about the "Low Tech" and "High Tech" target markets, their preferences, the reasons they are most likely to buy your products, and how those preferences change from year to year. A perceptual map will help you visualize how those preferences shift and progress in relation to your product's attributes. "Promotions" expenditures will impact the awareness your markets have about your product: Does your target market know you exist? "Sales" expenditures will impact the distribution and availability of your product: Does your target market have access to those products? You will also be able to compete based on the payment schedule you offer your customers. For example, your products may be more attractive if you allow your customers to pay in 60 days rather than in a 30-day time period. A part of the process will be to create a sales forecast. The sales forecast may be one of the most challenging and frustrating tasks of all as you attempt to predict your performance and anticipate how your competitors will impact your market share. These business decisions and their outcomes will directly affect the performance and profitability of the business.

Marketing Performance

After marketing program decisions are made, owners and managers need to evaluate the result of their decisions. Standards of performance need to be set up so results can be evaluated against them. Sound data on industry norms and past performance provide the basis for comparisons against present performance. Owners and managers should audit their company's performance on a periodic basis, at least quarterly.

Spending more is not always better. The law of diminishing return states that investing additional resources may initially increase productivity, but after a certain point, spending more will result in a lower return per dollar invested. The concept of ***diminishing return***, also referred to as the ***rate of diminishing return***, states that adding additional investment beyond a certain threshold will not add proportional returns. Each additional dollar yield less return then the previous dollar. Spending money beyond this point does not yield as much as the amount spent prior to that point.

For example:

> You have discovered that the rate of diminishing returns applies to your promotion budget. Your research has determined that the first $1,500,000 invested buys 36% awareness. Spending an additional $1,500,000, for a total of $3,000,000, creates 50% awareness. Therefore, the second $1,500,000 you invest buys only 14% more awareness. The investment beyond $1,500,000 yields a lower return per dollar invested compared to the initial $1,500,000. The return of your promotional dollars diminishes beyond the initial $1,500,000 and will impact your decision regarding spending beyond this amount. Investing beyond $3,000,000 in a single year is just not worth it.

Diminishing returns may also be associated with other aspects of business, such as hiring too many employees and investing in additional plant and equipment that you will never use.

A Marketing Perspective

The key questions to determine marketing performance include:

-

- Do the products and services the company is offering provide value to customers?

- Are existing and potential customers aware of the products and services available from the company?

- Is it easy for the customer to purchase what he or she wants and at a competitive price?

- Do the employees make sure the customer's needs are truly satisfied and leave them with the feeling that they would enjoy coming back?

In Foundation™

Your marketing strategy will determine the price and the attributes of your products. This includes your product's performance, size, and reliability. You also have access to market research conducted on each of your target markets. This research is valuable and will enable you to understand what is important to your customers. You will know the range of what they are willing to pay for your products and how they want that product to perform. You also have to consider what products your competitors are offering: their prices and how their performance, size, and reliability compare with yours. Your product awareness and accessibility are other factors that influence your sales volume. Your marketing strategy, shaped by how well you understand your potential customers, will play a significant role in how successful you are in accomplishing your business objectives.

Chapter Summary Questions

Be able to answer these types of questions in these areas:

Marketing

1. Define the term "market."

2. Marketing is concerned with what?

Marketing Mix

3. What are the elements of the marketing mix—what are the "4Ps?"

4. What does distribution mean?

5. Why is it important to track the impact of a promotional and sales budget and what can be learned from tracking this data over time?

Marketing Research

6. What is the essential goal of market research?

7. What decisions does the R&D department address?

8. What is the primary function of the research and development department?

Marketing Strategy

10. What makes up a good marketing strategy?

11. What is a market-oriented strategy and why is it unique?

Target Marketing

12. What does target marketing involve?

13. What is market segmentation?

Build Your Understanding
Foundation Exercise 2 - *Understanding Your Customers*

Your most basic goal is to serve your customers in a way that makes your owners better off. To serve them, you have to know them; to understand who they are and what they want when they come to the market for electronic sensors. To build this understanding, your experts recommend a solid understanding of these resources:

- Team Member Guide - The Sensor Industry
- Team Member Guide - The Customer Survey Score

The Sensor Industry

Scanning this section, the information seems straight forward enough. All potential customers look at the same four things; price, age, reliability, and position (a combination of size and performance). However, research has discovered that your customers can be better understood as two different groups because:

- They have different expectations for each characteristic, and;
- They place a different importance on each characteristic.

However, it bothers you that the concept of "Low Tech" and "High Tech" customers seems too abstract. After all, that is just the marketing label for the group that they belong to. They don't know – and wouldn't care – what market segment they are in. They just want products that meet their needs.

Andrew's sales people keep careful records about customers' suggestions and you see that your product, Able, is being used by both Ford and Honda in their MAP sensors. Both companies are putting a lot of pressure on your sales people for lower prices. They don't want anything new or fancy, just an established product at a lower price. They are the perfect example of a Low Tech customer.

On the other end of the spectrum are customers who incorporate your sensors in remote environmental monitors for hazardous exploration. It appears that "hazardous exploration" includes oil / gas, deep-ocean, and even space exploration. None of these companies are talking about price—they want smaller, faster, newer, and more reliable sensors. They are typical High Tech customers.

Low Tech Customers: Automobile Manufacturers	High Tech Customers: Energy Exploration
 Courtesy of metalpix/Alamy	 Courtesy of pumkinpie/Alamy
MAP: Manifold Absolute Pressure sensors. In a car's fuel injected engine, provides information that maximizes efficiency of the air/fuel mix.	*Wireless remote sensors measure different environmental dimensions and transmit data continuously via an RF transceiver.*

You are ready to begin working through this section more carefully.

2. An Introduction to the Sensor Industry: Market Size and Growth

From the introduction to this section, you learn that the overall market is split 70% of the customers are "Low Tech" and 30% are "High Tech." However, High Tech is growing twice as fast at 20% for High Tech compared to 10% for Low Tech. You remember that you saw specific size and growth information on the FastTrack report; you find it on pages 5 and 6 of the FastTrack Report.

Low Tech: Market Segment Analysis (p.5)

Statistics	
Total Industry Unit Demand	5,040
Actual Industry Unit Sales	5,040
Segment % of Total Industry	70.0%
Growth Rate	10.0%

High Tech: Market Segment Analysis (p.6)

Statistics	
Total Industry Unit Demand	2,160
Actual Industry Unit Sales	2,160
Segment % of Total Industry	30.0%
Growth Rate	20.0%

What is important? FastTrack reports information from <u>last year</u>. This report presents historical data from last year. You will use last year's information to make decisions about the coming year. Because the market is growing, you will ALWAYS need to adjust the FastTrack "Unit Demand" by the growth rate. To make this information more concrete and useful, you take a couple of minutes to calculate the size of the market segments for all 8 years. (For example, to "grow" a number by 10%, multiply that number by 1.1 and to grow by 20%, multiply by 1.2.) Complete Table 2.1 - Segment Growth using these percentages for Low Tech and High Tech for future reference.

Table 2.1 - Segment Growth

Segment	Current	Growth	R1	R2	R3	R4	R5	R6	R7	R8
Low Tech	5,040	10%	5,544	6,098						
High Tech	2,160	20%								
Total	7,200									

Buying Criteria and Buying Criteria by Segment

After reading these sections carefully, you notice a couple of things.

1. Customers' expectations for Price, Age, and Reliability apparently don't change over time.
2. Customers' expectations for position (size-performance) change constantly (month-to-month)
3. Low Tech customers have different expectations (for position, price, age, and reliability) than High Tech customers
4. Low Tech and High Tech customers place different importance on each characteristic.

While this section is very general about what customers want, remember that FastTrack reported specific expectations and importance for both market segments based on last year's performance. Table 2.2 - Customer Buying Criteria presents this information from the FastTrack Report.

Table 2.2 - Customer Buying Criteria

Low Tech Market Segment *(Page 5)*			High Tech Market Segment *(Page 6)*		
1. Price:	$15.00-35.00	(41%)	1. Ideal Position Pfmn.: 7.4 Size 12.6		(33%)
2. Ideal Age:	3.0	(29%)	2. Ideal Age:	0.0	(29%)
3. Reliability/MTBF:	14,000-20,000	(21%)	3. Price:	$25.00 - 45.00	(25%)
4. Ideal Position Pfmn.: 4.8 Size15.2		(9%)	4. Reliability/MTBF:	17,000-23,000	(13%)

To make this information more concrete (and useful), take a moment to fill out the Table 2.3 - Customer Buying Criteria for these constant expectations (Position is next). The "Overlap" area identifies the values that satisfy both segments.

Table 2.3 - Customer Buying Criteria

	Low Tech	High Tech	Overlap
Price			
Age			
Reliability			

Positioning and the Perceptual Map

Product positioning on the perceptual map is an important concept. The sooner you master this understanding, the better off you will be. You decide to study all of the positioning material at the same time by accomplishing the following:

1. TMG: Positioning

2. TMG: Positioning Score

3. Log onto www.capsim.com and go to: Select Help > Manager's Guide > Demonstrations > Perceptual Map

4. TMG: Perceptual Map

At first, the perceptual map may seem confusing; but it is not that complicated. There are just three things you need to remember.

1. Size and performance are interrelated product characteristics. A small sensor that is slow has little value in the market. Similarly, a high performance sensor that is large attracts no buyers. In order to consider the interrelationship, performance and size are mapped onto the Perceptual Map grid.

2. Customers expect size and performance to improve constantly. From month-to-month and year-to-year, the size / performance combinations each market segments finds acceptable change.

3. All acceptable combinations of size and performance are not equally attractive to customers; each market segment has an "ideal" combination. The "ideal" combination changes at exactly the same rate as the acceptable combinations changes.

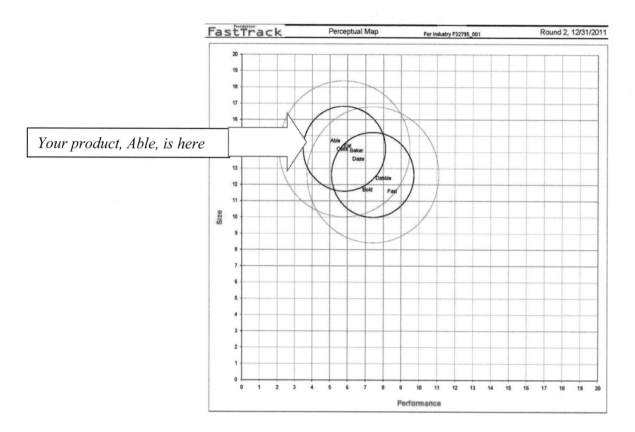

Market Expectations: Performance and Size (Positions on the Perceptual Map)
The segment center (which defines the acceptable combinations of performance and size) and the ideal spot (the size and performance combination most desired) are the same for the Low Tech market segment.

For the High Tech segment, the ideal spot is 1.4 units smaller and 1.4 units faster than the segment center. *(See figure 3.1 page 8 of TMG).* Because you know the segment center for each of the 8 rounds, you can also determine the ideal spot.

Performance and Size Expectations by Round
On the next page, Table 2.4 - Performance and Size Expectations by Round shows this year-by-year progression. Determine the "Ideal Spot" performance and size information for the High Tech segment.

An Introduction to Business

Table 2.4 - Performance and Size Expectations by Round

Round	Low Tech — Segment Center / Ideal Spot		High Tech — Segment Center		High Tech — *Ideal spot*	
	Perf.	**Size**	**Perf.**	**Size**	**Perf.**	**Size**
0	4.8	15.2	6.0	14.0		
1	5.3	14.7	6.7	13.3		
2	5.8	14.2	7.4	12.6		
3	6.3	13.7	8.1	11.9		
4	6.8	13.2	8.8	11.2		
5	7.3	12.7	9.5	10.5		
6	7.8	12.2	10.2	9.8		
7	8.3	11.7	10.9	9.1		
8	8.8	11.2	11.6	8.4		

Customers expect products to be smaller and faster every year (.5 units for Low Tech; .7 units for High Tech). But, the expectations change every month; Low Tech by .042 (.5/12) and High Tech by .058 (.7/12). So, for Low Tech to go from 4.8 & 15.2 to 5.3 & 14.7, the monthly change is shown in Table 2.5 - Size and Performance Expectations by Month below.

Table 2.5 - Size and Performance Expectations by Month

	Jan	Feb	Mar	April	May	June	July	Aug	Sept	Oct	Nov	Dec.
Size	15.16	15.12	15.08	15.03	14.99	14.95	14.91	14.87	14.83	14.78	14.74	14.70
Perf.	4.84	4.88	4.93	4.97	5.01	5.05	5.09	5.13	5.18	5.22	5.26	5.30

The Customer Survey Score

You recognize the importance of having a model of how the customers of a market segment make purchase decisions. The idea is simple; you know what product characteristics are important to your customers, what values they desire, and how important each characteristic is relative to the others. (Customer Buying Criteria are reported on FastTrack Market Segment Analysis pages 5 and 6 and in this document on page 2.) If you can systematically evaluate your product offering against the customers' expectations, you will know how "desirable" your product is to the customers in that segment. If you could use that same system to evaluate all of your competitors' products, you could predict sales (and market success) for all participants in the market. That would be powerful information to have.

To build an understanding, you start with the most simple scenario; a product that is not revised during the year. You decide to estimate January's Customer Survey Score (CSS) for your product Able. If your understanding is correct, it should be very close to December's CSS which you will find in the FastTrack Report on page 4, the "Production" page.

Attractiveness Score

Market research has determined an attractiveness score for each product attribute for both the Low Tech and High Tech segments. You will never have to "create" an attractiveness score. The attractiveness score will be provided to you based on this research. The attractiveness score multiplied by the importance results in the CSS points for each category. The summation of these areas equate to the Total CSS score. The following exercise illustrates this concept.

Estimating January's Customer Survey Score

To estimate a Customer Survey Score, set up a table (for each market segment) that has the product characteristics, the importance to the CSS (what percentage of the decision), the product's score (an evaluation of how close the current product offering is to the "ideal"), and the CSS points. You simple multiply the "importance" by the "attractiveness score" to give a weighted value for each. Table 2.6 - Customer Service Score Calculations allows you to calculate the CSS Points for the four product criteria below.

Table 2.6 - Customer Service Score Calculations

Market Segment	MTBF	Price	Age	Position	Total	
Importance	%	%	%	%	100%	*Customer buying criteria*
Attractiveness Score						*Tables and Graphs below*
CSS Points						*Multiply Importance x Score*

To evaluate your product, you have to know its current attributes. Using page 5 and 6 from the FastTrack Report (see next page) allows you to identify the attributes of your current product, Able, and evaluate them using the tables and graphs in the "Estimating a Monthly Customer Survey Score" (You will find an example of a FastTrack report in the appendices.)

Top Products In Segment

Name	Market Share	Units Sold to Seg	Revision Date	Stock Out	Pfmn Coord	Size Coord	List Price	MTBF	Age Dec.31	Promo Budget	Sales Budget	Customer Awareness	December Customer Survey
Able	17%	840	21-Nov-05		6.4	13.6	$34.00	21000	3.1	$1,000	$1,000	55%	18
Baker	17%	840	21-Nov-05		6.4	13.6	$34.00	21000	3.1	$1,000	$1,000	55%	18
Cake	17%	840	21-Nov-05		6.4	13.6	$34.00	21000	3.1	$1,000	$1,000	55%	18

Estimating Mean Time Between Failure Attractiveness

You know that your customers prefer a higher Mean Time Between Failure (MTBF). Full points (100) are awarded to the highest number in the range, and minimum points (1) to the lowest acceptable MTBF for each segment, shown in Table 2.7 - MTBF Attractiveness Scores below.

Table 2.7 - MTBF Attractiveness Scores

Low Tech	14,000	15,000	16,000	17,000	18,000	19,000	20,000
High Tech	17,000	18,000	19,000	20,000	**21,000**	22,000	23,000
Attractiveness Score	1	17	33	50	**67**	83	**100**

MFBF Contribution to CSS: Able has a MTBF of 21,000 hours

- For the Low Tech market, that is above the range so it would have a score of 100 points. From the buying criteria, MTBF makes up 21% of the decision. So for the Low Tech market, a MTBF of 21,000 hours contributes 100 x 21% or 21 points to the January CSS.

- For the High Tech market, 21,000 hours has a score of 67 points. From the buying criteria, MTBF makes up 13% of the decision. So for the High Tech market, a MTBF of 21,000 hours contributes 67 x 13% or 8.7 points to the January CSS.

Estimating Price Attractiveness

Your customers prefer a lower price, so you award full points (100) to the lowest price in the range, and minimum points (1) to the highest acceptable price for each segment. Because Figure 3.2 in the Team Member Guide on page 8 shows you that price appeal follows a classic demand curve, you adjust the scores to approximate the curve. The result is displayed in Table 2.8 - Price Attractiveness below.

Table 2.8 - Price Attractiveness

Low Tech	$15	$20	$25	$30	$35
High Tech	$25	$30	$35	$40	$45
Attractiveness Score	100	70	40	20	1

Price Contribution to CSS: Able is currently being offered at a price of $34.00

- For the Low Tech market, a price of $34 would probably contribute an estimated 5 points; and price is 41% of the decision. Price contributes 2.1 points (5 x 41%) to Low Tech's January CSS.
- For the High Tech market, a price of $34 would probably contribute an estimated 55 points; and price is 25% of the decision. Price contributes 13.75 points (55 x 25%) to the High Tech's January CSS score.

Estimating Age Attractiveness

Unlike reliability or price, the age of your product changes every month. If Able starts the year at 3.1 years old; it will be 4.1 years old next December. The monthly CSS score for age is estimated from Fig 3.3.

Table 2.9 - Documenting Age

	Jan	Feb	Mar	April	May	June	July	Aug	Sept	Oct	Nov	Dec.
Age	3.2	3.3	3.3*	3.4	3.5	3.6	3.7	3.8	3.8*	3.9	4.0	4.1

*__*Note:__ The application of a 10-point scale into 12 months means that the age does not significantly change in two of the 12 months, from February to March and from August to September.*

The Customer Survey Score is visually estimated from Figure 2.1 below.

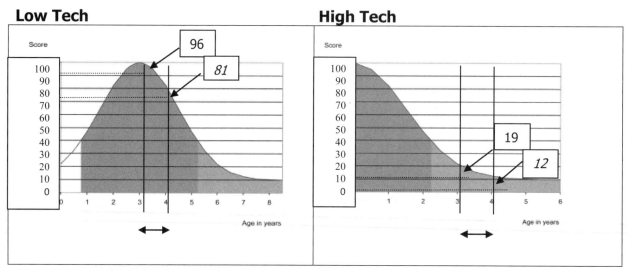

Figure 2.1 - Low Tech and High Tech Age CSS

Age Contribution to CSS

In January, Able's age is 3.2 years

- In Low Tech, an age of 3.2 would contribute 96 CSS points. Age is important to Low Tech customers contributing 29% to the CSS. So, in January, Able's age contributes 27.8 CSS points (96 x 29%) to the total Customer Survey Score.

    Note: By December, Able's age will only be contributing 23.5 points (81 x 29%).

- In High Tech, an age of 3.2 would contribute 19 points. Age is also important to High Tech customers contributing 29% to the CSS. So, in January, Able's attractive age contributes 6 CSS points (21 x 29%) to the total Customer Survey Score.

    Note: By December, Able's age will only be contributing 3.5 points (12 x 29%).

Estimating Position Attractiveness

The ideal position is literally a moving target – customers' expectations are changing from month to month. Also, because expectations for size and performance are interrelated, the *distance* between your product's position and customers' expectations (both for what is acceptable and for what is "ideal") is actually the hypotenuse of the triangle formed by the difference between your products position and the expected position, and difference between your products size and the expected size. While this is important to understand, you think it is too complicated to build into your decision making at this time. You opt for a simple visual examination and estimation using Figure 2.2 below.

Low Tech   **High Tech**

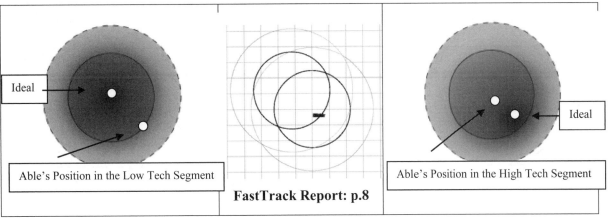

Ideal

Able's Position in the Low Tech Segment

FastTrack Report: p.8

Ideal

Able's Position in the High Tech Segment

Figure 2.2 - Positioning Scores

Position Contribution to January's CSS: Able has a size of 13.6 and performance of 6.4. Both ideal and acceptable positions are constantly changing. The "distance" from the ideal determines the CSS.

- The Low Tech ideal starts the year at 15.16 and 4.84. Able's current size is about 1.6 units smaller than the ideal and its performance is about 1.6 units faster than the ideal. It is on the edge of what is acceptable to the Low Tech customers. You estimate a CSS position score of 10 points. Position is not important to Low tech customers accounting for 9% of the CSS. So January's position contributes .9 points (10 * 9%).

    Note: Able's Low Tech position will improve over the course of the year. A size of 13.6 is only 1.1 units from December's ideal (14.70 and a size of 6.4 is only 1.1 units from the ideal of 5.3.

- The High Tech "ideal" position starts the years at 7.4 and 12.6. Able is 1 unit larger and 1 unit slower than the ideal point. However, Able's position is between the segment center and the ideal. Figure 2.2 suggests a fairly high concentration of customers in this position. You estimate a CSS position score of 54. Position is very important to High tech customers accounting for 33% of the CSS. January's position contributes 17.8 points (54 *33%).

> *Note: In High Tech, the ideal is moving away from Able's position. Able's size of 13.6 is 1.7 units larger than December's the ideal of 11.9 and a performance of 6.4 is 1.7 units slower than the ideal of 8.1*

These scores for Able are recorded in the **Table 2.10: Able's January Customer Survey Score** below.

TABLE 2.10 - Able's January Customer Survey Score

Low Tech	MTBF	Price	Age	Position	Total
Importance	21%	41%	29%	9%	100%
Able's Attractiveness Score	100	5	96	10	
CSS points	21	2.1	27.8	.9	**51.8**

High Tech	MTBF	Price	Age	Position	Total
Importance	13%	25%	29%	33%	100%
Able's Attractiveness Score	70	55	21	54	
CSS points	8.7	13.75	6	17.8	**46.25**

CSS Adjustments

The "base score" calculated in the table above has to be adjusted. For example, investments in awareness and accessibility also influence the total CSS score.

Assessing Awareness and Accessibility: According to the TMG on pages 9-10, both awareness and accessibility reduces the score based on this formula:

(1 + Awareness Rating) / 2 = Awareness CSS Impact

(1 + Accessibility Rating) / 2 = Accessibility CSS Impact

For example:

> If you have 55% awareness, that means 55% of your potential customers received your promotional materials and know about your product. The corollary is that 45% of customers are not aware of you. However, all customers engage in some research of their own. Of the 45% who did not receive your promotional materials, half (or 22.5%) discover your product through their own search. At decision time, 55% got your message and 22.5% discovered you through their own search process. Adding these figures together indicates that 77.5% of the customers know about your product.

$$(1 + .55) / 2 = 77.5\%$$

> **Note**: *The remaining 22.5% who didn't know about your product and did not consider it for purchase are a potential source of sales growth.*

Awareness is concerned with ***before the sale***. Using the formula, having 55% awareness reduces the CSS score by 22.5% for both Low and High Tech markets:

> Low Tech: 22.5% of 51.8 0 is a loss of 11.65 points
>
> High Tech: 22.5% of 46.25 is a loss of 10.40 points

Accessibility is concerned with ***during and after the sale***. Having 40% accessibility reduces the CSS score by 30% for both segments:

> Low Tech: 30% of 51.8 is a loss of 15.5 points
>
> High Tech: 30% of 46.25 is a loss of 13.9 points

Attributes in the Rough Cut: CSS adjustments

All products that fall within the ROUGH CUT parameters for position, price, and reliability will still be considered for purchase. However, if the products attributes are outside the FINE CUT parameters (all of the parameters you have been using so far), the TOTAL CSS is significantly adjusted.

For example:

> If your product is priced at $36, price would contribute 0 points to your CSS score for the Low Tech market AND the adjusted score would lose another 10% of the base score. Ouch!

Customer Survey Score Adjustments

These Customer Survey Score adjustments apply to products positioned in the rough cut:

- ***Pricing*** outside the range loses about 10% (of the base CSS score) per dollar.

- ***MTBF*** set below the range loses about 20% (of the base CSS score) per 1,000 hours.

- ***Positioning*** outside of the fine cut circle is a 1% loss if it is just over the line, a 50% loss if it is halfway, and a 99% loss if it is on the edge of the rough cut circle.

Additional customer survey adjustments, for Accounts Receivable for example, will be discussed in Chapter 4.

Build Your Understanding
Foundation Exercise 2 Questions

1. The information in the "Statistics" table from the FastTrack Report (pages 5 and 6), allows you to calculate "Total Industry Unit Demand" for the next year.

Statistics	
Total Industry Unit Demand	6,098
Actual Industry Unit Sales	6,098
Segment % of Total Industry	66.2%
Growth Rate	10.0%

How many units could be sold in the Low Tech market segment next year?

2. Given the "Customer Buying Criteria" from the FastTrack Report (pages 5 and 6), you should be able to identify customers' "ideal product" characteristics for the coming year.

Customer Buying Criteria		
	Expectations	Importance
1. Ideal Position	Pfmn 8.8 Size 11.2	33%
2. Age	Ideal Age = 0.0	29%
3. Price	$25.00 - 45.00	25%
4. Reliability	MTBF 17000-23000	13%

If you were designing a new product for the High Tech market segment, what product characteristics would be "ideal" for customers? *(Remember: The FastTrack provides information from last year.)*

3. Given the "Customer buying Criteria" and "Products" table from the FastTrack Report (pages 5 and 6), you should be able to identify your product's current characteristics and compare them to customers' expectations.

From FastTrack Report - Low Tech page 5

Top Products In Segment

Name	Market Share	Units Sold to Seg	Revision Date	Stock Out	Pfmn Coord	Size Coord	List Price	MTBF	Age Dec.31	Promo Budget	Sales Budget	Customer Awareness	December Customer Survey
Able	23%	1,375	9-Nov-10	YES	5.3	14.7	$35.00	20000	3.1	$2,000	$2,000	100%	28
Cake	19%	1,140	19-Jan-11		5.7	14.2	$28.95	17000	3.3	$925	$925	56%	20
Baker	18%	1,118	8-Mar-11		6.5	14.1	$33.40	19800	2.1	$1,350	$1,350	77%	23

How does Able's current price compare to customer's expectations in the Low Tech segment?

4. Given the "Customer Buying Criteria" tables, your current product's characteristics, and a way to determine the "attractiveness score", you should be able to fill out the CSS table and calculate the base CSS for a product.

Table 2.12 - Calculating Customer Survey Scores

Low Tech	MTBF	Price	Age	Position	Total CSS
Importance					100%
Attractiveness	100	5	96	10	
CSS points					

Using the "Attractiveness" scores given in the table above, calculate Able's Total Customer Survey Score.

Build Your Understanding
Foundation Exercise 3 - *Marketing Operations*

While it is necessary to understand who your customers are and what they want, it is not enough. Every decision that you make has trade-offs. If you lower your price, your customers are happy and they will buy more sensors from you; that is excellent. However, you will make less money on each product you sell; that is not excellent. When you offer High Tech customers a product that is "ideally" positioned, they are attracted to your product; but the cost of the materials that go into your product increase accordingly.

To build this understanding, your experts recommend a solid understanding of the following:
- Team Member Guide – Operations: Research and Development
- R&D and Product Invention Demonstrations (www.capsim.com – Help > Manager's Guide)
- Round 1: Rehearsal Simulation
- Team Member Guide – Operations: Marketing
- Marketing Demonstration (www.capsim.com – Help > Manager's Guide)
- Round 2: Rehearsal Simulation

Operations- Research and Development
After a careful reading of the section, you are impressed by how important the information is and decide to do a comprehensive review of the decisions and their trade-offs. As always, you want to be sure that you understand the simple ideas completely, and then build an understanding of the complex ways in which those simple decisions interact.

The Research and Development (R&D) function allows you to manage the product- or products-that your company is offering in the market. You can offer a product that is designed to meet the needs of Low Tech customers. It will have different characteristics than a product that is designed to meet the needs of High Tech customers. Your product, Able, is currently selling to both market segments, but no single product will excite customers in both segments for very long.

You have three options in managing your product offering(s). You can:
1. Revise an existing product (one that is currently offered in the market)
2. Introduce a new product
3. Discontinue an existing product

Whenever you order a change to an existing product (or introduce a new product), an R&D project is begun. One of the most important things about an R&D project is how long it will take. Project length is important because it determines how much the ***project*** will cost and when the improved ***product*** offering will be available. You list the relationships as you understand them:
1. The bigger the change in the product, the longer the R&D project will take. This makes intuitive sense. If you are making a small change to an existing product, you know a lot about it already and it won't take long to revise. If you are offering a radically different product, there will be many more "unknowns" to consider and it will take longer to resolve them.

2. If you have more than one R&D project underway, each will take longer than if there was only project in process.

3. The higher the automation of the assembly line, the longer the R&D project will take. R&D projects not only change the product, but also the requirements for producing (manufacturing) the product. The more specialized the equipment used in the manufacturing process, the longer it will take to reconfigure the equipment for the revised product.

4. The longer the R&D project lasts, the more it is going to cost. R&D projects incur expense at a rate of about $1,000,000 per year. For example, a 6-month (1/2 year) project will have an R&D expense of $500,000, a 9-month project (3/4 year) will cost $750,000, and an 18-month project will cost $1,500,000.

5. If a product begins the year and is already involved in an R&D project, you will not be able to schedule another project for that product in that year. Project scheduling is so important to success that schedules (and the resource commitments they require) can only be set once a year at the beginning of the year. Therefore, if a product is already in the process of being changed, you can't order your R&D staff to change it again until the current project is completed and the next scheduling cycle is started.

6. The "time in market" is probably the most important consequence of R&D project length. R&D projects make products more attractive to customers. Because attractive products sell more, the sooner you improve your product, the longer amount of time you have to sell it. Conversely, the longer your project takes, the longer your less attractive product will be on the market. If your R&D project takes 18 months, it means that you are offering your less attractive product and will sell fewer products during those 18 months.

Managing your products

After viewing the R&D Demonstration (www.capsim.com > Help > Manager's Guide > Demonstration > R&D) and completing the Rehearsal Round 1, it strikes you that the model of your company provided in the Foundation Spreadsheet is also an excellent tool for exploring the trade-offs of the product design decisions. For instance, you can change one product characteristic at a time and see how long the project will take until it is available, shown by the revision date. You will also be able to assess the change in the cost of materials and the change in the overall product attractiveness.

Trade-offs: MTBF

Your product, Able, currently has a MTBF of 21,000 hours. You change the MTBF in the R&D page (and do not change any other specification) and record the Revision date and R&D cost (from the R&D worksheet), the Material Cost (from the Production worksheet), and the predicted demand (from the Marketing Worksheet) in Table 2.14 below.

Table 2.14 - Revision and Demand Predictions

Change Able's MTBF to:	How long to revise?	R&D Cost to Revise	Material Cost to Revise	Predicted Demand
21,000			*$16.04*	*1,122*
20,000	15 Jan	$40K	$15.74	1,101
19,000	29 Jan	$80	$15.44	1006
18,000	13 Feb	$120	$15.14	913

Look for the relationships in Table 2.14. For example, what is the impact for every 1,000 hours change in MTBF?

1. How long does this revision take?
2. What is the R&D cost?
3. How much does the material cost change?
4. How much will demand change?

Trade-offs: Position

Able has a performance of 6.4, a size of 13.6 and a material cost of $16.04 (per unit). Based on that position, review the information in Table 2.15 and its impact on the length of time, R&D costs, and material costs.

Table 2.15 - Revision Costs

Position		How long to revise?	R&D Cost to Revise	Material Cost to Revise
Perf	Size			
5.4	14.6	25 September	$744	$12.54
5.9	14.1	3 May	$340	$14.54
6.4	*13.6*	*- Able's Current Position -*	*0*	*$16.04*
6.9	13.1	3 May	$340	$16.44
7.4	12.6	25 September	$744	$17.24

In general, what are the implications for every .5 unit change in performance and .5 unit change in size?

1. How long does this revision take?
2. What is the R&D cost?
3. In what ways does the material cost change with every change in position?

Trade-offs: Age

Managing your product's age is very different than managing any other characteristic. There is not an "age" cell in the R&D worksheet. You can only change your product's perceived age by changing its position on the perceptual map – by changing its performance and size. Because age is an outcome of repositioning, managing age does not have any direct impact on the cost of the R&D project or any direct impact on material cost.

However, age does have a very big impact on the CSS and how attractive your product is to your customers. For both Low Tech and High Tech customers, age is the second most important characteristic and determines 29% of the Customer Survey Score. For Low Tech customers, position only contributes 9% of the CSS. Age is a much more important determinate of its "attractiveness." As presented in Figure 2.1, if your Low Tech product's age is between 2 and 4, you will never have an age score of less than 80. If the age is younger than 2 or older than 4, the score drops very quickly. However, if you reposition your Low Tech product whenever its age is 4, then the "age at revision" will be cut by half – 4 years becomes 2 years – it is perfect! Make that change and then don't revise the product for another 2 years so the next revision occurs just as it approaches an age of 4 again.

Product Management for the Low Tech Market - *Thinking strategically*:

You realize that you are onto something important here. A heuristic (or "rule of thumb") for managing a Low Tech product is that you should reposition your product whenever that product is 4.0 years old. Its "age at revision" will be 2.0. After revision, it will be 2 years before the product is old enough that you have to reposition it again (first year- it will age from 2-3, second year it will age from 3-4; at 4 years old, you revise).

In the Low Tech market, the ideal spot drifts by .5 unit smaller and .5 unit faster every year. In two years, the ideal spot moves one unit smaller and one unit faster. A strategy for managing a Low Tech product is to position your product on (or near) the ideal spot. You reposition your product every other year (in whatever year the age will be 4.0), and you make your product one unit smaller and one unit faster.

You decide to test your idea and open Foundation Spreadsheet. In the R&D worksheet, you decide to position Able as a product for the Low Tech Market.

1. First, you change the MTBF to 20,000 which is the top of the range what Low Tech customers find the most attractive, but is also relatively costly to produce. By reducing MTBF, you will save $.30 on the cost of materials used in production. With no change in demand, if you sell 1,000,000 units lowering the MTBF will result in a $300,000 increase in profits.

2. Reposition Able to the ideal spot for Round 1 (the first year that you are running the company). In Exercise 2, you found the ideal spot to be a performance of 5.3 and size of 14.7.

3. With those changes, notice that the revision date is November 9th. Able will be available from January 1st to November 9th under its original specifications, with performance of 6.4, size of 13.6, and an MTBF of 21,000 (material cost of $16.04 per unit.) Able is 3.1 years old on January 1st and ages to 4.0 years old by November 8th. On November 9th, a new- improved- revised Able is introduced to the market. Able is "ideally" positioned for the Low Tech customer (performance of 5.3, size of 14.7, and an MTBF of 20,000). This new configuration has a material cost of about $12.00. It's perceived age is 2.0 on November 9th and probably about 2.1 at the end of the year.

    > ***Note:*** *The CSS (the demand for your product) in October will be based on Able's original specifications while the CSS in November will be based the revised specifications. Therefore, the demand for Able at these two points in time will be very different.*

4. In the second year (Round 2), you will not make any changes to Able – the MTBF is perfect and the age will go from 2.1 to 3.1 years old. However, in the third year (Round 3), Able will age from 3.1 to 4.1 years old when it will be time to reposition again. In Round 3, the ideal spot is 1 unit faster (6.3) and one unit smaller (13.7) than it was in the first year. Those specifications would be the starting point for your repositioning because AGE is more important to manage than positioning it on the ideal spot. Hopefully, you can position it a little smaller and faster than the Round 3 ideal (so its CSS improves over time).

From Foundation Spreadsheets - R&D Decisions

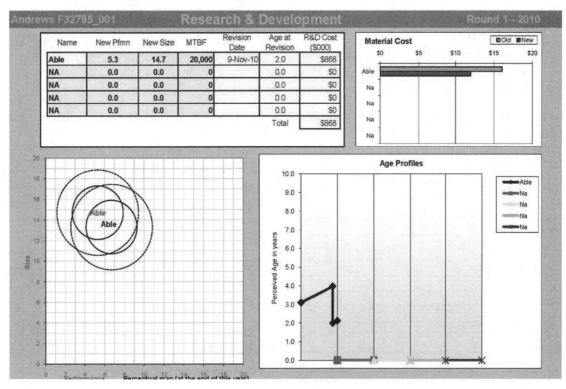

Product Management for the High Tech Market - *Thinking strategically*:

For High Tech customers, managing your product offerings require a different strategy. The two characteristics that are most important are positioning and age. You look at Able and decide that it would be difficult to make Able a good High Tech product because you can *either* reposition it to the ideal spot *or* try to keep the age as close to 0 as possible. But you can't do both.

From Foundation Spreadsheet - R&D Decisions

Able	8.1	11.9	21,000	19-Apr-11	2.2

If you wanted to manage Able's position for the High Tech market, putting it on the ideal spot (changing performance from 6.4 to 8.1 and size from 13.6 to 11.9) results in a revision date of 19 April of **next** year. The age profile doesn't change this year; Able ages from 3.1 to 4.1 year old. Next year, Able ages from 4.1 to 4.4 on 18 April, and then the age is cut in have to 2.2. By the end of that year Able's age will be about 2.9 years old. Not great; not even good.

Able	6.5	13.6	21,000	17-Feb-10	1.6

If you wanted to manage Able's age for the High Tech market, making the smallest change possible (changing performance from 6.4 to 6.5) results a revision date of 17 February at which point its AGE is cut in half from 3.2 to 1.6. By the end of the year, Able's age will be about 2.6 years old. And, it is a long way from the ideal spot. Not great; not even good.

The only way to have a great product for the High Tech market is to introduce a new product. **Inventing Sensors** and the on-line demonstration, **Product Invention at** www.capsim.com (Help > Manager's Guide > Demonstrations) provides insight. To determine what product characteristics your sensor should have, you decide to review the information about the Customer Survey Score and the expectations of the High Tech Customers.

You start by deciding on a name. In your industry, all of the product names start with the same letter as the company name. Since you run Andrews, you choose "AceX."

You want to design a perfect product, so you go to the Customer Buying Criteria for the specifications. Reliability is easy; you choose an MTBF of 23,000. Position is a little bit harder. The ideal spot is changing month-to-month and year-to-year and you know that it takes more than a year to invent a new product.

Customer Buying Criteria		
	Expectations	*Importance*
1. Ideal Position	Pfmn 8.1 Size 11.9	33%
2. Age	Ideal Age = 0.0	29%
3. Price	$25.00 - 45.00	25%
4. Reliability	MTBF 17000-23000	13%

The ideal spot for Round 1 is given in the table. If it takes a year, then AceX won't be available until Round 2. In Round 2, the ideal spot is .7 units faster (the ideal performance of 8.1 in Round 1 changes to 8.8 in Round 2) and .7 units smaller. *(The ideal size of 11.9 changes to 11.2 in Round 2).*

From Foundation Spreadsheets - R&D Decisions

Name	New Pfmn	New Size	MTBF	Revision Date	Age at Revision	R&D Cost ($000)
Able	6.4	13.6	21,000		0.0	$0
ACE X	8.8	11.2	23,000	17-Aug-11	0.0	$1,635
NA	0.0	0.0	0		0.0	$0
NA	0.0	0.0	0		0.0	$0
NA	0.0	0.0	0		0.0	$0
					Total	$1,635

Note: You make a mental note that it also takes a year to build a factory to produce your new product AceX. You would also order construction of the factory this year so it would be ready by 17-August-2011 .

With the decisions you have entered into the model, you only have one product, Able, available for the first year. In the second year (Round 2), you will have only Able available from 1 January until 16 of August. From 17 August until 31 December, you will have 2 products, Able and AceX. AceX will be a nearly perfect product on 17 August. Its position is very near the ideal spot. At "0" years old, it is the perfect age. Throw in a MTBF of 23,000 hours, and AceX is all that a High Tech customer could want.

However, by 31 December the situation is starting to change. The ideal spot is drifting away from your current position and AceX is .4 years old. You are losing ground on the two most important product characteristics. It is clear that you will have to reposition a High Tech product every year in order to keep it on (or near) the ideal spot and to keep the age as young as possible. Since the ideal spot for the High Tech market changes by .7 units faster and .7 units smaller every year, that is how much you would change your product specifications.

Operations - Marketing

Carefully review the available resources:

- Team Member Guide - Section 4.2: Operations - Marketing
- Marketing Demonstration (www.capsim.com – Help- Manager's Guide-Demonstrations)
- Round 2: Rehearsal Simulation

It becomes clear that you will have to play with this information in order to build a complete and useful understanding of the marketing decisions.

Trade-offs: Price

You know the basic trade-offs with price. If you charge a higher price, you will make more money on every unit that you sell; but you will sell fewer units. If you charge a lower price, you will sell more units; but make less money on each one. Although you have not yet reviewed the accounting information, you know that you have been given 2 performance targets that will be directly affected by price – contribution margin and profit.

You decide on a quick preview using the Marketing worksheet in the Foundation Spreadsheet. You enter a price and it generates an estimated demand. From this forecast, you can create a production scheduled. When you do this, the spreadsheet does several things to help you plan for the future. Inputting this information creates proforma statements, which are future statements based on your forecast, which gives insight into the following:

- Revenue – The money received from the sale of product
- Contribution Margin – The amount left over after you pay the cost of producing the products you sold (Revenue - Cost of the Goods Sold) and this is reported as a percentage of Revenue
- Net Income – Revenues minus all expenses are recorded in the pro-forma income statement.

You think that that makes sense, but decide to review the relationships to be sure you have a solid understanding. You are currently selling Able at a price of $34. At that price, the model predicts you will sell 1,122(000) units. Revenue would be $38,148 ($34 x 1,122). At that level of production, each unit cost you $26.50 (from the Production report). If you can sell them for $34 and they cost you $26.50 to make, each one that you sell contributes $7.50 to your profitability. The $7.50 that is left over represents 22.06% of the sale price. For every dollar of sales, you have $.22 left over after you pay for the cost of producing the product you sold. When you subtract all of the expenses, your profit is $2,521(000) as shown in Table 2.16.

Table 2.16 - Determining Net Income

Price	Units Sold	Revenue	Contribution Margin	Net Income
$34	1,122	$38,148	22.06%	2,521

The proforma Income Statement automatically does this for you based on your projections.

Table 2.17 - Determining Net Income+

Price	Units sold	Revenue	Contribution Margin	Net Income
$30	1,353	$40,599	9.7%	(288)
$31	1,295	$40,130	13.0%	585
$32	1,236	$39,561	16.1%	1,302
$33	1,179	$38,896	19.1%	1,947
$34	1,122	$38,148	22.1%	2,521
$35	1,065	$37,288	24.7%	3,027
$36	906	$32,625	28.6%	3,033
$37	745	$27,560	30.7%	2,449
$38	581	$22,061	32.4%	1,562
$39	412	$16,060	33.9%	427
$40	236	$ 9,444	34.9%	(1,007)

From studying the table, you realize that you would charge a different price depending on your goals. What price would you charge to optimize:

- Demand (units sold)?
- Revenue?
- Contribution margin?
- Profit?
- Profit given that you also need a contribution margin above 30%?

Trade-offs: Promotion Budgets and Awareness

The **promotion budget** is an advertising and market communications budget. Your company uses a measure called "awareness" to gauge the effectiveness of your promotional efforts and determine how many customers know about your product.

From year to year, a third of the customers who got your message last year have forgotten about your product this year. Therefore, this formula applies:

Last Year's Awareness - (Last Year's Awareness x .333) = Starting Awareness

For example:

> If you had 90% awareness last year, a third of those, or .333, will have forgotten about you. You will begin the next year with 60% awareness.

$$90\% - (90\% \times .333) = 60\%$$

If a sensor had 50% awareness at the end of last year, it will start with an awareness of approximately 33% for the next year. Therefore, this year's promotion budget would begin from a starting awareness of 33%. It follows this formula:

Last Year's Awareness + ((1 - Last Year's Awareness) /2) = New Awareness

For example:

> Your investments in Promotion have created a 60% Awareness level. This means that 60% of all your potential customers have received your message. You recall that when calculating the Customer Survey Score, that all customers engage in some independent search and that about half (50%) of those potential customers who did NOT receive your message will discover your offerings anyway. So, if you have achieved 60% awareness, 60% of the market got your message. Of the 40% who did not get the message, half (or

20%) learn of you on their own. Therefore, 80% of the customers in the market will consider your products when making the purchase decision.

$$60\% + ((1 - 60\%) / 2) = 80\%$$

The awareness created by your investments in promotion is described by the graph on the right, illustrating the diminishing returns of investing at level when the curve begins to flatten. If you have 100% awareness, you will still have to invest about $1,400(000) a year to maintain that level of awareness. If you have 100% awareness and 33% forget from one year to the next, $1,400(000) will create an additional 33%; exactly replacing what was lost. If you invest more than that, you will not be using your resources in the most efficient manner.

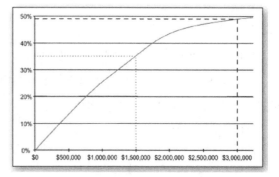

Trade-offs: Sales Budget and Accessibility

The **sales budget** is basically a distribution and after sales service budget. The effectiveness of the sales budget is measured by Accessibility; the percentage of customers who can easily interact with your company. Accessibility is reported on pages 5 and 6 of the FastTrack Report.

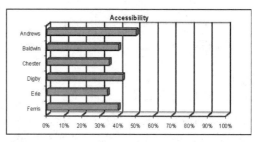

Like awareness, half of the customers who do not have easy "access" will find you through their own initiative in the purchase process. Like Awareness, you lose 33% accessibility every year. Unlike awareness, accessibility really requires 2 or more products in a segment to get to 100% accessibility .

General rules of thumb that help guide investments in the Sales Budget are:

1. If you have only one product in a segment, the "accessibility" created with investments in sales are similar to, but less effective than, the return modeled in the graph for the promotion budget. Similar in that it follows the same pattern of diminishing returns. Less effective because each dollar doesn't create *as much* additional accessibility.

2. If you have two or more products in a segment, the total invested in the promotion budgets for those products hits diminishing returns at $4,500 ($2,250(000) for each of 2 products) and requires a total of $3,300(000) (or $1,650(000) for each of two products) to maintain 100% accessibility.

Therefore:

*   **Awareness:** Once you reach 100% in awareness, you can invest $1,400(000) to maintain 100% awareness. *(If you invest $2M each year, for example, it is realistic to reach 100% awareness within several years.)*

*   **Accessibility:** Once you have 100% in accessibility, you can invest $1,650(000) to maintain 100% accessibility. *(It will be difficult to reach 100% accessibility within the "8-years" that you will manage your company . Invest to stay in the top ranked position.)*

Build Your Understanding
Foundation Exercise 3 Questions

Be able to answer these types of questions in these areas

R&D projects

1. What decision does the R&D department address?

2. What influences how long an R&D project will take?

3. What would the R&D expense be for a project that took 4 months?

4. If an R&D project takes longer than one year, what do you know about the ability to make changes for that project until after the revision date?

Product Design Trade-offs

5. What product design decisions will increase the cost of materials?

6. How does material cost change as a function of positioning on the perceptual map?

7. What factors influence the demand for your product?

Product Management

8. Given either an R&D worksheet or a Market Analysis Report (p. 5 or 6 from FastTrack) you should be able to alter the specifications of products to meet the needs of either the High Tech or Low Tech customers.

9. What changes would you make to Able to make it a better product for High Tech Customers?

10. How could a High Tech product, such as AceX, be altered to make it more appealing for Low Tech Customers?

11. In making decisions for round 3, should Ferris revise product Fast? If yes, what changes would they make to the Fast (ignoring price) to make it the best possible product for the High Tech Segment?

Marketing Management

Given a Market Analysis Report (page 5 or 6 from FastTrack) you should be able to address these types of questions for High Tech or Low Tech customers.

12. Price is the most important consideration when competing in the Low Tech market. Able's price is at the top of the Low Tech market's acceptable range. Why is Able's December Customer Survey the highest?

13. How much should Able invest in their Promotion budget for the next year?

14. If Ferris wanted product Fast to have 100% awareness in Round 3, how much would they have to invest in their Promotion budget for that round?

15. What percentage of the Low Tech Market Segment knew about product Baker when making purchase decisions in the reported year?

Build Your Understanding
Foundation Exercise 4 - *Forecasting Sales*

Determining how many units you think you are going to sell in the coming year is the most difficult decision—and one of the most important—that you will make in managing your company. It is also the only decision that maintains a high level of uncertainty throughout your entire tenure as the CEO of this company. To build your understanding of forecasting, you are going to have to carefully read TMG Section 9. Forecasting and use the FastTrack Report from Round 2 to work through the examples of the different forecasting methods.

Overview

Forecasting involves making guesses about the future (how many units of your product that will sell in the coming year) based on past information. You have a wealth of information about what happened last year in the FastTrack Report. The problem is that things change—and sometimes things change a lot. You take a minute and review the information available and how it might change over time.

1. You have good information about the size of the market segments. You know exactly how much they will grow from year to year. (Statistics - reported on page 5 and 6 of the FastTrack Report)

2. You have good information about customers decision process; how they evaluate your product and make their purchase decisions. You know exactly how customer's expectations will change from year to year. (Customer Buying Criteria - reported on page 5 and 6 of the FastTrack Report)

3. In "Units Sold," you know how many units your products sold and how many units your competitors' products sold last year in each market segment. You don't know how many you or your competitors will sell next year because the product offerings will change. (Top Products in Segment Table - page 5 and 6 of the FastTrack Report).

4. You have two valuable pieces of information in the market share report; how many units you sold as a percentage of the whole segment (Actual Market Share) and how many you would have sold *if each customer had gotten his or her first choice* (Potential Market Share). Why would a customer not have been able to make his or her first choice? Because you or your competitors did not produce enough units to meet the demand for the desired product (called "stocking out").

In the example to the right, Andrews's potential share is 26% and its actual share is about 22%. An estimated 4% of the market wanted to buy from Andrews but could not because Andrews did not produce enough. If the market was 1,000,000 units, that means that Andrews could have sold 40,000 more units than they did (1,000,000 * 4%). Who got those sales? Those units were sold by your competitors with an "Actual Share" greater than their "Potential Share."

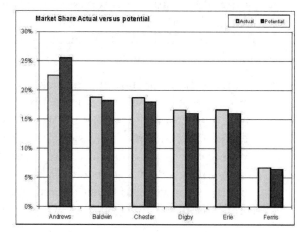

In this case, Andrews helped all of their competitors by "sending" customers to them. Baldwin, Chester, Digby, and Ferris each had sold about 8,000(000) units to customers who would have preferred doing business with Andrews. The Market Share Actual versus Potential" information is available on pages 5 and 6 of the FastTrack Report. Detailed information about market share is provided on page 7 of the FastTrack Report.

5. The December Customer Survey Score (DCSS) provides good information about how well your product meets customers' expectations compared to all others *at the end of the year*. You know if (and how) your Customer Survey Score (CSS) will change over each of the next twelve months, but not how your competitors CSS will change. (DCSS are reported in the Top Products in Segment table - page 5 and 6 of the FastTrack Report).

6. In the Production Information table (page 4 of the FastTrack Report), you have some limited information about new products entering the market in the next year. Because you don't know product specifications, you will have to guess whether it has been designed for the Low Tech or High Tech segment. You know which company is introducing a new product and, if they have a clear strategy like only competing in the High Tech segment, you may be able to guess in which segment the product will best perform. You also know how long it is going to take for that product to be introduced because of the Revision Date. You know that if the new product is similar to the old, the project time will be shorter. If the new product is very different than the old, it will take longer.

From the example on the right, AceX is so long to the market that it must be very different than Able. Since Able is Low Tech, a good guess is that AceX is probably designed for High Tech. Erie and Ferris's new products are more similar to their existing product, so the new product might be in the same segment as the existing. But you won't know for certain until the products come out.

Name	Primary Segment	Units Sold	Units in Inventory	Revision Date	Age Dec.31
Able	Low	1,630	0	9-Nov-10	3.1
Acex		0	0	17-Dec-12	0.0
Eat	Low	1,201	93	15-Jan-11	3.3
East		0	0	14-Mar-12	0.0
Fast	High	1,134	207	10-Oct-11	1.7
Feast		0	0	20-May-12	0.0

There appear to be two sources of "uncertainty" in this information which includes:
1. **Some of the information has to be adjusted.**
   The FastTrack Report provides information about last year. Demand grows from year to year. Products age from month to month. Ideal positions drift. Much of this information has to be adjusted for the coming year; the year you are making decisions about.

2. **Some of the information is a guess.**
   This is the major source of uncertainty. For instance, for the coming year, you do not know the changes in product offerings that will be available to customers. This is an important guess because each customer's decision process is driven by a *comparison*—they compare your product offering with your competitors' product offerings. Sales levels are driven by how much better or worse your product is relative to your competitors. Unless you study your competitors' decisions obsessively, it will be difficult to predict how your competitors' product offerings will change. It is safe to assume, however, that they will change and get stronger every year.

These forecasting techniques are important because you will use your sales forecasts to:
1. Set a production schedule
2. Establish a "worst case" scenario for sales so you can manage the risk of financing
3. Establish the need for investment in your capacity to manufacture product.

You have two goals for each of the forecasting techniques:
1. To master the technique of making a forecast – your educated guess.
2. To understand the quality or "goodness" of the guess.

Section 9.1 Basic Forecasting
You notice that what Section 9.1 refers to as basic forecasting involves two different techniques, "market growth" and "market share" forecasting.

Market Growth Estimate
The logic underlying the Market Growth forecast is that if the market will be 10% bigger next year, it is reasonable to assume your sales will be 10% bigger next year. To calculate the forecast, take last year's sales and grow them by the growth rate of the market. To try this forecast, use the information for product Daze (a competing product offered by Digby) from FastTrack Report pages 5 and 6: Market Segment Analysis. In the table, enter
- The number of units sold
- The growth rate for that Market Segment.
- Grow the number of units sold:
  Multiply Low Tech units sold by 1+ growth rate of 10%, which equals 1.1
  Multiply High Tech units sold by 1+ growth rate of 20%, which equals 1.2
- Add the two Market Growth estimates together

	Units Sold	Growth	Future Market Size
Low Tech			
High Tech			
Total			

The limitation of this forecasting method is that it doesn't use any information except last year's sales and growth. It fails to take into account any factors that would have influenced last year's sales. For instance, if you did not produce enough last year and stocked out of product, this forecast would not produce enough next year. If last year's sales were great in the beginning of the year and fell off by the end of the year, then this technique would predict more sales than you would get. If last year's sales were poor in the beginning of the year and were strong by the end of the year, then this technique would predict fewer sales than you would get.

This forecasting method also ignores information about the coming year. Changes to your product, changes to competitors' products, or new product offerings could all significantly influence sales and yet are ignored by this method.

Market Share Estimate
In the Basic Forecasting section, the Team Member Guide instructs you to use the "Potential Market Share" if your product stocked out (didn't product enough to meet the demand). After

thinking about it for a minute, you realize that you should use the market share estimates **whenever** there is a difference between your potential and actual market share.

The logic behind the calculation is simple. Both market segments will be bigger next year, so grow the reported demand (last year's) and get DEMAND (next year's demand). If you did get (or would have gotten) 18% of last year's market, then it is reasonable that you would get 18% of next year's market. To try this forecast, use the information for product Able from FastTrack pages 5 and 6 - Market Segment Analysis and page 7 - Market Share Report..

For forecasting sales to the Low Tech market use information from FastTrack page 5:
- Calculate DEMAND for Low Tech products next year (last year's demand *1.1).
- Enter it into both tables
- Enter Able's "Actual share" (from chart or use page 7) in the Actual table (top one)
- Multiply "Actual Share" by DEMAND to get the "Actual estimate" enter it into the Actual Market Share Table
- Enter Able's "Potential share" (from chart or use page 7) in the Potential table (bottom one)
- Multiply "Potential Share" by DEMAND to get the "potential estimate"
- Enter it into the Potential Market Share Table

A forecast for High Tech market sales will use information from FastTrack page 6:
- Calculate DEMAND for High Tech products next year(last year's demand *1.2).
- Enter it into both tables
- Enter Able's "Actual share" (from chart or use page 7) in the Actual table (top one)
- Multiply "Actual Market Share" by DEMAND- to get the "actual share estimate" enter it into the Actual Market Share Table
- Enter Able's "Potential share" (from chart or use page 7) in the Potential table (bottom one)
- Multiply "Potential Market Share" by DEMAND to get the "potential share estimate"
- Enter it into the Potential Market Share Table

Add the two Actual Market Share estimates

ACTUAL	DEMAND	"Actual" Share	"Actual" Estimate
Low tech			
High tech			
Total			

POTENTIAL	DEMAND	"Potential" Share	"Potential" Estimate
Low tech			
High tech			
Total			

The Actual Market Share estimate and the Basic Forecasting (Market Growth) estimate would be very close because they do exactly the same thing; take what was sold last year and "grow" it at the same rate as the market grows. If you use either for a product that stocked out, you will most likely underestimate sales for the coming year.

The "Potential Market Share" is what you would have sold if every customer had gotten their first choice. If you underestimated sales last year and didn't produce enough- you stocked out. In that case, your POTENTIAL market share should be greater than your ACTUAL market share. In that situation (Potential > Actual) then you should always forecast sales using your potential market share.

What if your ACTUAL market share was greater than your POTENTIAL market share? In that case, customers would have tried to buy their sensors from a competitor but not been able to (because the competitor stocked out). You were their second choice (or third, or forth). How do you forecast sales then? Your Actual Market Share estimate (and Market Growth estimate) would <u>overestimate</u> your sales for the coming year—unless your competitor still doesn't produce enough products to meet demand in the coming year. In this case, you have to determine whether your competitor will improve their decision making or not.

If the "Actual" and "Potential" market share are exactly equal, this method offers no advantage over the Market Growth method (and would produce the same forecast). However, if "Actual" and "Potential" shares are different, this method incorporates information about customers' preferences that were satisfied—or not satisfied—because of last year's production levels. In some situations, this is a huge improvement. Market share estimates do <u>not</u> take into account changes that will happen in the coming year; changes that you make to your product, changes that your competitors make to theirs, and new products that will be introduced into the market.

Qualitative Assessments
You already have a very comprehensive model of how customers make their purchase decisions. Every month, customers identify the products that meet their minimum expectations (which your market research staff calls the "rough cut"). They then evaluate those products against their buying criteria (the fine cut). They make adjustments to their evaluation based on credit terms (Accounts Receivable which we will address in a future chapter), Awareness, Accessibility, and if any characteristic is outside the fine cut.

Sales levels are directly and closely correlated with how well your product is rated *relative* to how all of the other products are rated. This evaluation is captured in the monthly Customer Survey Score (CSS).

The FastTrack Reports December's CSS (DCSS) for each product at the end of each year. You can use this information to forecast sales for the coming year. The logic of the calculation is simple. Your market share (percentage of the market that will buy from you) is your CSS as a percentage of the total CSS of all products in the market.

From the "Top Products in Segment" tables on pages 5 and 7 of the Fast Track report:

- Enter Able's DCSS in the table below.
- From those same tables, add the DCSS for all of the products and enter it in the table.
- Divide Able's DCSS by the Total DCSS and enter it. This is your projected market share.
- From the "Statistics" table on pages 5 and 6, take last year's "Total Industry Unit Demand" and increase it by the "Growth Rate" (1.1 for Low Tech, 1.2 for High Tech)
- Enter these figures as DEMAND.
- Multiply DEMAND by your market share (percentage) and that is your estimate for your sales in each segment.
- Add the estimates together and that is your estimate for Able's total sales.

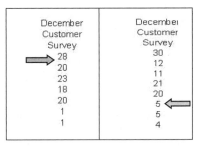

	Able's DCSS	Total DCSS	Percentage (Able/Total DCSS)	DEMAND	Estimate
Low Tech					
High Tech					
Total					

Unlike the basic forecasting methods, this method incorporates all of the changes to all of the products that occurred in the past year. It forecasts based on relative product attractiveness as of the moment you are making your decisions (December 31st for the coming year). It does not, however, take into account changes in product offerings that will happen in the coming year.

To do that, you would have to do a month-by-month estimate of the CSS for all products in each segment and use that to forecast sales.

All of the forecasts you have made are based on past information; what has already happened. However, you are forecasting the future; what has yet to happen. You know that your competitors are going through the same process that you are. They are following a strategy to entice customers to do business with them, and not you. They are seeking to capture resources and harness them so that they can compete more effectively. You have to adjust your forecast of the future to incorporate what you think will happen. This involves incorporating your improvements and your predictions of how your competitors will improve in the coming year(s).

Month to Month Customer Survey Score Forecasting

Assume AceX had a DCSS of 25. It started the year with an age of .9 and a position that lags the ideal spot. It's MTBF is 23,000, its price is $45.00, its awareness is 82% and its accessibility is 60%. Because AceX is a High Tech product, you know you will reposition it to the ideal spot every year. You will cut the price to $42.00 and plan on investing enough to get your Awareness to 100% and Accessibility to 75%. The price cut and the increase in Awareness and Accessibility give you a bump in your January CSS. At the same time AceX's age is increasing, its position is moving farther away from the ideal spot every month. This results in a net gain of about 3 points. But that gain erodes from there until the Revision Date in July. In July, being on the ideal spot and reducing the age from 1.4 to .7 gives a big seven point bump to the score. AceX immediately begins to age and the ideal spot moves away; slowly eroding the score.

An Introduction to Business

⇩

	Jan	Feb	Mar	Apr	May	June	**July**	Aug	Sept	Oct	Nov	Dec
Able	28	27	27	26	25	24	**31**	30	30	29	29	28

Even though there is a lot of movement in the score month to month, Able starts the year with a CSS of 28, it ends the year at 28, and the average score is a 28. This may not always be the case.

It is also important to remember that the "value" of a CSS of 28 changes depending on competitor's offerings. You construct a scenario in which AceX is one of 4 products competing in the High Tech market, but Ferris introduces two new and very attractive High Tech products on August 1st.

The CSS and AceX's market share are modeled in the table below.

	Jan	Feb	Mar	Apr	May	June	July	Aug	Sept	Oct	Nov	Dec
AceX	28	27	27	26	25	24	31	30	30	29	29	28
Fast	32	32	31	30	34	34	33	36	36	35	35	34
Daze	22	22	21	21	20	19	19	25	25	24	24	23
Dabble	23	23	22	22	21	21	20	20	19	18	23	23
Fabulou								41	41	40	40	39
Furious								41	41	40	40	39
Total	105	104	101	99	100	98	103	193	193	186	191	186
AceX	27%	26%	27%	26%	25%	24%	30%	16%	16%	16%	15%	15%

Notice that in the first 5 months, AceX's market share fluctuates. In July, AceX has a big jump in share because it has an earlier revision date than the competing products. However, the real news this year is that the market is completely transformed in August when two new products enter the competition for sales. In July, Ferris had one product and 32% of the market. By December, Ferris has 3 products and 60% of the market. In that same period, your company Andrews lost half of your sales, even though your product improved!

Something about this doesn't seem right. For example, if Apple introduced a new phone—the *aPhone* that was exactly like the *iPhone*—customers wouldn't be fooled. You call your marketing manager and she confirms your original analysis. Within some wide boundaries, electronic sensors are commodity products. You will sell more in any segment if you have two products than if you have one. In fact, she tells you, you can expect all competitors to aggressively introduce new products and this strategy will erode Andrews' market share unless you are an aggressive innovator also.

Forecasting With Incomplete Information
In this process, you notice how difficult it is to forecast sales for a new product. AceX will be introduced in the middle of December and that just isn't enough time in the market to do anything. So, to help build your understanding, you invent a different fictional product introduction - Ablest - that will be introduced on July 1st. Forecasting will be difficult for the first year because you do not have any information about its past performance. In the second year, forecasting will become somewhat easier but you will forecast for a whole year based on a half year's performance. You decide to think about them one at a time.

New Product Forecasting

Company Andrews has a new High Tech product called "Ablest" that will be introduced to the market on July 1, 2011. Ablest's size and performance are on the ideal spot for Round 3 (you should be able to determine what that is) and the MTBF is set at 23,000. On July 1st, it is 0 years old. At the end of the year, it will be .5 years old. How many units do you think it will sell?

The best information that you have is last year's FastTrack Report. Here you will see that the product "Fast" is the most attractive product in the High Tech market. Ablest will be younger, more reliable, and better positioned than Fast. (Even if Fast is revised, Ablest will still be better because of its young age.) To forecast sales for Ablest, the best information you have available is the information about Fast.

There are some adjustments that you will need to make. First, at the end of the year, Fast was outside the rough cut circle for the Low Tech market. It sold 408 units to Low Tech customers and in round 2, Fast was repositioned. (It had a revision date October 10, 2010.) Best guess: Fast sold those 408 units BEFORE it was repositioned. You should probably NOT use Fast's Low Tech sales in forecasting Ablest's sales. Calculate a forecast using Fast's Actual Market Share:

	DEMAND	"Actual" Share	"Actual" Estimate
High Tech			

There is another important adjustment. Foundation's sales are awarded on a month by month basis. The actual Market Share estimate that you just calculated is based on Fast being available for sale for a full 12 months. Ablest is only available for 6 months. You will have to adjust your forecast to accommodate the number of months that Ablest is available. In this case, you have to cut the forecast in half.

To help visualize, a simple example is provided. Assume your forecast is that Fast would sell 1,200 in 12 months. That is 100 units a month.

Jan	Feb	March	April	May	June	July	Aug	Sept	Oct	Nov	Dec
100	100	100	100	100	100	100	100	100	100	100	100

Assuming this is an accurate forecast for Ablest, sales would also be 100 units a month—but only from July1 through December 31. Ablest's total sales would be 600 units.

Jan	Feb	March	April	May	June	July	Aug	Sept	Oct	Nov	Dec
						100	100	100	100	100	100

Another Adjustment Based on Time Available

Then you move on to the NEXT year which is 2011. (Round 3 FastTrack and Round 4 decisions) You assume that the forecast was fairly accurate and Ablest sold 600 units. The demand in the High Tech Market for 2011 (Round 3) was 3,732 units. Selling 600 units gives Ablest an Actual Market Share of 16%. (Assume its potential market share was also 16%). Ablest's December Customer Survey is 39.

Fast sold more products, had a higher market share, but its December Customer Survey is now 27. What is going on? How do I forecast Ablest's sales for the next round (Round 4)? Ablest sold 600 units in 6 months. It is reasonable to assume that in 12 months, Ablest could have sold 1,200 units. If being available for sale for 6 months gave them a 16% market share, it is reasonable to assume that had they been available for 12 months, they would have gotten a 32% market share. Ablest's information—adjusted FROM the time it was available TO the time it will be available—is the best information to use in forecasting future performance.

Worst Case / Best Case and the Proformas

The model of your company (in the Foundation Spreadsheet) allows you to enter your decisions in all of the functional areas: R&D, Marketing, Production, and Finance. When you enter your decisions, the model adjusts the information it is providing to give you the "best guess" of the outcomes of your decisions. You only make one entry—Your Sales Forecast—that is not a decision, it is merely a guess.

From Foundation Spreadsheet - Marketing Decisions

NAME	Price	Promo Budget	Sales Budget	Computer Prediction	Your Sales Forecast	Gross Revenue Forecast	Variable Costs	Contrib. Margin Forecast	Less Promo & Sales
Able	$35.00	$2,000	$2,000	1,654	1,630	$57,050	$34,814	$22,236	$18,236
Acex	$0.0	$0	$0	0	-	$0	$0	$0	$0
Na	$0.0	$0	$0	0	-	$0	$0	$0	$0

The Foundation Spreadsheet uses the number in the "Your Sales Forecast" cell to determine **projected** outcomes and generate the proforma statements. In the coming exercises, you will use sales forecasts to make a variety of decisions; including how many to have available for sale. The number of units available defines a range of acceptable sales levels to meet your inventory management goals).

Enter the bottom of that sales forecast range (your worst case) before you make your financing decisions. Now enter the top of that range (your best case) to make your production decisions.

After you have entered your sales forecast into the Foundation Spreadsheet, click on "calculate" and that will show you how successful you will be in the market *if you could sell that number of products*.

Build Your Understanding
Foundation Exercise 4 Questions
Be able to answer these types of questions in these areas

General Forecasting

1. What information is available to help you forecast sales in Foundation?

2. What are sales forecasts used for? What benefit do they offer in decision making?

Forecasting Techniques: General

For each of the three forecasting methods, Market Growth, Market Share, and Customer Survey Score, you should know how to calculate the forecast and the limitations of the "guess."

3. If you sold 1,250 units in the Low Tech market segment last year, how many would you expect to sell next year if your sales grew exactly as much as the market segment? (market growth forecasting)

4. Fast's "Actual" is greater than its "Potential" market share. What is the danger of using the actual market share in forecasting next year's sales?

5. AceX was introduced to the market October 1st of this year. In 3 months, it captured 8% of the market share. Assuming that there are no radical changes in the market, what market share would you expect AceX to have in the coming year?

Forecasting Techniques: Using FastTrack Report information

You should know how to locate the necessary information in the FastTrack Report, calculate the sales forecast, and understand the limitations of the "guesses" for each of the three forecasting methods; Market Growth, Market Share, and Customer Survey Score.

6. Using the information provided and the "market growth" method, what is Cake's sales forecast for the coming year?

7. Using the information provided, how many units would Baker sell next year if each customer got his or her first choice in sensors?

8. According to the information provided, Able stocked out last year. How many could they potentially have sold?

9. Using the Low Tech customers' most current evaluation of Daze's "attractiveness," what would you expect Daze to sell next year in that segment?

10. You have a new product, called Abler, coming into the High Tech Market on April 1st. It will have almost the same characteristics as Ferris' product "Furious". Using the DCSS forecast, what would you expect Abler's sales to be next year?

An Introduction to Business

Chapter 3

Accounting:
A Business Information System

Accounting tracks, summarizes, and reports business operations in a way that assists with performance assessment and allows for better decision making.

Key terms to look for:

- Assets
- Balance sheet
- Cash flow
- Contribution margin
- Dividend
- GAAP
- Gross margin
- Income statement
- Liabilities
- Liquidity
- Net income
- Owners' Equity
- Retained earnings

A company has a responsibility to its stakeholders—a diverse group of people with different needs from the company. This group includes the:

- Owners
- Employees
- Customers
- Citizens (and the government that represents their interests)
- Creditors and financial institutions

These groups use accounting information to determine the degree to which the company is meeting its responsibilities. Accounting helps managers monitor the operations of the business and report their financial conditions to those inside and outside of the business. Managers can assess the performance of production, marketing, and finance decisions, and they may rely on accounting information to detect inefficient use of resources. Optimizing the use of resources—time, materials, and money—may result in greater efficiency and therefore generate greater earnings.

The accounting system of a business generates information about the economic consequences of a company's activities. It is the historical summary and analysis of an organization's financial condition. These activities are identified, measured, recorded, and retained, and then communicated in a set of accounting reports, or statements. Management accounting provides vital information about a company to internal users; financial accounting gives information about a company to external users.

Management Accounting

Management accounting helps managers plan, operate, and control a company's activities. The information provided through management accounting gives people working for a company vital business information. Managers need this information to help them compete in a world market in which technology and methods of production are constantly changing. Accounting is one of the critical tools of information management.

The management accounting system provides information for managers inside the company. It is free from the restrictions of outside regulation and can be expressed in the form that is most useful for managers. Information can be reported in dollars, units, hours worked, products manufactured, numbers of defective products, or the quantity of contracts signed. Management accounting has to produce information that is relevant to specific segments of the company, products, tasks, plants, or activities. The sole objective of management accounting is to provide information that enables managers to make more informed and effective decisions.

Financial Accounting

Financial reports provide a source of information about the company's performance. Financial accounting involves the identification, measurement, recording, accumulation, and communication of economic information about a company for external users to apply to their decisions. External users are people and groups outside the company who need accounting information to decide whether or not to engage in some activity with the company. These users include individual investors; stockbrokers and financial analysts who offer investment assistance; consultants; bankers; suppliers; labor unions; customers; local, state, and federal governments; and governments of foreign countries in which the company does business.

Generally Accepted Accounting Principles

Over the years, a set of broad guidelines for financial accounting has evolved within the United States called the "generally accepted accounting principles," or GAAP. For financial reports to be useful, companies must follow specific rules delineated by the GAAP. These principles have been developed to ensure that information reported is relevant, reliable, material, and valid.

The generally accepted accounting principles are the currently recognized guidelines, procedures, and practices that are used for financial accounting in the United States. These principles must be followed in the external reports of all companies that sell stock to the public and by many other companies as well. The GAAP cover such issues as how to account for inventory, buildings, income taxes, and capital stock; how to measure the results of a company's operations; and how to account for the operations of companies in specialized industries, such as banking, entertainment, and insurance industries. Many GAAP pronouncements are complex and technical in nature, and these principles do change. They are modified as business practices and decisions change as the Internal Revenue Service (IRS) makes new rulings and as better accounting techniques are developed.

Without these agreed-upon principles, external users of accounting information would not be able to understand the meaning of this information. Accounting is the language of business decision making and you can think of the GAAP as the agreed-upon rules of "spelling and grammar" for business communication. These rules provide a consistent basis for understanding and communicating about the financial aspects of business activities.

Management Activities

To help ensure the success of the company, managers use accounting information as they plan, operate, and control the activities of their business. These three processes are explained below.

Planning

Management begins with planning. Planning establishes the company's goals and the means of achieving these goals. Managers use the planning process to identify what resources, such as technological, human, and material, that the company needs to achieve its goals. They use the planning process to set standards, or "benchmarks," against which they later can measure the company's progress toward its goals. By periodically measuring the company's progress against those standards, managers identify when and how the company needs to make adjustments. Because the business environment changes so rapidly, planning is an ongoing process and must be flexible enough to deal with change.

To be effective in the planning process, managers have to consider the characteristics of the environment external to the organization. This includes the economic system, the political climate, the relative health of the monetary system, and the strength of the markets in which they operate. Managers must also create and communicate these plans in the social context of the organization. A plan is good only if everyone believes in it. Accounting information plays an important role in capturing what has taken place in the past as a basis on which to create a compelling and measurable view of the company's future.

Operating

Operating refers to the set of activities that enable the company to conduct its business according to its plan. A company's operating activities ensure that products or services get made and sold as planned and on schedule. This involves gathering the resources and employees necessary to achieve the goals of the company, establishing organizational relationships among departments and employees, and working toward achieving the goals of the company.

In the process of operating a company, managers and work teams must make day-to-day decisions about how best to achieve these goals. Accounting information gives them valuable data about a product's performance. With this information, they can decide which products to continue to sell and when to add new products or drop old ones. If the company is a manufacturing company, managers and work teams can decide what products to produce and whether there is a better way to produce them. Accounting information enables managers to also make decisions about how to establish product prices, whether to advertise and how much to spend on advertising, and whether to buy new equipment or expand facilities. These decisions are ongoing. The results and outcomes of these decisions are reviewed, and that information is used to make the next set of decisions.

Controlling

Controlling is the management activity that measures actual operations against standards or benchmarks. It provides feedback for managers to correct deviations from those standards, and to plan for the company's future operations. Controlling is a continuous process that attempts to prevent, detect, and correct problems as quickly as possible. Planning, operating, and controlling all require information. The company's accounting system provides much of the quantitative information that managers use.

Accounting Support for Management Activities

Management accounting involves the identification, measurement, recording, accumulation, and communication of economic information about a company for internal users in management decision making. Internal users include individual employees, work groups or teams, departmental supervisors, divisional and regional managers, and "top management." With the help of the management accountant, these internal users use this information to help them make more effective decisions.

The reports that result from management accounting may forecast revenues, predict costs of planned activities, and provide a business analysis based on these forecasts. By describing how alternative actions might affect the company's profit and solvency, these forecasts and analyses help managers plan.

Managers use accounting information to make day-to-day decisions about what activities will best achieve the company's goals. Management accounting helps managers make these decisions by providing timely economic information about how each activity might affect the organization. Accounting information also plays a vital role in helping managers control the operations of the company. Managers use revenue and cost estimates generated during the planning and decision-making process as benchmarks and then evaluate the company's actual revenues and costs against said benchmarks.

The deviation between the forecasted and actual numbers has to be explained. Either the forecasting process has to be improved or operational decisions need to be adjusted.

Management accountants provide information designed to meet the specific information needs of the manager. This involves selecting the appropriate information to be reported, presenting that information in an understandable format, interpreting the information when necessary, and providing the information when it is needed for the decisions that are being made.

Management accounting also varies widely from company to company and its responsibilities and activities continually evolve in response to the need for new information brought about by the changing business environment. In response to that environment, the Institute of Management Accountants (IMA) publishes guidelines for management accounting called Statements on Management Accounting, or SMAs. SMAs are nonbinding (they are not rules that must be followed), but management accountants turn to SMAs for help when faced with new situations.

In order to see how a company's accounting information helps managers in their planning, operating, and evaluating activities, consider the following three key management accounting reports that relate to budgets, cost analyses, and manufacturing costs.

1. **Budgets**

   Budgeting is the process of quantifying managers' plans and showing the impact of these plans on the company's operating activities. Managers present this information in a budget (forecast). Once the planned activities have occurred, managers can evaluate the results of the operating activities against the budget to make sure that the actual operations of the various parts of the company achieved the goals established in the plans. For example, a company might report a budget showing how many units of product it plans to sell during the first three months of the year. When actual sales have been made, managers will compare the results of these sales with the budget to determine if their forecasts were "on target" and, if not, to find out why differences occurred. Budgets are powerful planning and control devices.

2. **Cost Analysis**

   Cost analysis is the process of defining the costs of specific products or activities within a company. A manager will use a cost analysis to decide whether to stop or continue making a specific product. The cost analysis would show that product's contribution to profitability at different levels of sales. Assigning (or defining) costs to products and activities is a complex activity. Every decision maker in the company has to be familiar with the way relevant costs are assigned in order to make appropriate decisions. Consistency in this reporting process is critical to ensure this information is accurate and has meaning.

3. **Manufacturing Cost Reports**

   As we mentioned above, managers must monitor and evaluate a company's operations to determine whether its planned goals are being achieved. Accounting information can highlight specific "variances," or differences, from plans, indicating where corrections to operations can be made if necessary. A manufacturing cost report might show that total actual costs for a given month were greater than total budgeted costs; however, it might also show that some actual costs were greater while others were less than budgeted costs. The more detailed the information, the more useful it will be managers as they analyze why these differences occurred.

Internal and External Uses of Accounting Information

Both internal and external users need accounting information to make decisions about a company. Since external users want to see the reported results of management activities, these activities are discussed next, followed by how accounting information supports management activities and external decision making.

Presenting Accounting Information

Accounting information prepared for the external user may differ from that prepared for the internal user. Accounting information that helps external users with decisions such as whether or not to extend a bank loan to a company may be presented differently from the information a manager within the company needs. For instance, if a bank is deciding whether to make a loan, it will consider the likelihood that a company will repay the loan. Since this likelihood may depend on current and future sales of its products, the bank may want to evaluate the sales budget that managers developed as part of the planning process.

Many external users evaluate the accounting information of more than one company and need comparable information from each company. For example, a bank looks at accounting information from all of its customers who apply for loans, and it must use comparable information in order to decide to which customers to make loans. This need for comparability creates a need for guidelines or rules for companies to follow when preparing accounting information for external users. In addition, some external users may have a legitimate need for information generated for internal decision makers also.

Basic Financial Statements

Profit, commonly referred to as net income, is the difference between all the cash and credit sales of a company and its total costs, or expenses. Solvency is a company's long-term ability to pay its debts as they come due. As you will see, external users analyze the financial statements of a company to determine how well the company is achieving its two primary objectives.

Financial statements are accounting reports used to summarize and communicate financial information about a company. Financial statements are commonly recognized communication tools that enable people to assess the financial state of an organization.

A company's accounting system produces three major financial statements:

1. Balance sheet

2. Income statement

3. Cash flow statement

Each of these statements summarizes specific information that has been identified, measured, recorded, and retained during the accounting process.

Balance Sheet

A company's balance sheet summarizes its financial position on a given date. A balance sheet lists the company's assets, liabilities, and owner's equity. It is much like a snapshot or where the company's wealth is at a given point in time. The balance sheet is also called a statement of financial position.

Assets

The economic resources that a company owns and that it expects will provide future benefits to the company. Anything <u>owned</u> or under the direct control of a company is an asset.

Liabilities

The company's economic obligations (debts) to its creditors, including people outside the company, such as banks and suppliers, as well as the employees within the company. Anything that is *owed* by a firm is a liability.

Owners' Equity

The owners' current investment in the assets of the company includes the owner's original contribution to the company and any earnings (net income) that the owner leaves in the company. Owners' equity is also called stockholders' equity.

A balance sheet is arranged into accounts. The value of the asset accounts will always equal the value of the liabilities and owners' equity accounts. This defines the basic accounting equation and is expressed as:

Assets = Liabilities + Owners' Equity

The following page describes the key components of a balance sheet in the standardized sequence.

Balance Sheet – *Order and Definition of Terms*

Balance Sheet	
Assets	This includes the "stuff" or economic resources that the company has use of and from which it can expect to derive future economic benefit.
Current Assets	Assets that can (will be) converted to cash within the year
Cash	Currency readily available to the business.
Accounts receivable	The amount your customers owe because they purchased from you on credit.
Inventory	The value of the products (merchandise) that have been acquired for sale to customers and are still on hand.
Total current assets	These are the assets used to operate your business—an important part of working capital.
Fixed Assets	Assets that have a long-term use or value, including land, building, and equipment.
Property, plant and equipment	The purchase price that you paid for the land, buildings, and equipment that you use to create your products or services.
Accumulated depreciation	How much of the value of your plant and equipment you have used up while operating your business over time.
Total fixed assets	The net value of your property, plant, and equipment.
Total Assets	The value of all of the assets (stuff) of your business.
Liabilities and Owners' Equity	Where the money came from to get the assets. It accounts for who has claims against the assets of the company.
Liabilities	These are "loans," or debt contracts.
Current Liabilities	The loans that have to be paid back within a year.
Accounts Payable	The amount that you owe your suppliers for materials (inventory) that you purchased on credit.
Current debt	The loans (part of a long-term loan) to be paid back this year.
Total current liabilities	The debt that you have to pay back within one year.
Long-term liabilities	The loans (or debt contracts) that have to be paid back at some point in the future (in more than a year's time).
Total liabilities	The amount of other people's wealth you are renting the use of, as if you were using their money on contract.
Owners' Equity	The value of the owners' investments in the company.
Common Stock (paid-in capital)	The value of what the owners "paid in" as a direct investment in the company. (in a corporation, the sale of stock)
Retained earnings	The portion of owners' profits that they choose to reinvest in the company.
Total owners' equity	This is the owners' claim against the assets of the business—or the value of owning the business.
Total Liabilities and Owners' Equity	This will always equal Total Assets—as liabilities and owners' equity account for where the money came from to acquire the assets.

The "Snapshot"

The balance sheet describes an economic picture of a company at one point in time. This snapshot statement describes the "structure" and current financial condition of the company at a specific point in time. The balance sheet presents a picture of a company and allows you to:

- Compare pictures of two different companies at one point in time and describe the difference, and;

- Compare pictures of the same company at different points in time and describe how it has changed.

Assets are the "stuff" you can use in a business. Your best business investment is to put your assets to work and keep them working. Assets include money, buildings, vehicles, equipment, and anything the business owns that has value. A related concept to assets is liquidity.

Liquidity

Liquidity refers to the ease with which an asset can be turned into something else, or which assets are the most liquid. Cash, for example, can be turned into inventory easily, while it is hard to turn a building into a fleet of trucks, so these are considered less liquid.

Business language uses the word "current" to mean "within one year."

Current Assets

Assets that can be easily converted to cash are called current assets or liquid assets. They include such things as cash, accounts receivable, and inventory.

Cash

There are several issues regarding cash management:

- With too little cash on hand, the business cannot pay your bills without selling something or taking out more loans.

- Too much cash on hand means that your assets are not working for the business as well as they might.

Accounts receivable

You have made sales, but instead of being paid in cash, you extend credit. It is like accepting an "IOU." The issues involved with allowing someone to pay you after they have received the product or services include:

- How long does it take to collect the amount owed? (This is the receivables period.)

- How much do you lose on customers who do not pay their bills?

- More accounts receivable this year than last indicates either that there is a more liberal credit policy or there are more sales.

- The greater the accounts receivable, the less cash there is on hand.

Inventory

The tangible quantity of goods and materials on hand is referred to as inventory. Inventory, in whatever form, is generally categorized into three areas:

Raw materials inventory: When you purchase materials or component parts to create the product you make, those are raw materials inventory. For example, a candle factory purchases wax and wicks as raw materials.

Work-in-process inventory: When you are in the middle of producing or assembling a product for sale at any point in time, materials and labor committed to creating that product are referred to as "work-in-process" inventory.

Finished goods inventory: These are the finished products you have on hand, ready for sale.

Inventory Issues

Managing the appropriate level, or range, of inventory is difficult.

- When there is **too much inventory** that you are unable to sell, particularly if those goods could become obsolete, significant amounts of cash are tied up in products that may not sell for full price. If the products are not desirable, you may have to sell them at a discounted price or keep them around for a long time. This is expensive because it ties up cash. As a result, you may lose money, and you may eventually run out of cash.

- When there is **too little inventory,** such as in a situation where you are out of inventory, customers want your product but are unable to access it. They may forgo the purchase or, even worse, buy it from one of your competitors.

Fixed Assets

Fixed assets are things the firm owns that they will use for more than one year. They may include equipment, buildings, and vehicles. The value of the company's property, plant (factories, offices, etc.), and equipment is the investment the company has made in itself. It is the "capacity" of the company to create products or services. It is listed at its purchase price. The fact that they are "fixed" assets suggests that they do not have much liquidity; that is, they may take a while, more than one year, to sell these assets and turn them into cash.

Accumulated Depreciation

Fixed assets have a limited life. Trucks need to be replaced, buildings need repair, and equipment wears out. Depreciation is the process of recognizing that as you use your building and equipment to create products or services, the value of your fixed assets decreases. These assets are being used up or consumed. Accumulated depreciation is the total amount of value that has been used up since the initial purchase of the building and equipment.

Total Fixed Assets

Subtracting accumulated depreciation from fixed assets are the total fixed assets. This is sometimes listed as **property, plant, and equipment**. Total fixed assets are the current "accounting" value of your property, plant, and equipment. It represents the purchase price minus how much of it you have used up over time. This is *not* necessarily the same as the "market value" of your plant and equipment, which is the amount you would receive if you were to sell it right then. Companies with large accumulated depreciation have aging (old, out-of-date, or used-up) facilities. These fixed assets are worth much less than those that have been recently acquired.

Total Assets

At a given point in time, total assets are the value of all of the "stuff" you own in your business. It includes both the facilities and the operations at that time. Looking at total assets is a common way of assessing how "big" or what "size" a company is.

Liabilities and Owners' Equity

The money to invest in your company's assets and activities has to come from somewhere. In fact, it can come from only two sources; an investment from the owners' investments (owners' equity) or loans (liabilities). Providing money to fund the assets of a company also gives the "providers" a claim against those assets. Owners' claims and debt claims are quite different from one another and companies develop financing strategies to manage these. Financing strategies are plans using debt or owners' investments to operate and grow the company. These strategies consider the differences between the owners' claims and debt claims, the goals of the company, and the nature of the industry in which they are competing.

Liabilities

Liabilities are a form of a "debt contract." You have a contract that allows you to use someone else's wealth in exchange for some "consideration." For most debts, the consideration is an interest payment. This is the "rent" you pay to use someone else's money. A debt contract is for a specific period of time (length of the loan) and you have to return the wealth, or pay back the loan, at the end of the period. Borrowing money increases the amount of cash you have on hand but does not increase your profitability. Paying back your loans decreases the amount of cash on hand, but does not decrease your profitability.

Current Liabilities

Current liabilities are debts that you have to pay back within the year. Along with current assets, they account for the money it takes for you to operate your business for a given time. Together, current assets and current liabilities are called working capital.

Accounts Payable

Any good supplier wants you to buy from them, not from someone else. To make it easier and more attractive to buy, the supplier may offer you the use of their products or materials without payment for a certain number of days. The balance in this account is the amount that you owe to your suppliers for the materials (inventory) that you purchased on credit and have not yet paid for. This is referred to as buying on terms, and those terms specify the number of days that you have access to these products before having to pay for them. The phrase "net 30" for example, means that you do not have to pay for the products until 30 days after the day you received them. It is attractive for businesses to pay their bills as late as possible, without incurring expensive interest charges, so they can optimize their use of available cash.

Current Debt or Current Liabilities

The balance in this account is the amount of debt. This includes short-term loans, which are due in a year, or the current part of a long-term loan that needs to be paid back this year.

Total Current Liabilities

Current liabilities are the debts that you have to pay back this year. In general, it is extremely important that you have enough cash (or combination of cash and other current assets) to be able to meet your debt (contractual obligations) for the coming year.

Long-Term Liabilities

Loans, or debt contracts that you have longer than one year to pay back are referred to as long-term liabilities. These may include the more than one year part of *long-term bank loans* or *bonds*, which are loans that you take directly from the market.

Total Liabilities

This accounts for how much of other people's wealth you are using, or renting, on contract. This number represents the total amount of the company's debt. If you divide this number by total assets (or total liabilities and owners' equity) it will tell you what percentage of the assets was funded by debt. This is referred to as the "debt-to-assets ratio" and can be a valuable measurement tool for determining how your total debt compares to your total assets.

Owners' Equity

Owners' Equity is a measure of the value of the owners' investments in the company. Generally, accounting systems keep track of how much the owners pay in (out of their own pockets) and how much of the wealth created in the owners' name, or profits the company creates, is reinvested in the company. Therefore, Owners' Equity is the owners' claim against the assets of the business or the value of owning the business itself. Owners' Equity answers the question: After all debts are paid, how much of the assets do the owners actually own?

Common Stock or Paid-in Capital

Common Stock, also referred to as Paid-in Capital, is the owners' investment in the company through the purchasing some portion of the company. In a corporation, this is the money the business receives from the sale of stock. To increase the balance in this account, you have to sell more stock.

Preferred Stock

Preferred stock is a type of stock with a higher claim on the assets and earnings than common stock. Preferred stock generally has a dividend that must be paid out before dividends to common stockholders and the shares usually do not have voting rights.

Retained Earnings

The amount that owners reinvest in the company is called retained earnings. When a company makes a profit, it belongs to the owners of the company. Profits can be given to the owners to use in whatever way they want. An owner can decide to do one of two things with profits.

1. They can be reinvested back into the company, which is called **retained earnings.**

2. They can make a payment out of profits, which is called a **dividend.**

The balance in the retained earnings account is the value of the profits the owners choose to reinvest in the company. The balance in this account and all of the dividends ever paid will equal all of the profits made by the company. In both cases, if profits are kept as retained earnings or shared with owners as dividends, the money comes from profits the business made.

Book Value

The *book value* of an asset is the value of that asset on the balance sheet or the "books" of the company. In a corporation, if you divide the Owners' Equity by the total number of outstanding shares, it calculates the book value. This gives you the value of the claim that each share has against the assets of the company.

Book Value = Owners Equity / Number of Shares Outstanding

The book value is not necessarily the same as the actual fair market value, which is the amount the asset could be sold for on the open market. At some point, the book value may only represent salvage or scrap value, after all the depreciation has been taken. At that point, the asset is considered to be "off the books." That does not mean the asset does not have value to the company, it just means that the asset has no value (or only scrap/salvage value) on the balance sheet. If the asset is still "functional," the company may continue to use it.

Total Liabilities and Owners' Equity

This is the value of all of the loans and investments that have been made in the company. Because it describes where the money came from to fund the assets and it describes the claims against the assets of the company, it will *always equal* the value of the total assets of the company.

Two of the accounts are so important that they require additional explanation. The income statement explains the activity in the retained earnings account. This is an owners' equity account that records revenues and expenses. The cash flow statement explains activity in the cash account, or in an asset account.

Income Statement

A company's income statement summarizes the results of its operating activities for a specific time period—often one year—and shows the company's profit for that period. It shows a company's revenues, expenses, and net income (or net loss) for that time period. The income statement tracks revenues and expenses.

Revenues are the total of the prices charged to a company's customers for the goods or services the company provides to them.

Expenses are the costs of providing the goods or services.

Net Income is the excess of revenues over expenses, or the company's profit; a net loss arises when expenses are greater than revenues.

These amounts include the costs of the products the company has sold (either the cost of making or purchasing these products), the costs of conducting business (called operating expenses), and the costs of income taxes, if any. The result impacts net income as profit or as loss.

The income statement is a description of the activity in transactions that affect the retained earnings account. These activities are the operating transactions that define the owners' change in wealth. The income statement tells a story about the activity of a company over a period of time. It describes the sales and all of the expenses and defines how much profit was created. Because it is a story of activity, these numbers can be used to measure how well you are doing and to assess the "goodness" of your decisions in the market.

The following page describes the key components of an income statement.

Income Statement - *Order and Definition of Terms*

Income Statement		
Revenue		Funds that come into the company from the sale of goods or services. These can be sales that are in cash or on-account.
Variable Costs		Costs that vary with the level of activity—the more products you make, the greater the total cost.
	Material costs	The cost of the materials (raw material and component parts) that are used in the products you sold.
	Labor costs	The cost of the labor (human resources) used to produce the products sold.
	Inventory carrying costs	The costs (warehousing, insurance, etc.) of having inventory available for sale but not yet sold.
	Total Variable Costs Cost of Goods Sold (COGS)	This is the cost of making the products sold.
Contribution Margin		The difference between the revenue brought in by sales and the cost of making the products for sale. This difference is what is left over to operate your business and as profit.
Period Costs		Those costs that are fixed over a period of time. These do not vary with the level of activity.
	Depreciation	This figure recognizes the amount of value that operating a business "uses up" in the plant (factory) and equipment.
	Research and Development (R& D)	The investment the company makes in developing new products or improving existing ones.
	Marketing expense	The investment the company makes in advertising, selling, and distributing products.
	Administrative expense	The cost of running a business; legal expenses, accounting services, etc.
	Total Period Costs	The costs of operating your business over a period of time
Earnings Before Interest and Taxes (EBIT), or Net Margin		Revenues minus variable costs (contribution margin) minus period costs.
	Interest expense	The rent you pay to use other people's wealth. This is the expense of your financing strategy.
	Taxes	The tribute you pay to the government as a citizen of a society.
Net Income		Revenues minus variable costs minus period costs minus interest expenses and taxes. This is synonymous with profit, earnings, "return," and "bottom line." Creating net income for its owners is the reason a business exists.

Revenue

Revenues are the funds coming into the company from the sale of its products or services. It does not matter if the sales are for cash or credit (accounts receivable). Revenue is calculated by:

Price (per unit) * Units Sold = Revenue

For instance, if you sold 1,000 products at a price of $45 per unit, your revenue is $45,000.

Variable Costs

Variable costs are costs that are directly related to making the *products that you sell*. For instance, if the products you were making were electronic sensors, you would want to know how much each unit costs to make. If you add all of the variable costs together, you determine a "cost per unit." For example, if it cost $12.00 for the materials and $8.00 for the labor to transform the materials into the finished product the cost per unit is $20.00. Your total variable costs would be equal to the unit cost multiplied by the number of units sold.

$20 cost per unit x 1,000 units = $20,000 Total Variable Costs

This is the "cost of goods sold, "or COGS. In a period of time, you might make more than you sell and would "spend" more money than is recognized as an income statement expense. An easy way to remember this is that it represents the ***cost of goods sold***, not the cost of goods produced. If you divide the total variable costs by price, you get a percentage of every sales dollar (revenue) that goes into making the product. The lower the percentage of the cost of goods, the more efficient the company is at making products.

Contribution Margin

The contribution margin is shown on the income statement. The contribution margin number is determined by total revenues minus the variable costs.

Total Revenue - Variable Costs = Contribution Margin

In the previous example, the contribution margin would be:

$45,000 - $20,000 = $25,000

The total contribution margin is $25,000 and this can also be calculated as a per-unit number. If the price per unit is $45 and cost per unit is $20, the per-unit contribution margin is $25. (If you multiply the per-unit information by the number of units sold, you get the contribution margin on the income statement.)

If you divide the contribution margin by revenue, you can express contribution margin as a percentage of each dollar sold that remains after you pay for the cost of making the products that were sold.

$$\$25,000 \,/\, \$45,000 \;=\; 55.56\%$$

$$-\,or\,-$$

$$\$25 \text{ per unit} \,/\, \$45 \text{ per unit} \;=\; 55.56\%$$

Therefore, after the variable costs for the units sold have been paid, 55.56 cents out of every dollar of sales remains within the business.

Gross Margin
Gross margin is a related concept to contribution margin, but also recognizes depreciation expenses:

$$\textbf{Total Revenue} - (\textbf{Variable Costs} + \textbf{Depreciation}) \;=\; \textbf{Gross Margin}$$

By including depreciation, gross margin includes the complete cost of making a product; the cost of material, labor, and the consumption (or using up) of the equipment. The higher the gross margin, the more efficient the company is in its production. Gross margin is often expressed as a percentage of sales using the formula below.

$$\textbf{Gross Profits} \,/\, \textbf{Net Sales}$$

Period or Fixed Costs
Period costs, also referred to as fixed costs, include depreciation expenses, research and development expenses, and administrative expenses. These costs do not change regardless of the sales volume. Examples of period or fixed costs include research and development, promotion, sales and administrative expenses.

Depreciation Expenses
Depreciation expenses are expenses assigned to the consumption of the value of facilities and equipment. Depreciation is unique in that it is a non-cash expense. It does not cost anything, but it lowers both net income (profit) and taxes. Depreciation captures the value of the asset that was "used up" over a period of time. Each year, this expense "accumulates" on the balance sheet.

Sales, General and Administrative Expenses (SG&A)

The category of Sales, General and Administrative Expenses, also referred to as SG&A, captures the fixed expenses associated with research and development, marketing, promotional and sales expenses, and general administrative expenses. Together, these expenses make up the ongoing costs of being in business. They are the cost of creating, developing, marketing, and selling products. These also recognize the expenses of making decisions. Managers need to gather information about their environment, their markets, their customers, and about their operations in order to make effective decisions.

Earnings Before Interest and Taxes (EBIT)

EBIT is a measure of how profitable you are before subtracting the cost of your financing strategy; that is, your interest payments.

Interest

Interest payments are the rent you pay on your loans. Generally, the more loans you have, the more risky you are, and the higher interest rate you pay. The interest payment that you have to pay is a function of how much money you owe, how long you are borrowing it for, and the rate of interest you are paying. In general, the interest payment is the cost of your financial strategy. The interest, or "rent," you pay on a loan is an expense for having access to money and is an expected part of doing business. Interest is a business expense that reduces your profitability.

Net Income

Net income is the profit a firm creates by engaging in transactions. It is the firm's revenues minus all expenses. The net income generated by a company belongs to the owners of the company. The owners can choose to use this created wealth for personal purposes (that is, take it out of the company) or use the wealth to make the company bigger and more competitive (that is, reinvest it in the company). Because the goal of a business is to make a profit, the net income figure is used in several measures of business success:

Return on Sales - ROS:
A measure of how much profit was created for every dollar of sales.

ROS = Net Income / Sales

Return on Assets - ROA:
A measure of how much profit was created for the assets gathered.

ROA = Net Income / Total Assets

Return on Equity - ROE:
A measure of how much profit was created with owners' investments.

ROE = Net Income / Owners' Equity

Earnings Per Share - EPS:
A measure of how much profit was created for each share of stock.

EPS = Net Income / Number of Shares Outstanding

We will talk more about these and other financial ratios in Chapter 5.

The Cash Flow Statement

A company must have cash to operate. The cash flow statement provides a unique view of the company's cash position. It answers the question: Do we have enough cash to pay our financial obligations when they are due?

A company's cash flow statement summarizes its cash receipts, cash payments, and net change in cash for a specific time period. The cash receipts and cash payments for operating activities, such as products sold or services performed and the costs of producing the products or services, are summarized in the "Cash Flows from Operating Activities" section of the statement.

The cash receipts and cash payments for investing activities are summarized in the cash flows. Investing activities include the purchases and sales of assets such as buildings and equipment. The cash receipts and cash payments for financing activities, such as money borrowed from and repaid to banks, are summarized in the Cash Flows from Financing Activities section of the statement.

Cash flow is an important measure of a company's financial health and cash flow is crucial to an entity's survival. The Cash Flow Statement is often used by analysts to gauge financial performance. Companies with ample cash on hand are able to invest the cash back into the business in order to generate more cash and profit. Having ample cash on hand will ensure that creditors, employees and others can be paid on time. If a business or person does not have enough cash to support its operations, it is said to be insolvent, and a likely candidate for bankruptcy should the insolvency continue.

The cash flow statement will also be addressed in the next chapter along with working capital.

Annual Reports

A company may publish its income statement, balance sheet, and cash flow statement, along with other financial accounting information, in an annual report. A company that is publicly traded, where stockholders have purchased shares of the company, is required to publish an annual report by the Securities and Exchange Commission to communicate their financial performance.

For example, you can the annual report for The Walt Disney Company at:

http://corporate.disney.go.com/investors/annual_reports.html

Applying the Information

The ability to read and understand financial statements is valuable in understanding the financial status of any business that makes this information available. Once you have a basic understanding, the standardization imposed by the Generally Accepted Accounting Principles enables you to review and interpret almost any organization's financial statements, such as those presented in an annual report. This will be an important skill as you look at the financial information of a potential employer, an investment opportunity, or for your own business.

Chapter Summary Questions

Be able to answer these types of questions in these areas:

Accounting

1. Who relies on accounting information?

2. What is cost analysis?

3. What are the three basic financial statements?

Balance Sheet

4. Give an example of a current asset.

5. What is a fixed asset?

6. Give an example of a current liability.

7. What is an example of a long term liability?

Income Statement

8. What does an Income Statement tell about a company's performance?

9. What is the difference between variable costs and period (or fixed) costs?

10. What is a dividend?

Cash Flow

11. What is the purpose of the Cash Flow Statement?

12. What type of insight does the Cash Flow Statement provide to a business?

Build Your Understanding
Foundation Exercise 5 - *Accounting Numbers*

Determined to start deliberately, you decide to look at the financial documents for the year that has just ended. Although you are comfortable with accounting information, you believe it is a good idea to review—in the simplest terms—what each piece of information tells you.

The Balance Sheet Statement

Your Balance Sheet is a statement of the financial condition of your company. You have always considered it to be a "snap shot" of your company at this moment in time. Assets are the "stuff" the company owns and has control over. These assets are the things that you have at your disposal to create electronic sensors your customers will want, but in a way that creates a profit.

Refer to the Balance Sheet on page 84. To start the year, you have $5,593,000 in *cash*. With Total Assets worth $20,852, you have 26.8% of your assets in cash. It seems like a lot and, for now, you are content. You know that this cash can be turned into inventory (more sensors) or it could be used to upgrade your factory. You can do this by either increasing the capacity of your factory or improving the machinery so you could make your sensors at a lower cost.

You also have $3,353,000 in *accounts receivable*. You know that accounts receivable is the account that keeps track of sensors that you sold last year, but haven't yet been paid for. Your customers owe you this money. You know that your receivables policy is that your major customers have 30 days to pay for the sensors they buy from you. Last year, you sold 1,200,000 sensors at a price of $34 each. The current balance in your accounts receivable, or A/R, would represent 99,000(000) sensors sold at $34 that you haven't received the cash for yet. This makes sense as it is about 1/12, or one month, of the total.

You have a balance of $2,353,000 in the *inventory* account. The inventory account keeps track of sensors that you are either in the process of making or that you have made but not yet sold. You remember that right now it is costing you just a little less than $27 to make each sensor. That would mean that you have about 87,000 sensors in the warehouse ready to be sold ($2,353/$27).

You currently have one factory, your *Plant and Equipment,* and the value is $14,400,000. Your predecessors invested this much to create a factory that can produce 800,000 units a year (with no overtime) with an automation level of 3. (This is a measure of your ability to efficiently produce sensors and the sensor industry uses a standard rating of 1 [lowest] to 10 [highest].)

Accumulated depreciation is the recognition that running the factory "uses up" some of the value. You know that you are currently using a 15 year straight line depreciation method; meaning that every year the depreciation expense on your income statement is 1/15 of the value of your investment in your factory. One fifteenth (1/15) of $14,400,000 is a depreciation expense of $960,000 a year. The accumulated depreciation of $4,848,000 represents about one third (1/3) of the initial investment in the factory, which suggests this factory has been in use about 5 years.

The current accounting value of your factory (*total fixed assets*) of $9,552,000 represents the $14,400,000 initial investment and depreciation recognizing 5 years of use ($4,848,000). All told, you have control over $20,852,000 worth of assets. This equates to your *Total Assets.*

Where Did That Money Come From?

The money to operate and grow your company can only come from two places: debt and owners' investments. On the Balance Sheet, the *liability accounts* represent different kinds of debt. *Owners' Equity* accounts are the investments made by the owners of the corporation.

Accounts payable are a type of short term "loan" from your suppliers; those companies from whom you buy the component parts used in the production of your sensors. You will have to pay your suppliers $2,855,000 within the next 30 days for materials already received.

The *current debt* account keeps track of loans that have to be paid back in the coming year. This is also known as current liabilities. It can include loans from the bank, the infamous "Big Al", or the face value of any bonds that mature in the coming year. You are glad that you have no current debt at this time.

Long term debt (or long term liabilities) keeps track of money borrowed by issuing bonds. You currently have three bond issues ($866,667; $1,733,333; $2,600,000) for a total of $5,200,000. All bonds are 10 year contracts.

There are two owners' equity accounts; *common stock* and *retained earnings*. The common stock account keeps track of the money the corporation's owners paid "out of pocket" to purchase the stock. Your stockholders paid in $2,313,000 to purchase 2,000,000 shares of stock. The average price for a new share must have been about $1.16. What a bargain! Those shares trade now trade at $11.88.

The *retained earnings* account keeps track of profit that has been retained for use in the company. You never forget that the profit you create belongs to the owners of the company—in your case the stockholders. Their profit can be paid out to them, in the form of a dividend payment or it can be retained in the company. Owners have given you money for one reason—so that you can make them "better off." If you retain earnings (profits) for use in the company, you have to use them to make your owners wealthier. In the past 5 years, the company has made $10,485,000 in profits that the owners have chosen to retain for use in the company.

The total value of the owners claim (*total owners' equity*) is $12,798,000. Wait a minute, your explanation to yourself is getting too fancy. Let's try again. You have control over more than $20M worth of stuff. If you subtract the $8M the company has borrowed, the owners value is more than $12M. If you split that equally among the 2,000,000 shareholders, each share of stock has a "book value" of $6.49.

Another look at the balance sheet shows that 38.6% of your assets are currently funded by debt and 61.4% of the company is funded through owners' investments.

The *balance sheet* shows what resources you have and where they money came from to pay for those resources. The *income statement* describes how you used the resources last year to create wealth (make a profit)

ANDREW'S FINANCIAL STATEMENTS

BALANCE SHEET		Total	
ASSETS			*Common Size*
Cash	$5,593		26.8%
Accounts Receivable	$3,353		16.1%
Inventory	$2,353		11.3%
Total Current Assets		$11,299	54.2%
Plant & Equipment	$14,400		69.1%
Accumulated Depreciation	($4,848)		-23.2%
Total Fixed Assets		$9,552	45.8%
Total Assets		**$20,852**	100.0%
LIABILITIES & OWNER'S EQUITY			
Liabilities			
Accounts Payable	$2,855		13.7%
Current Debt	$0		0.0%
Long Term Debt	$5,200		24.9%
Total Liabilities		$8,055	38.6%
Owner's Equity			
Common Stock	$2,313		11.1%
Retained Earnings	$10,485		50.3%
Total Equity		$12,798	61.4%
Total Liabilities and			
Owners' Equity		**$20,852**	**100.0%**

INCOME STATEMENT	Total	*Size*
Sales	**$40,800**	**100.0%**
Variable Costs		
Direct Labor	$12,138	29.7%
Direct Material	$20,240	49.6%
Inventory Carry	$282	0.7%
Total Variable Costs	**$32,660**	**80.0%**
Contribution Margin	**$8,140**	**20.0%**
Period Costs		
Depreciation	$960	2.4%
Sales General &Admin:		
Research & Development	$0	0.0%
Promotions	$1,000	2.5%
Sales	$1,000	2.5%
Admin	$637	1.6%
Total Period Costs	**$3,597**	**8.8%**
Net Margin	**$4,543**	**11.1%**
Other EBIT	$4,543	11.1%
Short Term Interest	$0	0.0%
Long Term Interest	$641	1.6%
Taxes	$1,365	3.3%
Profit Sharing	$51	0.1%
Net Profit	**$2,485**	**6.1%**

The Income Statement

Last year, your company had total **_revenues_** of $40,800,000. This money came from the sales of 1,200,000 sensors at $34.00 each. There are a lot of decisions that affect how much revenue you can generate. Certainly the price matters. You can get more revenue for each sensor you sell if you raise the price. But if you raise the price, you might not sell as many sensors. The characteristics of your product will affect revenue (sales). In general, the smaller, faster, and more reliable your sensors; the more your customers will like them. The money you spend in your promotion and sales budgets will also increase revenue.

Variable costs are those costs whose total cost gets bigger with the more sensors you sell. Considered together the variable costs are sometimes called _"**Cost of Goods Sold**"_ because they only recognize the material and labor costs that are incurred making the sensors that you sold that year- these numbers do NOT account for the sensors you made but didn't sell. Variable costs are tied to the cost of materials that go into the sensors and the cost of labor incurred in the production process. If you talk about the variable cost for each sensor, the material cost plus the labor cost, this is referred to as the **_unit cost_**.

Last year, you sold 1,200,000 sensors. For each of those sensors, the materials used in them cost $16.87 and therefore, your total **_cost of materials_** for the 1.2M sensors was $20,240,000. If you make your sensors smaller, faster, or more reliable; the cost of materials will increase.

For each sensor, the **_cost of labor_** was $10.12. To produce 1,200,000 sensors, the total cost of labor was $12,138,000. You can decrease your labor costs by investing in better equipment/machinery for the factory. "Better" is increasing the level of automation. Every level of automation you invest in lowers your labor cost by $1.12.

Inventory carrying costs are the additional expenses incurred when you have inventory in the factory. It is calculated at 12% of the cost of inventory left at the end of the year. From the Balance sheet, you know that you have $2,353,000 of inventory left at the end of the year. 12% of that figure is $282,000.

If you add all of the variable costs, you get $32,660,000. This is the cost of producing the goods that you sold. If you subtract your cost of goods sold (total variable cost) from the revenue you generated when you sold those goods, you get the contribution margin. You sold sensors and generated $40,800,000 of revenue. However, those sensors cost you $32,660,000 to produce. After you have paid for the cost of the goods you sold, you have $8,140,000 left over- that will contribute to your profitability. This number is your **_contribution margin_**. These numbers are measures of how efficiently you are manufacturing the products you sell. For a manufacturing firm, these numbers are very important and are talked about in three ways:

1. **The total numbers:** $40,800 in revenue minus $32,660 cost of goods sold provides a contribution margin of $8,140.
2. **The per unit numbers**: A price of $34 minus the variable cost per unit of about $27.22 ($16.87 [material] plus $10.12 [labor] plus $.24 [carrying cost]) provides a contribution margin of $6.78 per unit.
3. **Percentages (expressed as a dollar of sales):** A total of 29.7% of your sales dollar goes to pay for labor, 49.6% to pay for materials; for a total of 80% of your sales dollar going to cost of goods sold. This leaves 20% of the sales dollar to contribute to your overall profitability.

In more common language, for every $1.00 of sales revenue, you are spending almost 30 cents on labor and almost 50 cents on materials. For every dollar of sales, you have a cost of goods sold of 80 cents; leaving you 20 cents towards being profitable. When you were hired, your board of Directors made it clear that they expected a minimum 30% contribution margin. You have your work cut out for you.

To improve your contribution margin, you can:
   a. **Raise your price:** But fewer people will purchase at a higher price.
   b. **Lower your material costs:** Although you will need to check the production report to be sure, the only way is to make your produce less attractive—bigger, slower, less reliable. A strategy sure to lose sales!
   c. **Reduce your labor costs:** You can invest in greater production efficiency by increasing the automation for your equipment or greater capacity to lower overtime.

From your contribution margin, you subtract some of the costs of being in business for the year. Because these tend to be "fixed" over the course of the time period (in this case a year), they are referred to as period costs.

Depreciation is the recognition that you are "consuming" your investment in your factory every year. This $960,000 is the yearly recognition of "using up' the value of your fixed assets. This is a unique number on the income statement because it is not paid to anyone; it is a non-cash expense.

The next group of expenses is called SG&A, or Selling, General, and Administrative Expenses. *Research and development,* or *R&D,* are expenses are the expenses you incur when your engineers improve your product. You are concerned that your company didn't invest any money improving the product last year.

The *promotion expense* is what the company spends on advertising. Another way to think of this money is creating awareness in customers that your product exists. You can only sell products to people who are AWARE of your offerings. Last year, the company invested $1,000,000 in creating awareness of the product—you wonder how much awareness (measured by what percentage of the market) did they possess. The *sales expense* is what the company spends on getting your sales representatives to contact your customers. You can only sell products to people who have ACCESS to your sales representatives. Again, the company invested $1,000,000 last year to create access to your product—you wonder how much access (what percentage of the market) was realized. *Administrative expenses* are estimated at 1.5% of the sales; this is simply administrative overhead.

You have total period costs of $3,597,000. This represents 8.8% of your total sales (or almost 9 cents of each $1 dollar of sales). If you subtract this from your Contribution Margin ($8,140-$3,597), you get $4,543,000 for your net margin or Earnings Before Interest and Taxes (EBIT). You started with sales revenue and subtracted the cost of making the goods sold (sensors), which left contribution margin. From the contribution margin, you subtracted out the costs of being in business—the costs that are fixed for the year. You are left with your Earnings before you make your interest payments (cost of your financing decisions) and taxes (your burden as a citizen).

Interest payments are the rent you pay to use other peoples' money. Short term loans tend to be to the bank (although you have heard rumors of your company having to take out short term emergency loans from "Big Al" a reputed loan shark). Your predecessor must have paid off all of the short term debt because the balance in the current debt account is $0, and so the company didn't pay anything in interest on short term loans last year.

Long term interest payments are payments that you have to pay on your bonds (your long term debt). You currently have $5,200,000 of bonds outstanding (about 25% of your total assets are funded by bonds). Your company paid $641,000 in interest on bonds- a little more that 12% interest.

Other income statement observations include:

- The company pays a 35% income tax on their income after interest has been subtracted. *EBIT* was $4,343,000 minus $641,000 is $3,902,000 in taxable income. 35% of that is $1,365,000. Ouch.

- A part of the employee contract is that your company has a *profit sharing* program to share its profits with employees (after taxes have been paid). This year that profit sharing pool is $51,000.

- Last year, the company's *net income* was $2,485,000. This is *profit*. Creating profit—creating wealth—is a major reason the company was organized and why it does business.

- The company created $2,485,000 profit on $40,800,000 worth of sales. That is a return on sales *(ROS)* of 6.1%. This means that a little more than 6 cents of every $1 of sales is profit.

- The company created $2,485,000 profit using assets worth $20,852,000. That is a return on assets *(ROA)* of 11.9%- or for every $1 of assets, the company created a little less than 12 cents profit.

- The company created $2,485,000 profit on owners' investments of $12,798,000. This is a return on equity *(ROE)* of 19.4%. This means that for every $1 the owners have invested, the company created 19.4 cents profit.

- The company created $2,485,000 profit for a corporation that has 2,000,000 share of stock outstanding. This represents *earnings per share* of $1.24. In other words, for every share of stock outstanding, the company created $1.24 profit in this past year.

Build Your Understanding-Foundation Exercise 5 Questions

The Balance Sheet Survey: FastTrack Reports, Page 3

Balance Sheet Survey	Andrews	Baldwin	Chester	Digby	Erie	Ferris
Cash	$9,812	$12,070	$8,715	$13,236	$8,978	$7,313
Accounts Receivable	$4,690	$5,642	$3,220	$5,925	$2,892	$3,587
Inventory	$0	$3,216	$2,591	$4,016	$1,883	$5,639
Total Current Assets	$14,502	$20,928	$14,526	$23,177	$13,754	$16,540
Plant and equipment	$37,440	$32,569	$32,692	$33,015	$32,070	$25,300
Accumulated Depreciation	($8,142)	($8,036)	($8,047)	($8,021)	($7,930)	($7,200)
Total Fixed Assets	$29,298	$24,533	$24,645	$24,994	$24,140	$18,100
Total Assets	$43,800	$45,461	$39,171	$48,171	$37,894	$34,640
Accounts Payable	$2,523	$4,060	$1,841	$4,236	$1,415	$2,770
Current Debt	$1,867	$6,134	$6,364	$7,880	$5,679	$7,936
Long Term Debt	$7,333	$11,858	$11,755	$11,488	$11,828	$7,751
Total Liabilities	$11,723	$22,053	$19,960	$23,604	$18,922	$18,456
Common Stock	$8,323	$5,212	$4,436	$4,376	$5,109	$3,224
Retained Earnings	$23,754	$18,196	$14,775	$20,191	$13,863	$12,960
Total Equity	$32,077	$23,408	$19,211	$24,567	$18,972	$16,184
Total Liabilities & Owner's Equity	$43,800	$45,461	$39,171	$48,171	$37,894	$34,640

1. How large or how "big" is company *Chester*?

2. How could you tell if a company had taken an emergency loan from the Balance Sheet?

3. What is the value of the sales that *Digby* has already made but hasn't been paid for yet?

4. What is the value of sensors *Ferris* has in stock?

5. Which company "stocked out" (had no units of their product left in the warehouse) this year?

6. How much did *Erie* spend to buy the factory and machinery (new)?

7. How much is *Erie's* factory and machinery worth today?

8. How much money has *Baldwin* borrowed that has to be paid back in the next year?

9. What is the total value that company *Baldwin* has in long-term debt?

10. Which company has the greatest amount of debt?

11. How much money has company *Ferris* accepted as cash investment from owners?

12. If company *Digby* has disbursed a total of $6,000 in dividends since the start of the company, how much total net income have they generated (cumulative profit)?

13. What is the value of the net income that has been re-invested (kept) in company *Erie*?

14. How much money has *Chester* borrowed that doesn't have to be paid back this year?

15. What is the value of all of the resources that you (*Andrews*) have under your control to use to create more wealth?

16. How much of the assets under your control were financed by loans in dollars?

17. How much of the assets under your control were financed by owners' investments in dollars?

An Introduction to Business

The Income Statement Survey: FastTrack Reports, Page 3

Income Statement Survey	Andrews	Baldwin	Chester	Digby	Erie	Ferris
Sales	$57,063	$68,647	$39,174	$72,090	$35,191	$43,645
Variable Costs (Labor, Material, Carry)	$33,831	$49,914	$28,052	$50,932	$24,537	$31,496
Depreciation	$1,920	$2,171	$1,820	$2,201	$1,703	$1,267
SG&A (R&D, Promo, Sales, Admin)	$5,882	$5,979	$4,032	$6,830	$3,962	$5,740
Other (Fees, Write Offs, TQM, Bonus)	$250	$354	$330	$325	$367	$195
EBIT	$15,180	$10,229	$4,940	$11,802	$4,622	$4,947
Interest (Short term, Long term)	$958	$1,938	$1,938	$2,054	$1,892	$1,679
Taxes	$4,978	$2,902	$1,051	$3,412	$956	$1,144
Profit Sharing	$185	$108	$39	$127	$35	$42
Net Profit	$9,060	$5,281	$1,912	$6,210	$1,739	$2,082

1. Which company had the greatest amount of revenue in the reported year?

2. What is company's *Digby's* contribution margin?

3. If *Chester* had one product and charged $30, how many sensors did they sell last year?

4. How much did *Baldwin* spend to manufacture all of the sensors they produced last year? (this is a trick question... the income statement only reports cost of the goods that you sold)

5. How much did *Baldwin* spend to manufacture all of the sensors they sold last year?

6. What is the value of the machinery that *Ferris* used up making their products last year? (Did this decrease their cash? Did they have to pay anyone that money?)

7. How much did *Andrews* spend on product development, marketing and administrative expenses last year?

8. How much did *Erie* pay in interest?

9. Which company had the greatest amount paid in interest?

10. How much did *Chester* pay in taxes?

11. How much profit did Digby earn?

12. Which company created the most wealth in the past year?

13. What percentage of your sales was profit?

14. What percentage of your sales was left over after you paid for making the product (material-labor-inventory carrying costs)?

Build Your Understanding
Foundation Exercise 6 - *Customer Survey Score Adjustments*

The Customer Survey Score that was discussed in Chapter 2 is determined by several factors. Adjustments to these factors will change this score. As a review:
- Pricing outside the range loses about 10% (of the base CSS score) per dollar.
- An MTBF set below the range loses about 20% (of the base CSS score) per 1,000 hours.
- Positioning outside of the fine cut circle is a 1% loss if it is just over the line, a 50% loss if it is halfway, and a 99% loss if it is on the edge of the rough cut circle.

Your evaluation of Able for January shows that all product attributes are within the range of the "Fine cut" and the final score does not need to be adjusted for having attributes in the "Rough Cut."

Rough Cut CSS Adjustments

	Total	A/R	Awareness	Accessibility	Rough Cut	CSS
Low Tech	51.8	-4.1	-11.65	-15.55	0	20.2
High Tech	46.25	-3.8	-10.4	-13.9	0	18.1

December's CSS for Able was 18 for Low Tech segment and 16 for the High Tech segment. You have some confidence that you understand the basic process because your estimates were relatively close.

A change in the Accounts Receivable policy can also change the Customer Survey Score. For example, assume that product Fast had a base Customer Survey Score of 80 points for the High Tech market. The 30 days A/R policy reduces the score by 8% of the base. Using the FastTrack report for High Tech, what is the adjusted CSS? (All product characteristics fall within the "fine cut.")

CSS Adjustment

FAST	"FastTrack Score" Percent (PCT)	"In Reality" PCT +[1/2 (1-PCT)]	Adjusted Factor = 100% - "in reality"
Awareness	85%	85% + (1/2 (15%)) = **92.5%**	100%- 92.5% = **7.5%**
Accessibility	38%	38% + (1/2 (62%)) = **69%**	100% - 69% = **31%**

The 30 day lag for Accounts Receivable reduces the base score by 8%. *(This information is provided in the question and it came from page 9 of the Team Member Guide.)* This 8% of 80 represents a reduction of 6.4 points off the CSS.

A total of 85% of the high tech customers received Ferris' promotional materials and were "aware" of product Fast. That means 15% did not receive the advertisements. Of that 15%, half of the customers (7.5%) find out about Fast through their own search. In reality, 92.5% of customers are aware of Fast when they make their decision. That means that 7.5% of them did not know about the product when making their decision. That is the adjustment factor for the CSS that you need to subtract; 7.5% of 80 or 6 points from the base.

Only 38% of customers have access to Ferris' sales people. That means that 62% do not have access. Half of them, or 31%, initiate contact through their own initiative. Therefore, 69% of the market has access to Fast. The adjustment factor is the 31% who do not have access to the sales staff and 31% of 80 equals 24.8. This hurts!

The CSS of 80 is reduced 6.4 points because of the Accounts Receivable policy, 6 points because of Awareness, and 24.8 points because of Accessibility. That leaves an adjusted Customer Survey Score of 42.8.

CSS Adjusted Score

Base Score =	A/R	Awareness	Accessibility	Rough cut	CSS
Adj. (% of Base)	8% of 80	7.5% of 80	31% of 80	0	
Points **Base: 80**	6.4	6	24.8	0	**42.8**

Build Your Understanding
Foundation Exercise 6 Questions

1. Given the "Customer Buying Criteria" tables, your current product's characteristics, and a way to determine the "attractiveness score", you should be able to fill out the CSS table and calculate the base CSS for a product.

Low Tech	MTBF	Price	Age	Position	Total
Importance					100%
Attractiveness	100	5	96	10	
CSS points					

Using the "Attractiveness" scores given in the table above, calculate Able's base CSS. *(Refer back to your work in Foundation Exercise Questions 2 on page 40.)*

2. Given the "Base score" and a way to determine the adjustments for A/R, Awareness, Accessibility, and product characteristics that are in the Rough Cut, you should be able to calculate an adjusted (or final) CSS for a product.

If you lost 4% of your base score because of your A/R policy and your awareness and accessibility were both at 50%, what would your adjusted CSS be? (Assume that there were no adjustments for product characteristics being outside the "fine cut" expectations.)

	Base	A/R	Awareness	Accessibility	Rough Cut	CSS
Product	**51.8**					

Production:
Improving Productivity and Performance

Production involves the efficient management of resources, including people and equipment, to successfully produce and provide quality products and services.

Key terms to look for:

- Benchmarking
- Capacity
- Carrying costs
- Economies of scale
- Human resources
- Materials requirement planning
- PERT chart
- Quality control
- Raw materials
- Supply chain management
- Total quality management
- Work-in-process inventories

Production is the process by which a company produces finished goods and services. This act of making products that will be traded or sold commercially is based on decisions about what goods to produce, how to produce them, the costs to produce them, and how to optimize the mix of resource inputs used in their production. Production information can then be combined with market information (like demand) to determine the quantity of products to produce and sell at an optimal price point. This process might involve the work, ideas, and plans of the design engineers, the production manager, the plant manager, the plant superintendent, their crews, and any other department actually involved with producing the product.

Production can take the form of mass production, when a large number of standard products are created in a traditional assembly line process, or it can be a more specialized process, as when individual or small quantities are created.

Therefore, production is the conversion of inputs into outputs. It is a process that uses resources—such as cash, labor and raw materials—to create a commodity attractive for a market. This can include manufacturing, storing, shipping, and packaging. Because it is a flow concept, production is measured as a "rate of output per period of time." There are three basic aspects to the production process:
1. Quantity of the commodity produced
2. Form of the good produced
3. Temporal and spatial distribution of the commodity produced

A production process can be defined as any activity that increases the similarity between the pattern of demand for goods and the quantity, form, and distribution of these goods available to the marketplace.

Production plays a key role in the objective of a manufacturing-based business to maximize profits. Profit maximization is the process by which a firm determines the price and the output level that returns the greatest profit. There are several approaches to accomplish this goal.

The "total revenue minus total cost" method relies on the fact that profit equals revenue minus cost, and the marginal return method (marginal revenue minus marginal cost) is based on the fact that total profit in a perfectly competitive market reaches its maximum point where marginal revenue equals marginal cost.

A business needs a production process whenever it provides products or services. This involves a series of tasks where resources are used to create a product or service. This process involves planning, procuring goods to produce the products, and assigning and organizing tasks to make those products available for sale. It is important to differentiate production from operations. **Operations** describe the activities needed to keep the company producing through a function or series of functions to carry out a plan, while **production** involves the actual process of creating goods and services.

Production management seeks to develop an efficient, relatively low-cost and high-quality production process of creating specific products and services. Production management can contribute to the success of both manufacturing firms and service-oriented firms. The profits and value of each firm are influenced by its production management process.

The primary resources that firms use for the production process include:

Human Resources: Employees and their skills involved in the production process

Raw Materials: Cost of goods to create the products

Capacity: The annual production capabilities of the facilities, technology, machinery, and equipment

These resources cost money. Employees need to be paid, materials have to be purchased, and building and production facilities take time and money to be ready for production. The objective is to use these resources in the most efficient manner possible. This will enable the organization to take advantage of higher production levels producing more units at a lower cost per unit.

Bang & Olufsen   *A business profile*

For more than 80 years, Bang & Olufsen has created sound systems that combine cutting edge audio and entertainment technology with an emotional appeal. The challenge is to contribute to the continued growth of Bang & Olufsen by further refining and utilizing production skills that have enabled them to become one of the largest and most innovative loudspeaker manufacturers in the world. Bang & Olufsen's approach to product development and production focuses on both tradition and constant renewal. "We never forget that technology should work for people, not the other way around. We utilize only tried and tested technologies, innovatively integrated into products that offer viewing and listening experiences beyond expectations, that are a pleasure to use, and that invite you to approach, touch, and look at, even when it is turned off."[4]

Economies of Scale

Economies of scale may be one objective of an efficient production process. *Economies of scale* occurs when the cost of each good produced decreases as the volume produced increases. This reduction in cost per unit occurs when the initial investment of capital is shared with an increasing number of units of output, and therefore, the cost of producing a good or service decreases as production increases. Variable costs—those associated with the number of goods produced—and fixed costs—costs that do not change regardless of volume—are monitored throughout this process. As output increases, fixed costs remain the same, and variable costs on a per-unit basis typically decline as production volumes increase.

For example:

> The cost to print 50 business cards is $25, or 50 cents for each business card. However, if you were to place an order to print 500 business cards, the total costs is $50, reducing the cost per card to 10 cents. The more business cards printed in each print "run" the lower the cost per individual business card.

---

[4] Source: www.bang-olufsen.com

Another example:

A company is currently in a situation with economies of scale where their initial fixed investment of $1 million is spread over 2,000 customers and their average fixed cost per unit is $500:

$$\$1,000,000 \ / \ 2,000 \ = \ \$500$$

If that same organization has now grown to 2,500 customers, their average fixed costs decrease as they spread these costs over a larger customer base to only $400 per unit.

$$\$1,000,000 \ / \ 2,500 \ = \ \$400$$

In both examples, the result is a lower unit cost. Therefore, economies of scale are particularly critical in industries with high fixed costs, also known as capital costs. A common example is a factory. With an initial fixed investment in machinery, one worker, or unit of production, begins to work on the machine to produce a certain number of goods. If a second worker is added to the production line, he or she is able to produce an additional number of goods without adding significantly to the factory's cost of operation. If the number of goods produced grows significantly faster than the plant's cost of operation, the cost of producing an additional unit is less than the unit before, and an economy of scale occurs. Economies of scale and the efficiencies this concept offers is another benefit companies seek through growth.

Scheduling Product Production

The role of scheduling product production is concerned with volume, production sequence, and the type of product to be produced. This responsibility lies with the production manager. Three elements of management—planning, organizing, and controlling—can clearly be seen in the tasks of the production manager.

A *master production schedule* determines when the products will be produced and in what quantities. Dates must be met, specified quantities must be produced on time, and costs need to be controlled to make certain this process goes smoothly and meets commitments. One tool to help with this process is a **PERT chart**. PERT stands for "Program Evaluation and Review Technique." This is a graphical representation that tracks production events with their respective time frames from start to finish. A PERT chart depicts the process and maps out the time it will require. A PERT chart can help to identify problems in the process before even it begins.

Inventory Control

As goods are produced, they also need to be managed. Inventory control is the process of efficiently managing inventory. There needs to be enough product available for sale, but there should not be too much product unnecessarily sitting in the warehouse that ties up cash. An efficient inventory control system minimizes the costs associated with inventory.

Companies must also manage their products as inventory is in the process of being created. This is described as **work-in-process inventory**, or products that are only partially completed but have required an investment of some type of resource. Products cannot be sold until they are complete, and monitoring the status of products still involved in production is important.

Another cost directly associated with inventory is carrying cost. **Carrying costs** are the costs of maintaining inventories. A popular method for reducing carrying costs is the just-in-time (JIT) inventory system. This system is based on having just enough inventory on hand to satisfy consumer demand. Product should always be available, but there is not an overstock of what is needed for the near future. JIT may be in conflict with economies of scale goals, however, so the organization needs to balance the use of these.

The just-in-time system is often associated with a materials requirement planning system that ensures that materials are available when needed. A **materials requirement planning** system or MRP helps to determine when the materials to produce the product are needed to meet production deadlines. As a firm develops a forecast for the demand for its products, it determines the time at which the materials need to arrive at the production site to meet the anticipated market demand.

The collection of partners—manufacturer, wholesaler, distributor, retailer, on-line sales site—is referred to as the supply chain. Efforts to improve the relationships among manufacturers and their suppliers are referred to as **supply chain management (SCM),** and its objective is to manage the connections between supply chain members in order to enhance efficiencies and reduce costs.

Supply chain management involves these five basic components:

1. **Plan:** *The strategic plan to manage all of the resources that go into meeting customer demand for your product or service*
2. **Source:** *The selection of the supplies that will deliver goods and services*
3. **Make:** *The manufacturing step involving scheduling, testing, packaging and preparing for delivery*
4. **Deliver:** *The logistics and timing of getting those products and/or services through the channel*
5. **Return:** *The "soft" link in the chain that supports customers returning product or have had problems with the experience*

Companies such as Toyota, General Electric, Apple and others have developed systems that have produced dramatic results. Cisco Systems and others have developed software and Web-based programs to assist organizations as they work to realize greater efficiencies in their supply chain process.

Quality Control and Total Quality Management

Quality is the degree to which a product or service meets the company's internal standards and satisfies customer expectations. Quality relates to consumer satisfaction and is a factor regarding the firm's current and future success. Quality control is the process of testing to determine if the product or service meets the performance and other set standards of the organization before it is sold. Techniques to monitor quality may include sampling, monitoring customer/user complaints, and looking to correct deficiencies.

In some cases, quality standards are set by agencies, such as the Food and Drug Administration (FDA) and the Consumer Products Safety Council (CPSC), or by industry associations. The standards imposed by these entities affect the design, performance, durability, safety, and many other attributes of how the goods will perform and function. Quality is also used as a competitive advantage to provide "perceived excellence" compared with other consumer choices on the market.

Several techniques are used to improve quality within an organization. *Quality circles* are small groups of employees who meet regularly to attempt to identify and solve problems involved in quality improvement. A more formalized process is the concept of *Total Quality Management (TQM)*.

Total Quality Management is the act of monitoring and improving the quality of products and services produced. This concept is primarily based on the work of W. Edwards Deming, an American statistician, professor, author, lecturer and consultant. He is perhaps best known for his work in Japan. Beginning in 1950, Deming taught top management in Japan how to improve design and service, product quality, testing, and sales through the application of statistics and other methodologies. Deming offered fourteen key principles to managers for transforming business effectiveness first presented in his book "Out of the Crisis." Although Deming does not use the term in his book, Deming is credited with launching the Total Quality Management movement. His work followed these guidelines:

- To provide managers and other employees with the education and training they need to excel in their jobs.

- To encourage employees to take responsibility and to provide leadership.

- To encourage all employees to search for ways to improve the production process.

Many firms create teams of employees to assess quality and offer suggestions for continuous improvement. This creates a form of cross-functional teamwork where employees with different jobs, responsibilities, and perspectives work together to improve the production process through enhanced quality.

Benchmarking

The process called ***benchmarking*** is another quality-improvement technique. Benchmarking describes a method of evaluating performance by comparison with another specified level achieved by another entity. Often, benchmarking involves studying highly successful companies in other industries. For example, Ford Motor Company studied and used the customer service performance levels of Eddie Bauer to improve its customer relations process. Benchmarking may also be used in conjunction with a TQM process.

Merritt Tool Company   *A business profile*

Owner A.P. Merritt, Jr. studied Toyota's lean manufacturing process to understand how he might apply these techniques to Merritt Tool, a 65-person parts manufacturer for the aerospace industry. His team of employees began looking for a way to streamline processes to improve efficiency and minimize waste. The results included a lower accident rate, higher quality, lower costs, faster delivery intervals, shorter setup times, fewer machine breakdowns, and a higher level of employee satisfaction.[5]

Technology

Many production processes have been automated, and robotics has become a significant factor in manufacturing throughout the world. From the simple machines of olden times to the intelligent machines of today, robotics has changed the face of industry, be it from automotive manufacturing to food processing. Machines and robotic equipment reduce the labor required in the production process and although these machines may be an expense at first, their ongoing use can reduce labor expenses in time due to the efficiencies they offer. Good planning is required to make certain that the automation process accomplishes the desired goals. This involves a thorough assessment of the required costs, the savings and benefits that may be realized, and the degree of "fit" within the organization and production process.

Improving Productivity

A healthy economy often correlates with consistent improvement in productivity. A common measure of productivity is expressed in dollar of output per hour worked. Production faces the standard challenges of increasing labor, material, and opportunity costs. It also must address the impact of uncertain world events, technological change, and the global labor market.

John Deer   *A business profile*

John Deere dominates the $23 billion U.S.-Canada market for farm equipment with 60 percent market share. Deere's strategy is to couple state-of-the-art machines with dealers who work so closely with farmers that they become virtual partners, often locking in customers over several generations. The Waterloo, Iowa manufacturing plant employs 5,600 people producing thousands of products each year for more than 130 countries.[6]

---

[5] Mark Albert, "This Shop Really Shines ..." *Modern Machine Shop*, January 2004, http://www.findarticles.com/p/articles/mi_m3101/is_8_76/ai_112862177.

[6] Gruley, Bryan and Shruti Date Singh, "Deere's Big Breen Profit Machine, Bloomberg Businessweek, July 5, 2012, http://www.businessweek.com/articles/2012-07-05/deeres-big-green-profit-machine.

Chapter Summary Questions

Be able to answer these types of questions in these areas:

Production Management

1. Discuss the primary resources involved in the production process.

2. What does "economies of scale" mean and why is that concept relevant in the production process?

3. What are the key advantages of just-in-time (JIT) manufacturing?

4. What do you consider to be the single most challenging aspect of the production process?

Quality Control and Total Quality Management

5. What benefits does TQM offer an organization?

6. What does benchmarking accomplish?

7. How does supply chain management impact the production process?

8. What are the potential benefits of effectively managing quality control?

An Introduction to Business

Build Your Understanding
Foundation Exercise 7 - *Production & Inventory Management*

Production management requires two different kinds of decision making
1. ***Operations:*** Operational decisions are those that run your company in the current year. Within a one year time horizon, many options are fixed. For instance, you can't build a new factory and you can't add a new product. Operational decisions involve making your best effort to meet your goals with available resources.
2. ***Investment:*** Investment decisions are those that help create the company that you want to be running next year. Investment involves creating capacities to compete differently.

Both operational and investment decisions are dependent upon one thing; accurate sales forecasting.

The sales forecast is an ***uncertain*** prediction. You are using knowledge of your customers' preferences and past performance information to predict future events. You have to adjust those predictions both by the changes you make to your product offering and by the changes you believe your competitors will make.

The sales forecast is also an ***important*** prediction because you will use it to make decisions that have significant consequences. The sales forecast:
- Determines the production schedule (how many to units of each product to produce)
- Determines capital investments (when and how much to invest in capacity)
- Establishes the financing requirements to operate and grow your business
- Is used to test the sensitivity of the company's overall performance in the market to different levels of sales.

Decision making under conditions of uncertainty and risk is the essence of operating in a competitive environment.

Fortunately, there are tools to help you manage the riskiness of each decision. This analysis will explore these areas:
- Inventory management goals;
- Production schedule, and;
- Investment decisions in capacity.

Sales Forecasting and Inventory Management
Manufacturing electronic sensors is what your company does. It is the reason the company exists. Determining how many sensors get produced is the single most important operational decision that the company makes. Why is it so important?

If you produce too few sensors (you don't make enough), then you will sell everything you produce; you "stock out". On the surface, that's sounds like a good thing. But it means that there were customers who wanted to buy your product but were denied that opportunity because you didn't make enough. Disappointed customers are not a good thing. Also, the reason you sell sensors is that it makes you better off. The more sensors you sell, the better off you are. When you don't make enough sensors, you are missing an opportunity to make more profit.

If you produce more sensors than you sell, then you will have a large build-up of sensors (inventory) in the warehouse. On the surface, that may sound positive; you will always have product available for sale and customers will not be disappointed. However, the aging inventory is will lose appeal and become obsolete if it stays in the warehouse too long. In addition, it costs money to store higher levels of inventory. The cost of carrying inventory for a year is about 15% of its value and that is an expense that reduces profitability. However, the biggest reason to manage inventory levels is that inventory ties up cash.

At the most simple level, the production process turns cash into electronic sensors. You take cash and purchase materials and labor. The materials and labor are combined in the factory to produce product.

For example:

> You decide to produce 2,000,000 units of your product Able. Each unit requires $15 of material and $10 of labor for a unit cost of $25. When you produce 2,000,000 units, you are converting $50,000,000 of cash into sensors. That is not a problem if you sell 2,000,000 units. But if you only sell 1,000,000 units, you will have $25,000,000 of cash turned into sensors that are sitting in the warehouse. That is $25M that can't be used to pay bills, or improve product, or put to any other legitimate business use.

Inventory Management Targets

How much is the right amount of inventory to have at the end of the year? When you were hired, the board established two inventory management goals for you to meet.
1. Never stock out; have at least one unit of inventory left at the end of the year
2. Do not have more than 60 days of inventory on hand at the end of the year.

What is 60 days of inventory? It is the amount of inventory you would sell in 60 days. Because you don't have control over how many you will actually sell, we are going to talk about 60 days of production instead.

To help visualize 60 days of production, a simple example is provided. Assume you want to produce 1,200 units of product Able in 12 months. That is 100 units a month.

Jan	Feb	March	April	May	June	July	Aug	Sept	Oct	Nov	Dec
100	100	100	100	100	100	100	100	100	100	100	100

Since a month has (on average) 30 days, 60 days of inventory is about 2 months. In this example, 2 months of inventory would be the 100 units produced in November and the 100 units produced in December. If you have 1,200 units available for sale, 60 days of inventory would be 200 units. 60 days is 2/12 of a year. For ease of calculation, 2/12 is 1/6 of a year. A convenient inventory management tools is this simple table (that is presented in a most confusing manner):

Available for Sale: X,XXX units

	Year End Inventory	Sales	
Least->	1	X,XXX-1	<-Most
Most->	X,XXX / 6	X,XXX- (X,XXX / 6)	<-Least

However, it is not at all confusing when you put in real numbers. You stick with the example that you want to have 1,200 units available for sale.

Available for sale: 1,200 units

Year End Inventory	Sales
1	1,200 - 1 = **1,199**
1,200 / 6 = **200**	1,200 - 200 = **1,000**

To meet your inventory management goals:
- What is the least you can have in yearend inventory? Since you never want to stock out, you want at least 1 unit left.
- What is the most you can have in inventory? Since you don't want more than 60 days or 1/6 of a year's worth of inventory, you don't want more than 1,200/6 or 200 units left in the warehouse at the end of the year.
- What is the most you can sell? If you have 1,200 available for sale and have one left in the warehouse, you would have sold 1,199.
- The least you can sell? If you have 1,200 units available for sale have 200 units left at the end of the year, you would have sold 1,000 units total.

If you have 1,200 units available for sale, you will meet your inventory management goal if you sell at least 1,000 but not more than 1,199. If you have 1,200 units available, you will meet your inventory management goal if you have at least 1 but not more than 200 in the warehouse at the end of the year.

Look at FastTrack Report on page 4, Production Analysis. Baldwin had 1,712 units of product Baker available for sale in Round 2; they sold 1,582 and had 120 left in inventory.

Name	Primary Segment	Units Sold	Units in Inventory
Baker	Low	1582	130

To determine if they would have met their performance target for inventory management, you can ask one of two questions:
1. What is the most – and least – they could have left in inventory at the end of the year?
2. What is the most – and least – they could sell and still meet their inventory management goals?

Available for sale:

Year End Inventory	Sales
1	1,712 - 1 = **1,711**
1,712 / 6 = **285**	1,712 - 285 = **1,427**

Did they meet their performance target for Inventory?
- To meet the performance target they would have to sell more than **1,427** but less than **1,711**. Baker sold 1,583 products, an amount that is within the acceptable range.
- To meet the performance target they would have to have at least 1 but not more than 285 left5 in the warehouse at the end of the year. They actually had 129 left in inventory and met their performance target.

This seems straight forward enough. It is the same target—the same standard—for inventory management. It is just expressed in two different ways; in terms of sales and in terms of units left in the warehouse. You decide to test your understanding a little more. Using the same FastTrack information, you ask the following:

- Would your company, Andrews, have met their performance target for inventory in the reported year? Why or Why not?

- What is the most that Daze could have left in inventory and still met their inventory management goal? Did they meet their performance target for Inventory?

Sales Forecasts and Production Schedules

There is one important concept that you have to understand to set your production schedule:

> *The number of units that you make available for sale should generate an inventory management range that captures your sales forecast.*

You start simply. You analyze all of the information available to you and decide that your BEST estimate is that you will sell 1,100 units of your product AceX next year. How many do you produce?

You want to choose a number that generates an inventory management range that is "centered" on 1,100 units. That way, if you sell more than you predict, you will still have some units left over. If you sell less than you predict, you won't have too many left over.

The inventory management range is 2 months' worth of inventory. If you want 1,100 to be in the "middle" of that range, you would to produce so that you would have made 1,100 units in 11 months. If you do that and you sell 1,100 units; you would still have one month's inventory left at the end of the year.

If you want an inventory management centered on 1,100 units; you would:
- Divide 1,100 (number to be in the center of the range) by 11 (number of months that you want to produce your target in). The result is 100 (your 1 month "cushion")
- Add the 100 to 1,100 to get 1,200. This is the number you want to produce.

To check, generate an inventory management table based on having 1,200 units available for sale.

Available for sale: 1,200 units

Year End Inventory	Sales
1	1,199
200	1,000

It is just like magic—only it is math. If you produce 1,200 units, your sales forecast of 1,100 units is right in the middle of the range (1,000 - 1,200). Your forecast is uncertain. If you have been too optimistic in your forecast, you can sell 100 units less (1,000) and still meet your goal. If you was conservative in your forecast, you can sell 99 units more (1,199) and still meet your goal.

For a more realistic example, consider product Baker. You used a market growth forecast to predict sales of 1,232 in the Low Tech segment. (1,120 x 1.1). Baker sold 463 units in the High Tech market, but those customers are going to have better options next year. You did another forecast using the December Customer Survey and predict selling 418 to the High Tech market. Combining your forecasts (1232 + 418) gives you a best guess of 1,650 units. How many should you have available for sale?

You want to pick a number so that you have 1,650 available in 11 months. If you divide 1,650 by 11, you have a monthly production schedule of 150 units. If you make 150 units a month for 12 months, you would have 1,800 units available. (That is the same as adding 1,650 = 150).

Available for sale: 1,800 units

Year End Inventory	Sales
1	1,799
1800 / 6 = **300**	1,800 - 300 = **1,500**

Your target of 1,650 is in the center of the "acceptable sales" range generated by having 1,800 units available for sale.

Note: You are using the clumsy language "having 1,800 available for sale" rather than "making 1,800" because the actual number you have to produce has to take into account the number of units left in inventory. In Able's case (on the right), you want 1,630(000) units available for sale.

Andrews F32795_001

Schedule	Able
Unit Sales Forecast	1,630
Inventory On Hand	123
Production Schedule	1,522
Production After Adj.	1,507

You start the year with 123(000) in the warehouse. Instead of scheduling production for 1,630 units; would schedule so that you would have 1,507 produced (1,630-123 = 1,507).

However, to really have 1,507 produced in a year, you have to schedule production for 1,522 so that your "Production After Adjustment" will be your target of 1,507. (There are several reasons you might not get all of the units you schedule for production. In this case it is because you have a 30 days Accounts Payable lag; and at 30 days, your suppliers withhold about 10% of the components you have ordered from them.)

Unfortunately, things are never as simple as dividing by 11. In most cases of forecasting sales, you get different predictions based on the forecasting techniques you are using. When you were forecasting Baker's sales, you actually had three fairly diverse predictions. Using one method, you had a prediction of 1,560 (which you thought would be low as they sold 1,583 last year). Another produced a guess of 1,723 (which you thought was too optimistic as Baker's High Tech sales would be hurt by the 3 new products entering the High Tech market. Your best guess, the prediction in which you had the most confidence, was 1,650. You were lucky that when you decided to have 1,800 available for sale, the inventory management range "captured" all three guesses. Remember, if you have 1,800 available for sale, you meet your inventory management goal if you sell at least 1,500 and not more than 1,799.

All three of your guesses were larger than 1,500 and smaller than 1,799. If they weren't in the range; you would have to make some decisions about the quality of your guesses.

You want to practice to be sure that you can apply this understanding properly. Using the Round 2 FastTrack Report information, forecast Able's sales for Round 3 using the following three methods:

1. The market growth forecast
2. The potential market share forecast
3. The December Customer Survey

Market Growth	Potential Market Share	December CSS

Using those forecasts, how many would you want to produce for Round 3? And using that number, complete the table below

Units available:

Year End Inventory	Sales
1	

Capacity Decisions

All of the production decisions discussed above assume that you have a factory that has the capacity to produce as many products as you need. When you assume control of the Andrews company, the factory for Able has the capacity to produce 800(000) units running one shift for a full year. If you operate at 100% overtime, you can produce as many as 1,600(000) units. If you look at the FastTrack Report for Round 2, you can see that if companies had NOT increased their capacity, they would face a situation where they could not make enough units to meet the demand for their products. That is a situation you do not want to find yourself in. To complicate matters, there are timing issues involved.

Consider the situation described in the Round 2 FastTrack Report for product Able. At the end of the second year of operation, Able had 1,630 units available for sale and sold them all.

Name	Primary Segment	Units Sold	Units in Inventory	Capac-ity Next Round	Plant Utiliz.
Able	Low	1,630	0	900	175%
Acex		0	0	600	0%

Looking at the market share potential in both markets, you calculate that Able could have easily sold 1,875 units in Round 2. However, Able's factory (with a capacity of 900 units) could have only produced 1,800 running 100% overtime. Able could NOT have made enough to satisfy demand in Round 2. You now realize you should have invested in additional capacity in Round 2. You certainly are going to have to invest in additional capacity in Round 3.

For Round 3, you think you can sell 2,000 units. However, "increases in capacity require a full year." So when you are making decisions about how much capacity you need to add in Round 3, you have to consider your sales forecast for Round 4 because Round 4 is when your new capacity will be available. Thinking two years ahead can be very helpful.

Forecasting 2 years out is highly uncertain. You grow your anticipated Low Tech sales by 10% (the segment growth rate) and get 1,918. When you look at the High Tech market, Able will NOT be a player in Round 4; you think you will get less than 200 units sales.

Physical Plant	
1st Shift Capacity	900
Buy/Sell Capacity	250
Automation Rating	6.5
New Autom. Rating	6.5
Investment ($000)	$8,000

Together, you believe that you will need capacity to produce at least 2,300 units operating at 100% overtime in Round 4. Half of 2,300 equal 1,150 units. (If you had capacity for 1,150 units running one shift, you could make 2,300 units running 2 shifts). You currently have capacity for 900 units, so you would have to add 250 units of capacity (1,150 – 900= 250).

You want to be sure that you can apply this understanding properly. Using the Round 2 FastTrack Report information, answer these questions:

1. What is Cake's sales forecast for Round 3?

2. What is Cake's sales forecast for Round 4?

3. Does Chester need to add capacity for product Cake in round 3? If so, how much?

Build Your Understanding
Foundation Exercise 7 Questions

Determine Inventory Management Targets

1. If you had 1,900 units of your product Able available for sale, what is the least you could sell and still meet your inventory management target?

2. Given the "Production Analysis" table (page 4 of the FastTrack report), did Chester meet its inventory management goal for product Cake?

Use Sales Forecasts to set a Production Schedule

3. If your best guess is that you will be able to sell 1,750 units of your product Abuser next year, what number should you make available for sale to put 1,750 in the middle of the inventory management range?

4. Using the FastTrack Report provided, forecast Able's sales using the following three methods: the December Customer Survey, Market Growth, and Potential Market Share forecasts.

Average Adjusted DCS	Market Growth	Potential Market Share

Using those forecasts, how many units would you want to make available for sale for the next year?

Using that number, complete the table below.

Units available:

Year End Inventory	Sales
1	

Use Sales Forecasts to Make Capacity Decisions

5. You are making decisions for Round 3. Based on your sales forecasts, you decide to make 1,750 units available for sale. You currently have a factory that has a capacity of 950 units with an automation rating of 4.5. Do you need to add capacity this year?

6. Using the FastTrack Report provided, forecast Daze's sales using the following three methods: the December Customer Survey, Market Growth, and Potential Market Share forecasts.

Average Adjusted DCS	Market Growth	Potential Market Share

Using those forecasts, how many would Digby want to make available for sale?

Does Digby need to add capacity for product Daze in the coming year? If yes, how much?

An Introduction to Business

Build Your Understanding
Foundation Exercise 8 - *Production Investments in Capacity and Automation*

A company competes in a market because they believe that they can attract customers to exchange with them and be better off as a result. For a manufacturing company, such as a company that produces and sells electronic sensors, success in the market requires producing quality products:

- That meet customer expectations (effective marketing)
- At the lowest possible production cost (efficient manufacturing)

Efficient manufacturing requires a concrete and specific understanding of two areas:
1. The costs of production, and;
2. The investments that allow you to control those costs.

You resolve to explore those relationships and build your understanding of how operating decisions are reflected on the income statement and so that you can better determine the effectiveness of those decisions. To build this understanding, your experts recommend a solid understanding of

- Team Member Guide - Section 4.3: Operations - Production
- Production Demonstration (www.capsim.com – Help > Manager's Guide)
- Round 3: Rehearsal Simulation

Production and Contribution Margin – *A Review*
The income statement is an accounting document that provides information about how much new wealth- or profit- the company is creating. A manufacturing company creates wealth by creating high quality products at as low a cost of production as possible and then selling them for as high a price as they can.

Because the income statement only recognizes the costs associated with products that are sold over a specific period of time, the contribution margin can be understood in two ways:
1. A total over a period of time. Revenue – Total Variable Costs (also called Cost of Goods Sold or COGS)
2. A "per unit" measure. Price per unit – cost of making the unit (unit cost)

This is more easily seen if you look at the way the income statement numbers are calculated.

Price	X units sold	Revenue
Unit cost	X units sold	- Total Variable Cost
Contribution margin(unit)	X units sold	Contribution Margin

Because the number of units sold is a constant, the relationship between Revenue, total variable cost and contribution margin is the same as the relationship between price, unit cost and contribution margin (unit). Contribution margin is usually reported as a percentage of price (for a per unit contribution margin) or of revenue (for the total contribution margin). It doesn't matter which because the percentages are the same.

Consider the income statement generated by selling 1,000 units at a price of $50 and a unit cost of $30:

$50 X 1000	$50,000
- $30 X 1000	- $30,000
$20 X 1000	$20,000

Calculated on a per unit basis, the contribution margin is $20/$50 or 40%. Calculated on the totals, the contribution margin is $20,000 / $50,000 or 40%. Notice that changing the number of units sold will change the size of the contribution margin on the income statement but it will not change the percentage. In the example, if 2,000 units had been sold the revenue would have been $100,000, total variable cost would have been $60,000, and the contribution margin would have been $40,000. The contribution margin as a percentage would still be 40%.

Contribution Margin as a Percentage is a Measure of Operational Efficiency
To improve the efficiency of your operations (make more profit on every unit that you sell), you need to improve your contribution margin. The only way to improve your contribution margin is to increase your price or to reduce your unit cost. In Foundation, your unit cost consists of two components; material costs and labor costs.

Drawing on your understanding of marketing management, you know that you can increase your contribution margin by raising your price or by lowering your material costs. (You can lower material costs by making your product bigger, slower, and less reliable.) You also know the trade-offs that are associated with those decisions.

ACTION	RESULT
Increase your price	• Lower monthly survey scores • Sell fewer units
Lower your material costs: • Make your product bigger • Make your product slower • Make your product less reliable	• Lower monthly survey scores • Sell fewer units

All of the options for improving the contribution margin through marketing management result in lower sales volume. That is not good.

The other option for improving the contribution margin is to lower labor costs. Labor costs per unit are determined by two things; automation and overtime.

Automation

Automation is a measure of how sophisticated the machinery used in the production process is. The idea is that as automation increases, work processes are altered so that human labor is made more efficient because workers are given more specialized machinery with which to do their jobs. A more cynical understanding is that as you invest in automation, you are replacing human workers with machines.

After reviewing these sections, there are three things you have to understand to use automation to help you meet your goals:
1. As automation goes up; labor costs go down
2. As automation goes up, R&D project times increase
3. Automation is expensive

Automation and Labor Costs

You are surprised at how good the cost information is for the whole industry. The base labor rate at the lowest level of automation (an automation rating of 1) is $11.20 per unit. The labor rate per unit is reduced by about 10% (of the base) for each level of automation. The overtime rate, or the second shift wage differential, is time and a half; or 1.5 times the base rate at each level of automation.

A useful understanding requires you to work out the labor cost details at each level of automation.

Automation Level	Base Rate	Overtime Rate
1	$11.20	$16.80
2	$10.08	$15.12
3	$8.96	
4	$7.84	
5		
6		
7		
8		
9		
10	$1.12	$1.68

The potential of increased automation exciting because it reduces labor costs. Your target is to manage your contribution margin. You decide to take time and think more about this important relationship.

Assume that you have developed a good product; it has the size, performance and reliability that meet your targeted customer's needs. You have set the price that will generate the volume of sales required to be successful. In this situation, the higher your level of automation (the lower your labor cost per unit), the greater your contribution margin will be. That means that your will make more profit on every one you sell.

That is a good start, but you need more details. You decide to calculate contribution margins at different levels of automation. To do this, set up a table and make some assumptions. You assume that your price is $35.00, your material cost per unit is $15.00, and you can sell 1,500(000) units. You set up a table that allows you to calculate the contribution margin (unit), the contribution margin as a percentage of price, and the total contribution margin at the different levels of automation (assuming 0% overtime so you can use the base rate at that automation level).

There are three calculations you want to do

1. Price – (material cost + labor cost) = Contribution Margin (unit)
2. Contribution Margin (unit) / Price = Contribution Margin (percentage)
3. Contribution Margin (unit) * number of units sold = Total Contribution Margin

Price	Material Cost	Automation Level	Labor Cost	**1** Contribution Margin (unit)	**2** Contribution Margin %	**3** Total Contribution Margin
$35.00	$15.00	1	$11.20	$8.80	25%	$13,200
$35.00	$15.00	3				
$35.00	$15.00	5				
$35.00	$15.00	7				
$35.00	$15.00	10	$ 1.12	$18.80	54%	$28,320

Increasing the contribution margin by investing in better machinery for your factory (increasing automation is better machinery) is an investment that, once it is made, results in greater profitability forever—or until the machinery wears out. So if you raise your automation enough to lower you unit cost by $2.24 in round 2, you will make $2.24 more profit on every sensor that you sell for the next 7 years. However, automation slows down product innovation, it increases the R&D cycle time, and it is expensive.

Automation and R&D Project Times
Figure 4.3 in the Team Member Guide on page 14 shows the relationship between automation levels and the length of R&D projects.

Low Tech products should be repositioned every second year. These customers expect that each year their products will be .5 units smaller and .5 units faster. At automation ratings of 8 or above, the R&D Project times get so long that repositioning might take more than one year. You can still manage your product at high levels of automation, but it requires careful planning with respect to timing.

An Introduction to Business

High Tech preferences are more demanding with expectations that products will be .7 units smaller and .7 units faster each year. Therefore, you must reposition your product every year (to keep its age young and positioned on the "ideal spot") to meet the needs of High Tech customers. You can see from the chart, that if you have automation much above 3 or 4; High Tech repositioning takes too long to meet both goals of having the ideal spot and the youngest age.

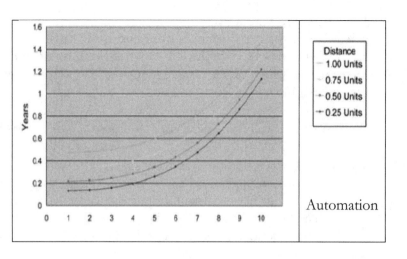

Investing in Automation

The enduring cost savings of automation are a good thing because automation requires a big investment; $4.00 per unit of capacity for every level of automation. So if you want to raise your automation by 1 level; say from an automation level of 3 to an automation level of 4, it will cost you $4.00 per unit of capacity. If you wanted to raise your automation 2 levels; from 3 to 5, it will cost you $8.00 per unit of capacity.

At the end of Round 2, Able has a capacity of 900(000) units and an automation rating of 6.5. If you wanted to raise the automation rating one level (from 6.5 to 7.5), how large of an investment would be required?

Physical Plant	
1st Shift Capacity	900
Buy/Sell Capacity	0
Automation Rating	6.5
New Autom. Rating	7.5
Investment ($000)	$3,600

Automation is $4.00 per level of automation per unit of capacity. You are raising your automation one level (so $4 per unit of capacity) and you have 900 units of capacity. This project would require an investment of $4 x 900(000) or $3,600(000). The Foundation Spreadsheet file calculates this investment in the Production worksheet. You notice that to increase automation one level, you do not enter "1.0," instead you entered in the desired automation level.

To test your understanding, you pose the following problem. You are creating a new product AceX and want to build a very efficient factory to produce it. Since AceX will compete in the High Tech market, you think that an automation level of 4 would be the best. You want your factory to have a capacity of 800(000) units.

1. How much will you have to invest in the machinery for ABLER's factory?

2. What will the labor cost per unit be if you are produce 800 units?

3. What will the labor cost per unit be if you produce 1,600 units?

Investment in Capacity

The other factor that influences labor cost is the capacity of your factory. The capacity of a factory is the number of units you can produce running one shift. How does capacity influence overtime? You can produce more than your first shift capacity; but every unit produced above your first shift capacity costs you one and a half times your base wage. This is standard across most businesses; overtime employees earn "time and a half". If your labor costs $10 per unit for the first shift, it will cost one and a half times that, or $15.00 per unit, for the second shift.

One way to avoid overtime is to have a large enough factory that you can produce all of the necessary units on the first shift. The major flaw with this strategy is that increasing capacity requires a significant investment. Expanding capacity requires two major expenditures:
1. The building, and;
2. The production machinery and equipment.

Whether you are building a new factory or expanding an existing facility, the size of the investment is directly proportional to the number of units of capacity you want to add. For example:
- The building requires an investment of $6.00 for every unit of capacity you wish to add.
- If you want to add 200(000) units of capacity, it will require an investment of $6.00 times 200(000) or $1,200(000) for the "addition" onto your factory.
- If you are adding a new product and building a new factory that has a capacity of 800(000) units, you will need to invest $4,800(000).

Investing in the building gets you a building—a big empty space. To make the building a factory, you have to put machinery in it. You have already done the investment analysis for machinery when you did the automation analysis. How expensive is it to add machinery? It depends on what level of automation and how many units you want to be able to build. For every unit of capacity you want to add, machinery costs $4.00 per level of automation.

You currently have a factory with a capacity of 800(000) units at an automation level of 3. How big of an investment was required to create that factory? Since it is $6.00 per unit for the building and $4.00 per level of automation per unit for the machinery, you can calculate the investment by following these steps:

Building	Machinery	Total
$6.00 x 800(000)	($4.00 x 3) x 800(000)	
$4,800(000)	$9,600(000)	$14,400(000)

Notice that to add capacity, you enter the amount that you want to add. Because this is a new factory, you are going from 0 units to 800 units of capacity.

The Foundation Web spreadsheet allows you to click the "calculate" button to determine the cost of this for you in the Production worksheet.

You enter 800 in Buy/Sell Capacity. If you wanted to go from 800 to 1,000 in the next year, you would enter the amount of capacity you wished to add; or 200 units. As you noticed before, the desired automation rating is what is entered. How do you account for this investment? It is recorded on the balance sheet under Fixed Assets as "Property Plant and Equipment."

Physical Plant	new factory
1st Shift Capacity	-
Buy/Sell Capacity	800
Automation Rating	-
New Autom. Rating	3.0
Investment ($000)	$14,400

You want to test your understanding a little more. Your current factory has a capacity of 700 units at an automation level of 4. What size investment would be required to bring the capacity to 1,100 at the same level of automation?

Selling capacity - Discounting a Sensor

If you find that the demand for one of your products has fallen and believe that it will not recover; you can sell some of your factory. If you find that the demand for one of your products has fallen and don't believe that it will never recover, you can sell all of your factory's capacity. When you do, you will recover 65% of your original investment.

Physical Plant	
1st Shift Capacity	1
Buy/Sell Capacity	(899)
Automation Rating	6.5
New Autom. Rating	6.5
Investment ($000)	($18,699)

An alternative phrasing: You will get back $.65 on the dollar. To sell capacity, enter a negative number (in Buy/Sell Capacity. The Foundation spreadsheet calculates (and reports) how much money you will receive for it.

If you sell **all of the capacity** for your product, FOUNDATION takes that as a liquidation order for that product. The product will disappear from the R&D worksheet in the next year. Any inventory that you have remaining in the warehouse is liquidated at one half the cost of production. "Liquidation" means that it is sold all at once but at ½ the unit cost. And advantage of this option is that you do not have to worry about your inventory — stocking out or having too much is no longer a consideration for this "liquidated" product.

If you **reduce capacity**, even if you downsize your factory so that you have only one unit of capacity remaining, the inventory in the warehouse is not liquidated. You can sell it using whatever pricing strategy is works in the market. This may be an advantage because you have the potential of making a contribution margin from the sale of these products. However, you are still responsible for managing your inventory with this choice. You may end up with too much inventory or you may stock out and you will be responsible for this outcome.

Build Your Understanding
Foundation Exercise 8 Questions
You should know...

Automation: Labor costs, contribution margins, and R&D project times

1. Assuming no overtime, if you raised your automation rate from 3 to 5, how much would your labor costs go down?
   Remember: Each level of increased automation changes your labor cost by $1.12.

2. If you raised your automation rating from 3 to 5, how much would that investment cost and what impact would that have on your labor rate?
   Remember: Each level of increased automation changes your labor cost by $1.12.

3. Assuming no overtime, if you raised your automation rating from 4 to 7, how much would your contribution margin per unit go up? If you had set your price at $30, how much would your contribution margin as a percentage of sales go up?

Calculate the required investment in automation

4. You are creating a new product AceX to compete in the High Tech market, you think that an automation level of 4 would be the best. You want your factory to have a capacity of 1,000(000) units. How much will you have to invest in the machinery for AceX's factory?

5. You have a production line for an existing product. The capacity is for 1,000 units with an automation level of 3. The per-unit cost of adding capacity is $6 for floor space and $4 per level of automation. If you increase the automation from 3 to 6 for the current capacity, what will that cost?

Calculate the required investment in capacity

6. Your current factory has a capacity of 700 units at an automation level of 4. What size investment would be required to bring the capacity to 1,100 at the same level of automation?

7. You are adding a new product and want the factory to have a capacity of 1,000 units at an automation level of 6. What size investment would be required to build this factory?

Determine the impact of reducing capacity and/or discontinuing a product

8. At the end of the year, you have 600 units of product ABYSS in left in inventory; each unit cost $20 to produce. Your gut reaction is that you need to discontinue this product. ABYSS's factory has a capacity of 500 units at an automation level of 6. If you decide to discontinue this product, how much money will you get for the factory? How much will you get for the inventory?

An Introduction to Business

Chapter 5

Finance:
Working and Investment Capital

"Cash is king" and is the single most critical asset in managing a successful business.

Key terms to look for:

- Accounts payable
- Bonds
- Book value
- Current ratio
- Debt-to-asset ratio
- Inventory management
- Leverage
- Line of credit
- Liquidity
- Principal
- Quick or acid ratio
- Stockholder's equity
- Working capital

The activities that you engage in to run your business are kept track of in your current assets and current liabilities accounts. Collectively, these are referred to as your working capital. Cash is the most liquid current asset and is critical to running your business.

In its simplest form …

When you operate your company, you turn cash into inventory and inventory into cash through the sales you make. However, to get the cash you need to create inventory, a company might purchase materials on account, referred to as accounts payable, or take a short-term loan from a bank. In order to generate sales, the company might sell on account to make the transaction more attractive. The working capital cycle, also known as the cash flow cycle, is the time between the payments of what a business owes (payables) and the collection of what a business is owed (receivables). Businesses need to manage the amount of time that funds are "tied-up" in order to reduce the amount of working capital needed for operations. This helps to make certain that there is adequate cash on hand to operate the business successfully.

Accounting Profit versus Cash Flow

Profits, also referred to as earnings or net income, and cash flow are two different concepts. Profits are defined by accounting rules for an income statement. An accrual accounting system is where the accounting system recognizes transactions when the agreement is made, not when the cash is exchanged. This is opposed to a cash accounting system where transactions are recognized when the cash is received. Income statements also include non-cash expenses such as depreciation. When using an accrual accounting system, it is possible for a company to be very profitable and still run out of cash. This may occur when a company is in a growth stage. It is showing a profit, but does not have the cash available to pay its debts. Without cash, the company can go out of business. In addition to managing profitability, the company also has to manage its cash flow: the cash receipts and cash disbursements, or payments, over time.

Working Capital Management

Net working capital is the difference between a business's current assets and its current liabilities. Working capital management involves the decisions related to operating the business. These decisions will involve the management of cash, accounts receivable, inventories, accounts payable, and short-term bank loans.

Working capital management is concerned with the day-to-day operations rather than with long-term business decisions. For example, plans for introducing new products to the market and plans for obtaining the facilities and equipment necessary to produce them are strategic in nature, as are the long-term financing needs of the firm. In general, long-term financing needs are best met through long-term sources of capital such as retained earnings, sale of stock, and the sale of long-term debt obligations (bonds). Working capital management policies address short-term (issues that occur within the business year) problems and opportunities.

There is a direct relationship between sales growth and current asset levels. For example, higher sales volume may be achieved only if production increases. Higher production, however, requires more money tied up in inventory. Additionally, if a firm buys on credit, its accounts payable increase and when it sells on credit, its accounts receivable increase. Therefore, higher sales require a larger investment in current assets, which requires greater financing. Unless something is really wrong, higher sales mean higher profits. To increase profits, you have to effectively manage your working capital.

The Working Capital Cycle

The working capital cycle includes all the activity between the first cash spent producing a product to receiving a cash payment for its sale. The first step is when the firm orders and receives the raw material, generating an account payable. The last step in the cycle happens when you receive the money owed to you from the sale of the product on credit, which is when the account receivable is paid off.

The working capital cycle is defined as the length of time between the payment of the payables and the collection of receivables. During this cycle, a business's funds are unavailable for other purposes. Cash has been paid for purchases but cash has not been collected from sales. Short-term financing may be needed to sustain business activities for this period. Since there is always a cost to such financing, a goal of any business should be to minimize the cycle. To achieve this goal three terms must be clearly understood:

1. **Production cycle** refers to the length of time between the purchase of raw materials, production of the goods or service, and the sale of the finished product.

2. **Accounts payable lag** is the time between the purchase of raw materials on credit and the cash payments made for the resulting accounts payable.

3. **Accounts receivable lag** is the time between the sale of the final product on credit and cash receipts for the accounts receivable.

Let's look at examples with different payable and receivable lags. In both examples assume it takes 40 days after an order is received to process the raw material into finished product (production cycle is 40 days).

30-Day A/P Lag: In the first example, the accounts payable lag is 30 days, and the receivables lag is 45 days. Your company receives the materials and starts to process it. Within 30 days after receiving the material, you have to pay your supplier (A/P lag); 40 days after receiving the material, you have inventory to sell. For 10 days, then, your cash is tied up in inventory that is not available for sale. If you deliver it to your customer on the fortieth day of the production cycle, your customer has 45 more days to pay for it. On that day, your cash has been tied up in inventory for 55 days (10 days before inventory was ready for sale and 45 days after).

45-Day A/P Lag: The second example has the accounts payable lag at 45 days, and the receivables lag at 30 days. Your company receives the materials and starts to process it. Within 40 days after receiving the material, you have inventory to sell. Within 45 days after receiving the material, you have to pay your supplier (A/P lag), For 5 days, you have inventory available for sale with none of your own cash tied up. If you deliver it to your customer on the 40th day of the production cycle, your customer has 30 more days to pay for it. On that day, your cash has been tied up in inventory for only 25 days. (You didn't have to pay your supplier for 5 of the 30 days after delivery).

As mentioned before, the working capital cycle represents the time in which working capital is "tied up" in covering production costs. If a business owner is able to shorten the cycle, the need for external financing and the resulting interest expense will be smaller, thus creating higher profits.

Cash and Marketable Securities

You need cash on hand to pay your bills; for example, to pay wages, buy raw materials, and pay taxes. The question is, how much cash should you have on hand? You need to be sure you can cover your day-to-day transactions. This amount is called the transaction balance. You might want to keep some extra cash on hand to take advantage of special bargains (a supplier's clearance sale of raw materials, for example), or to take advantage of discounts offered by suppliers for early payment of your bills (accounts payable), or as a precaution against emergencies (any unexpected expense). The cash held for such purposes is called *speculative cash balances*.

There are many advantages to having sufficient cash on hand and many problems when you do not have enough. Cash, however, does not work for you. Cash does not earn an explicit return. If you have too much cash on hand, you are not working your assets effectively and your cash is not being used in the most productive manner. As an alternative to holding large cash balances, many companies hold part of their liquid funds in short-term marketable securities. These instruments earn interest and can be very easily converted to cash. Some examples of such securities are:

- *Treasury Bills (T-Bills)* are short-term loans to the United States government with a smallest denomination of $10,000 and that mature in less than one year. Sold at a discount, the buyer pays an amount less than the face value of the T-Bill, but still receives the full amount when the bill matures.

- *Commercial Paper* is an unsecured loan to a large corporation with good and well-established credit ratings. These loans usually mature between 15 and 45 days (but it can be anywhere from 1 to 270 days).

- *Certificates of Deposit (CDs)* are short-term instruments issued by commercial banks. CDs are issued in denominations up to $100,000 and may be traded in the secondary market. They are insured by the Federal Deposit Insurance Corporation (FDIC).

Accounts Receivable and Credit Management

The profitability of a business is dependent upon its ability to successfully sell its products for more than it costs to produce them. Offering to "sell on credit" attracts customers and increases sales volume. However, there are costs to extending credit that must be understood. When a company sells products without receiving cash, an account receivable (A/R) is generated. You are "loaning" your customer the money to buy your products. Normally, a loan generates some value, usually an interest payment. An account receivable "loan" usually generates value in increased sales, not in a cash interest payment.

The total dollar amount of receivables is cash that is "tied up" and unavailable for other uses. This amount is determined by the volume of sales and the average length of time between a sale and receipt of the full cash payment:

Credit sales per day x Length of collection period = Accounts Receivable

For example:

> If a business has credit sales of $1,000 per day and allows 20 days for payment, it has a total of $1,000 x 20 or $20,000 invested in receivables at any given time. Any changes in the volume of sales or the length of the collection period will change the receivable position.

A credit policy refers to the decisions to grant, monitor, and collect the cash for outstanding accounts receivable. Four factors must be considered in establishing an effective credit policy:

1. Credit worthiness standards – *Can your customers pay you back?*

2. Credit period – *How long do they have to pay?*

3. Collection policy – *What you will do if they do not pay?*

4. Early payment discount - *Do you give them a discount if they pay early?*

Inventory Management

A firm's profitability depends on its ability to sell its products. A company has to have enough inventory to meet demand. How does a company know how much is "enough" inventory? They must forecast and develop sales for a period. Since sales depend on many factors outside of a business's control, inventory management is very challenging. Holding inventory levels at less than what is needed will cost the firm lost sales. On the other hand, holding inventory is expensive and involves costs such as storage and insurance expenses. Holding inventory ties up cash that cannot be used for other purposes. Excess inventory must also be avoided to maximize profits.

Typical questions in determining inventory levels include the following:

- How many units of particular products must the firm hold in stock?

- How many units must be ordered or produced at a given time?

- When should the order be placed?

As mentioned before, in determining how many units to have in stock, sales must be predicted and sufficient inventories held to satisfy the expected demand. Moreover, to prepare for potential sales increases, some level of "safety stocks" must also be held. The amount of safety stock is determined by comparing the cost of maintaining this additional inventory against potential sales losses.

The following ratios should help to determine the optimal number of each product to keep in your inventory:

Inventory Turnover Rate = Cost of goods sold / Inventory

Inventory Turnover Days = Number of days in a period / Inventory turnover rate

Ideal Inventory = Cost of goods sold / Industry average turnover rate

For example:

> Last year your business sold goods, which cost $100,000, and your average inventory for the year was worth $10,000. The inventory turnover rate for last year was $100,000/$10,000, or 10 times. Furthermore, the business's inventory turnover days were 360 days/10, or 36 days. These numbers indicate that during the past year, your inventory turned over 10 times and, on average, it took 36 days to sell the entire inventory. When compared with industry averages, the relative strength of your business's inventory management will be revealed. A low inventory turnover rate could indicate overstocking, while high inventory turnover days can represent slow sales.

If the average industry turnover rate is 12 times, your business's ideal inventory levels for the year should have been:

$$\$100,000 \, / \, 12 \, = \, \$8,333$$

This figure may be used as a guideline for determining inventory levels during the current year.

Inventory Carrying Costs

Total costs associated with inventory include the time value of capital tied up in inventories, storage and handling expenses, as well as insurance, taxes, and costs relating to obsolete inventory. These costs are generally referred to as the inventory carrying costs. Carrying costs increase as inventory levels rise.

Short-Term Liabilities

Short-term credit is any liability with an original payment period of less than one year. Major sources of short-term credit include payables (accounts payable, wages payable, taxes payable) and short-term loans. There are both advantages and disadvantages to using short-term credit.

Speed, flexibility, and lower costs are potential advantages of short-term credit. Increased risk to the borrower is considered a disadvantage. Generally, obtaining a long-term loan requires a longer period of time because of the need for a more thorough examination of the borrower's financial statements. Short-term credit, however, usually can be obtained fairly quickly. In addition, short-term credit generally requires a lower interest rate, which is more cost effective than long-term debt.

But even though short-term debt is often less expensive than long-term debt, short-term borrowers face the possibility of paying higher interest rates as their need for new loans develops over a period of time. Over time, there also exists a potential for interest rates to increase. Consequently, short-term borrowing subjects the borrower to uncertain interest expenses as compared with borrowers of long-term funds with locked-in interest rates.

Accounts Payable

Purchasing equipment and raw materials represents a large portion of total operating expenses. A small manufacturing firm may spend in excess of 70% of total sales purchasing raw materials and converting them into finished goods (COGS is 70% of sales and gross margin is 30%). In this type of case, accounts payable become an important source of financing in the short term. Managing prompt payments of accounts and keeping repayment cycles as short as possible make the company an attractive customer.

Short-Term Bank Loans

As a business grows, its needs for "nonspontaneous" sources of credit will grow as well. Commercial banks are major providers of short-term financing to businesses. When applying for a short-term bank loan, select a bank that best serves your needs, and then prepare for a successful loan application interview.

The provisions of a loan agreement must be clearly understood by the borrower if they are to know the true costs of the loan. Loan terms can include "hidden" costs or restrictions on business practices.

Line of Credit

A *line of credit* is an informal understanding between a bank and a borrower that a specific amount of funds is available for future financing purposes. A *revolving credit account* is a formal line of credit offered to larger businesses in exchange for up-front fees and standard interest payments. In return, the bank has the legal obligation to fulfill its commitments under the formal agreement. Some banks require their borrowers to maintain compensating balances, which usually are a certain percentage of the loan amount. Finally, a lender can require a borrower to pledge collateral as security to ensure repayment of the loan's *principal* and interest.

---

[7] Jenny Wonderling, "The Art of Business," Chronogram.com, April 2002, Web http://www.chronogram.com/issue/2002/04/business1.htm.

The Banker's Decision

Factors that your banker may evaluate in considering your loan application:

1. *Your character, integrity, and overall management skills.*

2. *Your company's track record; i.e., its sales and profits.*

3. *Your product and its relative importance to the market.*

4. *Your financial statements, preferably accompanied with a statement from a certified public accountant, (CPA).*

5. *A description of the purpose of the loan.*

6. *Your company's ability to provide data to the bank both accurately and in a timely manner.*

7. *The primary and alternative sources of repayment.*

Factors that your banker may look upon <u>negatively</u> in approving your loan:

1. *Accounts receivable past due, indicating that cash is coming too slowly.*

2. *Accounts payable abnormally extended.*

3. *Poor inventory operation, such as low turnover and large back orders.*

4. *High debt-equity ratio, signifying large outstanding loans.*

5. *Large withdrawals of profits by the company's officers/owners.*

6. *Attempts to borrow short-term funds to meet long-term needs.*

7. *Insufficient financial data.*

8. *Poor credit rating for principal business owners/officers.*

9. *Personal problems of executives.*

Investment Financing: Getting Money to Grow Your Business

Companies that are growing typically need more money to fuel their growth. They need money to develop new products, to buy new equipment, to launch new promotion campaigns, and to take advantage of opportunities in the market as they emerge.

Individuals or organizations who might provide money that will allow you to grow your business want something from you. It is an economic transaction that follows the rules of all economic transactions; people will only participate if they are made better off through the transaction.

There are basically two kinds of transactions that will allow you to get access to additional funds:

1. Taking out a loan (debt contract)
2. Taking on new owners.

Both of these transactions provide cash to help the business thrive. In all other ways, they are quite different.

For example:

> If I have money to invest, it represents wealth that I have created in the past and not yet consumed. I could use that wealth to buy tools that would allow me to create something of value that I could take to the market. This investment in myself would give me a greater ability to create wealth in the future. However, if I am not going to use it myself, I still want to put it to work. I want that money to work for me as hard as it can, 24 hours a day. I want it to work so I do not have to. One of the things I can do is let others use my money to create wealth that will come back to me in some form.

> If I am a person who has money to invest, what do I want out of the transaction? I want the highest return I can get for my money, and I want to be sure that I do not lose my money. The degree of certainty (or uncertainty) that I will get my money back is the "risk." In a market system, I have a lot of choices about how to put my money to work.

> I might be attached to my money and only want it to work in a safe and secure environment. If that is what I want, I would only "rent" my money to people who were going to use it conservatively. Maybe I would rent it to the government, which can guarantee its safe return. The problem is that everything else being equal (which it isn't) there are a lot of people willing to put their money out for a safe use. When there is a lot of money competing to be put to a safe use, it is easy for those "safe users" (for example, electric utilities or governments) to get the use of that money cheaply. For the person investing the money, therefore, the "return" is expected to be low.

> On the other hand, I might be willing to risk my money and give it to someone who will use it in a venture that just might not work out economically. It may represent a risk. For instance, I might put my money to work in a biotech firm. They always need more money to create useful mutant biological stuff. The problem is that at this point, a low percentage of biotech projects work out. However, the ones that do work out economically make huge amounts of money.

To rent your money or attract your interest, they have to offer you a high return on those funds.

The common rule regarding risk and return is:

The higher the risk, the greater the expected return.

Loans

A loan is basically a form of a rental agreement. If I were borrowing money from you, I would be renting the use of your money. The amount borrowed is the principal of the loan. At the end of that loan period, I would be expected to return your money in good condition. I am renting your money for a specific period of time (term of the loan) and paying you a fee for the use (interest) of that money. In most all business situations, the fee for using other people's wealth is a percentage of the money you are renting and called the interest rate.

In business, your venture's risk can be a function of the industry you are in, your strategy for competing in that industry, and your experience in serving this market. Your financing strategy, or the way you go about getting the money you need to grow your business, also influences your risk. The more debt you have the more risk you are exposed to. Debt involves a contract whose terms you must meet. If you do not meet your obligation (make your payment), the contract usually specifies a remedy. This may include your creditor's being able to force you to sell your assets until you can meet your contractual obligations. When this happens, you are in the process of going out of business. The greater the percentage of assets acquired by debt, the greater the possibility that you would be forced to sell key assets to meet your obligations.

In Foundation™

All companies in Foundation face the same level and type of market risk. Therefore, the proportion of your assets that are financed by debt determines your risk level. Your company's risk is measured by the debt-to-assets ratio. When your debt-to-assets ratio approaches 80%, the banks will not lend you additional funds, and they will charge you the highest interest rate possible. Keeping your debt-to-assets ratio at an acceptable level—below 80% in this case—will allow you to have access to more affordable capital that you can use to operate and expand your business.

Borrowing money increases the total value of your company and infuses cash into the business, but this money is not income. The transaction involves increasing the balance of your cash account and increasing the value of the appropriate liability account. Paying back the loan reduces the balance in your cash account (and the value of your company) and the balance in the appropriate liability account.

IMPORTANT NOTE:

Paying down the principal of a loan is not an expense. However, the interest that you pay to use or "rent" the money is a legitimate business expense. Interest expenses reduce the balance in your cash account and the balance in your retained earnings account. Because these interest payments comes out of retained earnings, it is a part of (and expensed on) the income statement and reduces your net profits. The more you borrow, the higher the interest rate and the higher the interest payment. Additional payments against the principal reduce both the principle amount due and the interest payments.

In Foundation™

You can borrow money in four ways:
1. Purchase inventory *(materials)* on credit from your suppliers *(short term)*
2. Take a short-term loan *(1 year)* from the bank
3. Take a long-term loan from the market *(selling a long-term debt called a bond.)*
4. Take an emergency loan *(a short-term loan that is very expensive!)*

Instead of going out of business or selling off your assets, you may be forced to take out an emergency loan. This is an expensive loan that you must pay back within the next year, and it drives your interest rates up. You want to avoid an emergency loan whenever possible by using solid financing strategies as you invest in your business.

Accounts Payable

When you purchase materials on account you increase the balance in your inventory account and you increase the balance in your accounts payable account. You are borrowing the use of materials from your suppliers to create products. When you sell the products, you will have the required cash to pay back your suppliers. As mentioned earlier, the amount of time you can use these materials for is called the Accounts Payable lag. As your A/P lag gets larger, your suppliers become more reluctant to provide more materials. If you do not have the materials, you cannot produce products, and the actual number of units produced may be limited by this restriction.

Short-Term Bank Loans

Banks are financial institutions that accept deposits and make loans. They fall into several categories, such as savings and loans, credit unions, thrift institutions, and commercial banks. Knowing the category in which they include themselves can tell you a lot about the kinds of loans these banks are interested in making. Savings banks are more experienced in dealing with consumer loans, such as home mortgages and automobile loans. Commercial banks have more experience and interest in larger business loans. Regardless of the type of institution, the most important point to keep in mind when dealing with a bank is that bankers seek to avoid risk. Their primary concern is always the safety of their funds. A bank will have a company fill out an application, document their financial history (past balance sheets and income statements), and submit a business plan to assess future potential financial success. In Foundation, your risk is determined by the percentage of assets that are financed by loans, primarily based on the debt-to-assets ratio.

Bonds

A bond is a form of long-term financing. When you borrow money from a bank, you sign a debt contract to use the bank's money for a certain period of time and to pay a specific rate of interest. You might have to pledge specific assets as security, or collateral, for the loan. If you should miss payments, the bank can force you to sell the asset and use that money to retire the loan.

Companies and government entities can develop a similar debt contract, but instead of borrowing money from a bank, they can borrow money directly from investors. These debt contracts are called bonds. Bonds are referred to as *securities* because they represent secured (or asset-based) claims for the investors. Stocks are another type of security. These are secured or asset-based claims against the company and both are traded in *securities markets*.

The debt contract is called an "indenture" and contains the critical information of a loan including answers to these questions:

- Who is borrowing the money?

- How much money is being borrowed?

- For what period of time?

- At what rate of interest?

- How and when is the loan going to be paid off?

- How will the loan amount be secured?

When you borrow money from a bank, you provide information in the loan application that helps the bank determine how likely you are to meet the terms of the contract. The bank uses this assessment to determine whether or not to loan you the money and how high an interest rate they should charge. The higher the risk of nonpayment, the higher the interest rate you have to pay.

It is impractical for every investor who might want to buy a bond (loan some money) to assess the risk of the company (or government entity) who is issuing the bond. Instead, a few well-established companies, such as Moody's and Standard & Poor's, will assess the company and the bond issue and assign it a risk rating. The ratings range from AAA, which is excellent, to D, which indicates the organization presents an exceptionally high level of risk.

Bond ratings progress from a rating of "excellent" to "very poor" in this order:

```
Bond Ratings
     Excellent      AAA        Low Risk
                    AA
                    A

                    BBB
                    BB
                    B

                    CCC
                    CC
                    C

                    DDD
                    DD
     Very Poor      D          High Risk
```

The lower the bond rating the higher the interest rate the issuing company expects to pay in order to attract investors. Companies get very concerned when their bond rating is degraded. It communicates a negative message to the financial community and to the market in general.

The Bond Market

When bonds are first issued, the company who wants to issue the bond has to get permission from the *Securities and Exchange Commission* (a federal agency). The company then typically goes through an **investment bank**. An investment bank is a financial institution that specializes in issuing and reselling new securities such as stocks and bonds.

The financial managers of the company and the investment bankers evaluate the reasons for the bond issue (what are they borrowing money for), how long they want to borrow the money for, how much money they want, and how much interest they expect to pay.

The investment bank then works to market the new bond issue. They contact big investors—such as banks, insurance companies, pension funds—to determine the willingness of the market to buy the bonds and to create a distribution network for the bond issue. The investment bank also *underwrites* (buys) a significant portion of the bond issue. This first sale of the newly issued security takes place in the **primary securities market**.

Because bonds are a secured claim, investors who own them can buy and sell them to other investors. These transactions occur in the *secondary securities markets (or exchanges)* or the "bond market." In the bond market, the bond (debt contract) can trade above or below the face value of the bond. In general, bond prices move in the opposite direction of interest rates—as interest rates fall, bond prices go up, and as interest rates rise, bond prices drop.

A bond is an investment whose return is specified in the debt contract. Consider a very simple example: A $1,000 bond that pays 10% interest per year for 5 years.

As an investor, you view the investment like this:

YEARS	"Bond A"
Year 1	$100
Year 2	$100
Year 3	$100
Year 4	$100
Year 5	$100 + $1,000
TOTAL	$1,500

Because this is a contract, this return on your investment does not vary at all. Suppose as an investor, you had the opportunity to choose between buying the 5-year, 10% bond or a new, 5-year, 15% bond (assume equal "risk or bond rating). If the two investments each borrowing $1,000 looked like this, which would you choose?

YEARS	"Bond A"	"Bond B"
Year 1	$100	$150
Year 2	$100	$150
Year 3	$100	$150
Year 4	$100	$150
Year 5	$100 + $1,000	$150 + $1,000
TOTAL	$1,500	$1,750

The rational investor would pick the investment with the higher return: "Bond B" paying 15% interest. However, if the investor who owned "Bond "A" was motivated, she might offer to sell it at $980. If she attracted no buyers, she might offer it at $960, then $940, and then at some lower price. The potential buyer would then be as well off buying "Bond A" as "Bond B." As the return on the alternative investment (interest rate of the other bond) goes up, the trading price of existing bonds goes down.

Consider the same scenario, but the alternative bond offers a 5-year, 5% return:

YEARS	"Bond A"	"Bond B"
Year 1	$100	$50
Year 2	$100	$50
Year 3	$100	$50
Year 4	$100	$50
Year 5	$100 + $1,000	$50 + $1,000
TOTAL	**$1,500**	**$1,250**

The rational investor would want to buy bond "A," as would other investors. The current owner of "Bond A" faces a situation where there are motivated buyers competing to buy his investment. The owner would then bid the price of a 10% bond higher than the face value ($1,000) because the return is better than any alternatives. At some price, say $1,120 for discussion purposes, the two investments would be equally attractive and would generate buyers. A $1,120 price for a bond that pays $1,500 would be about as attractive as a $1,000 price for a bond that pays $1,250.

Bonds are bought and sold every day on the bond market. At the end of a trading day, the information about the outstanding bonds, the value of their issue, their trading prices, yield, and the bond rating of the company are published in the financial press, as per the following example:

Company	Issue	Value	Yield	Close	S&P
Digby	10.8S2013	$4,347,878	10.3%	105.16	AA
	13.2S2014	$23,000,000	11.4%	115.48	AA

In this instance, the company "Digby" has two different issues of bonds outstanding.

The first bond "10.8S2013" is:
- An issue that pays 10.8% each year until the bond matures in 2013.
- One that when the series was issued, Digby received $4,347,878.
- Currently trading at 105.16% of its face value.
- Showing a face value of $1,000, so it would currently cost you $1,051.60 to purchase one of these bonds.
- One with a 10.8% return on a price of $1,051.60, so it's real return, or yield, 10.3%.

The second bond "13.2S2014" is:
- An issue that pays 13.2% each year until the bond matures in 2014.
- A significant issue, raising $23 million.
- Currently trading at $1,154.80 for a $1,000 face-value bond.
- Showing a purchase price of $1,154.80 on a 13.2% bond and providing a real yield of 11.4%.
- The company has an AA bond rating based on its current financial status.

Stockowner's Equity

When you sell shares of stock, you are selling ownership rights to a corporation. Owners, or stockholders, never have to be paid back, and you do not have to pay them interest on the money that they are investing in the company. However, owners have a claim against the assets and the wealth that is created in the form of net income, earnings, and profit by the company. That ownership claim *never* ends. This ownership lasts as long as the organization does, and the owners will continue to have a say in the management of the company.

Stock Market

When you own a stock, you are actually a part-owner of a corporation. As a shareholder, you have a "say" in how the company operates, although your voice may be just one among thousands of other shareholders.

Companies initially issue stock to raise capital to run their businesses, often motivated by the fact that they need more money. A corporation sells shares to investors in an organized fashion called a public offering, the first of which is its ***Initial Public Offering***, or ***IPO***. After the company's IPO, investors are free to sell their shares and buy more, but not from the company directly. Instead, shares are traded on organized stock markets like the New York Stock Exchange and NASDAQ.

A company can issue common stock or preferred stock. ***Common stock*** represents a simple share of ownership and each common stock share has one vote to cast when electing the corporation's board of directors. If the company were to go bankrupt, the corporation would have no financial liability to common shareholders, and those shares may become worthless.

Preferred stock is a form of stock that is traded at a far lower volume than common stock and has specific privileges. Preferred shareholders, often having some kind of history or relationship within the company, may receive higher dividends and have a first claim to assets if a company should go bankrupt.

Shares of stock are traditionally represented by a piece of paper called a stock certificate. Since shares of stock trade electronically, you may never actually see a physical certificate for the share that you own. The brokerage holds the shares on your behalf in what is known as a "street name" which is nothing more than a method of bookkeeping and has no effect on your ownership of the stock. Owning shares in street name is much more efficient and convenient, especially when it is time to sell the stock.

Like a bond, stocks are secured investments. They have a claim against the assets of the company. The company sells new shares of stock to potential owners through the *primary securities market* in a process similar to the way new bond issues are sold. The company meets with an investment banker who reviews the business strategy and specific plans for the money that is to be raised. The investment bank underwrites or buys, markets and distributes the new shares. Underwriters charge a commission and also make money by holding some of the shares until the price per share rises. Again, once stock has been issued, owners can buy from and sell to others on the **secondary securities markets** *(exchanges)* in "stock markets" in the United States and in numerous exchanges throughout the world. The company itself receives no cash for shares that are sold in the secondary markets, and every corporation wants to see its stock price increase for the benefit of its shareholders and the financial reputation of the corporation.

If you are a potential investor in a company (someone who is thinking about purchasing shares of stock in a company), you have choices about which company you might want to purchase shares in. You want to invest your money in a company that is going to work your money and create as much wealth for you as possible.

There are two ways in which your wealth increases by owning stock:

1. When the value of your shares increases as the stock price goes up
2. When the company distributes the profits it has created in the form of cash payments called dividends to owners out of net income.

Paying Dividends
When a company creates profit, the profit belongs to the owners. There are only two things that can happen with that profit:

1. It can be kept in the company as retained earnings
2. It can be distributed to the owners in the form of a cash disbursement or payment. If it is paid out to the owners, it reduces the amount of cash on hand.

For example:
> As an owner, you might wish to invest in a company that pays a regular dividend. If you were retired you might want to have 10,000 shares of stock in a company that regularly pays a four dollar per share dividend. You would know that every year, you would receive $40,000 in cash for me to live on. You would think about this dividend policy added to the value of the shares of stock you purchased and would consider this in deciding how much you might be willing to pay for that stock.

Value and Stock Claims

Interactions between buyers and sellers determines stock price. A potential buyer might consider three things in determining how much they would be willing to pay to own stock in a particular company:

- The value of the stock's claim against the assets of the company

- How much profit the company makes per share of stock

- How much of that profit is distributed to owners (in form of a dividend)

The value of this claim is determined by dividing the total owners' equity from the balance sheet by the number of shares outstanding. For instance, if the value of the owners' claim is $100 million and there are 2 million shares of stock issued and outstanding, then each share has a claim against the assets of the company worth $50. This is called the ***book value*** of the stock.

There are two ways to increase book value:

1. Increase the value of total owners' equity
2. Reduce the number of shares outstanding (buy back stock)

The easiest way to increase owners' equity is to make a profit and reinvest it, or retain it, in the company, which increases the value of the "retained earnings" account. If you sell more shares to increase the value of the common stock account, you have increased the value of total owners' equity, but you have also increased the number of shares you have to divide it by in order to get book value.

In general, current owners would prefer that you borrow money to grow the company, if you can afford the interest payments, rather than dilute the value of their claim.

Stock Reports

Large volumes of stock are commonly traded every day. At the end of the day, the transactions in the market are summarized so investors can study what has been happening and make informed decisions about future purchases.

Company	Close	Change	Shares	Dividend	Yield	P/E	EPS
Andrews	$51.29	$22.48	2,000,000	$2.00	3.9%	5.8	$8.88
Baldwin	$69.86	$21.09	2,157,790	$0.50	0.7%	5.6	$12.49
Chester	$41.26	$6.75	2,045,860	$1.00	2.4%	6.8	$6.04
Digby	$37.40	$10.60	4,096,380	$2.00	5.3%	8.1	$4.61
Erie	$15.82	($0.47)	3,209,871	$0.00	0.0%	18.0	$0.88
Ferris	$65.20	$24.76	2,339,022	$3.00	4.6%	6.0	$10.84

In the above table, the trading of six companies' stocks is summarized. Let's use the first one, Andrews, as an example:

Close

At the end of the trading day, buyers in the stock market determined that Andrews' stock was worth $51.29 per share.

Change

Because this is $22.48 higher than the close at the end of the last trading period, the last closing price was $28.81:

$$\$28.81 + \$22.48 = \$51.29$$

Shares

Andrews has 2 million shares of stock outstanding. Last year, they paid a dividend of $2.00 to each of those 2 million shareholders . Issuing these dividends reduces their cash by $4 million:

($2 x 2 million)

Dividend

The company decided to share all or part of the profits with the owners of the company. The dividend that was "declared" by those managing the company was $2.00 and each shareholder receives that amount for each share they own.

Yield

A yield of 3.9% is a comparison of the dividend amount to the closing price of the stock. The $2.00 dividend payment represents a 3.9% return (yield) on the $51.29 stock price:

$$\$2.00 / \$51.29 = .0389 \text{ or approximately } 3.9\%$$

Price Earnings Ratio – P/E

The Price/Earnings ratio, or the PE, measures how many times you would have to multiply the earnings to get the stock price. Andrews' stock is trading at 5.8 times as much as it earned in this one year.

Earnings Per Share – EPS

Each share of Andrews' outstanding stock (2 million) has earned $8.88 of net income (Earnings per Share). This indicates their total net income must have been $17.76 million (2 million x $8.88).

Financial Ratios and Ratio Analysis

Financial ratios are computed from an organization's balance sheet and income statement. Ratio analysis is a method of expressing the relationships between any two accounting elements. These ratios provide a convenient technique for performing financial analysis. Ratios can be used to compare to the company's past performance, to competitors' performance, and to the industry's overall performance.

Twelve key ratios help business owners assess the financial health of their company and they are categorized into these four areas.

1. Liquidity ratios
2. Leverage ratios
3. Operating ratios
4. Profitability ratios

The table on the next page "12 Key Ratios" summarizes these key ratios, how they are calculated, and what each ratio measures. Foundation consistently uses five of these ratios in the "Selected Financial Statistics" table.

In Foundation™

The "Selected Financial Statistics" section found on Page 1 of the FastTrack report focuses on five ratios including Return on Sales (ROS), Asset Turnover (Turnover), Return on Assets (ROA), Leverage, and Return on Equity (ROE). The "Stock Market Summary" table on page 2 of the FastTrack Report summarizes several important stock ratios including Earnings per Share. This ratio information is provided for the Andrews company and for all its competitors. These ratios offer insight into the financial performance of the Andrews company and how that performance compares to competitors within the industry.

Return on Sales: ROS = Net Income / Sales
Return on Sales is a measure of how much profit was created for every dollar of sales.

Asset Turnover: Turnover = Sales / Total Assets
The total sales generated in a particular year divided by the value of total assets for the same period is referred to as *asset turnover*, or in some cases, just as *turnover*. Asset turnover measures the amount of "activity" taking place in a business, or how active the assets are in regard to generating sales . The higher the use of these assets, such as the plant and equipment, the higher the level of this activity reflected in the asset turnover ratio .

Return on Assets: ROA = Net Income / Total Assets
Return on Assets is a measure of how much profit was created for the assets gathered.

Return on Equity: ROE = Net Income / Owners' Equity
Return on Equity is a measure of how much profit was created with owners' investments.

12 Key Ratios

Category	Ratio Name	Calculation	What it measures:
Liquidity Ratios	Current Ratio	$\dfrac{\text{Current Assets}}{\text{Current Liabilities}}$	A company's ability to meet short-term debt obligations
	Quick Ratio	$\dfrac{\text{Current Assets - Inventory}}{\text{Current Liabilities}}$	A company's ability to meet short-term debt obligations without including inventory.
Leverage Ratios	Debt-to-Total Assets Ratio	$\dfrac{\text{Total Debt}}{\text{Total Assets}}$	The percentage of funds that represent debt provided by creditors.
	Debt-to-Net Worth Ratio	$\dfrac{\text{Total Debt}}{\text{Tangible Net Worth}}$	What the business "owes" compared to what it is worth.
	Times Interest Earned Ratio	$\dfrac{\text{EBIT}}{\text{Total Interest Expense}}$	The extent to which earnings can decline before the company is unable to meet its annual interest costs.
Operating Ratios	Average Inventory Turnover Ratio	$\dfrac{\text{Cost of Goods Sold}}{\text{Average Inventory}}$	The number of times average inventory is sold out, or turned over, during the accounting period.
	Average Collection Period Ratio	$\dfrac{\text{Credit Sales}}{\text{Accounts Receivable}}$	The average number of days it takes to collect accounts receivables.
	Average Payable Period Ratio	$\dfrac{\text{Purchases}}{\text{Accounts Payable}}$	The average number of days it takes to pay its accounts receivable.
	Net Sales to Total Assets	$\dfrac{\text{Net Sales}}{\text{Total Assets}}$	A company's ability to generate sales in relation to assets.
Profitability Ratios	Return on Sales Ratio (ROS)	$\dfrac{\text{Net Income}}{\text{Total Sales}}$	A company's profit for each dollar of sales it makes.
	Return on Assets Ratio (ROA)	$\dfrac{\text{Net Income}}{\text{Total Assets}}$	A company's profit for each dollar of assets it owns.
	Return on Equity Ratio (ROE)	$\dfrac{\text{Net Income}}{\text{Owners' Equity}}$	A company's profit for each dollar of stockholder's investment in the firm.

Leverage

The concept of *leverage* measures how "big" of a company the managers have created using the owners' investments. Foundation applies another leverage ratio based on total assets divided by total owners' equity.

Leverage = Total Assets / Total Owners' Equity

This leverage ratio determines how the assets were purchased; through owners' equity or through debt. A larger total owners' equity and a lower dependence on debt is associated with a lower measure of leverage. A smaller leverage number indicates a lower dependency on using debt to purchase assets and that the owners <u>own</u> a greater portion of the assets. A larger leverage number indicates a greater dependency on debt.

For example, assume that owners have invested a total of $1 million. In this first example, the managers have created a company whose total assets are $1.5 million. The leverage ratio is 1.5.

$1.5 million / $1 million = 1.5

How could the managers create a $1.5 million company with owners' investments of $1 million? Remember, the accounting equation is:

Assets = Liabilities + Owners' Equity

One way they can accomplish this is by borrowing the $.5 million. The managers have created a company 1.5 times as big as the owners' investments by borrowing additional capital.

In the second example, the managers have created a company whose total assets are $5 million from the initial $1 million invested. Therefore, the leverage ratio is 5.

$5 million / $1 million = 5

Managers in this company used the initial $1 million investment to borrow an additional $4 million. They created a company five times as big as the owners' investments.

From a current stockholder's perspective, it is desirable to borrow money rather than to sell stock, as long as it makes economic sense. A stockholder would rather have the business borrow (and pay a reasonable interest rate) rather than have the business repeatedly sell stock which dilutes their ownership position. Leverage tracks this relationship.

In Foundation™

Rather than use one of the leverage ratios listed in the previous table, Foundation applies a leverage ratio that places total assets over total owners' equity. This suggests that it is more attractive for current stockholders if the company borrows money rather than sells stock, or issue equity capital. Borrowing avoids diluting stock value and also requires that long-term debt has a "reasonable" interest rate and that those funds are to be used wisely to benefit the company.

An Introduction to Business

Earnings per Share

Other ratios also provide insight for owners. The primary goal of a business is to make a profit for its shareholders. Owners are interested in how much new wealth (profit) the company makes per share of stock and desire the company to make as much profit as possible. Earnings per share, or EPS, is a ratio that calculates profit per share:

$$\textbf{EPS} \; = \; \textbf{Net Income / Number of shares}$$

If a company with 1 million shares of stock outstanding creates a net income of \$10 million, the EPS would be \$10 per share. Clearly, the way to maximize this number is to make as much profit as possible while keeping the number of shares as low as possible. In addition, remember that owners have a claim against all future profits of the company. The company made \$10 per share this year, an owner might anticipate earnings at least that good in the future. This anticipation of future earnings also influences how the value of a share is determined.

Other Important Ratios

Proper management and use of current assets and current liabilities is crucial to the health and survival of any small business. Three ratios allow a comparison of your business with your competitors' and to industry averages. These ratios also play an important role in the granting or denial of loan requests. Managers should calculate and monitor these financial ratios as part of their working capital management policy.

Current Ratio = Current Assets / Current Liabilities

Quick or Acid Ratio = (Current Assets - Inventory) / Current Liabilities

Total Debt-to-Total Assets Ratio = Total Debt / Total Assets

The Current and Quick ratios measure liquidity and reveal whether the firm can meet its debts for the coming year. The Debt-to-Asset Ratio shows the degree of financial leverage.

Smith's Home Furnishings   *A business profile*

This retail furniture store was in the middle of a rapid expansion program and opened several stores in a relative short period of time. It appeared that the business was thriving. Rather than paying for these new buildings, however, Smith's Home Furnishings was leasing them. They had also made arrangements with furniture manufacturers to allow the stores to have the manufacturers' inventory on the showroom floor without paying for it until it was sold. Smith's was a company that owned very few assets and had acquired a tremendous amount of debt. Due to this expansion, Smith's debt-to-assets ratio was much higher compared to acceptable industry standards, and as a result the business was forced into bankruptcy.

Using the Cash Flow Statement as a Management Tool

A business needs profits and, equally as critical, it needs cash. It is important that managers ensure that the business has sufficient cash on hand to purchase and pay for the materials, human resources and other expenses required to continue to produce goods and services. Cash keeps a business functioning.

As discussed earlier, there is a difference between profitability and cash flow. A business may be profitable and still have a negative cash flow—a difficult concept for many business owners to understand. This is because there are things that take cash "out" of the business that are not classified as expenses. These include payment of loan principal, payment of credit card principal, and when owners are paid through "draws" rather than through dividends. These transactions take cash out of the business yet they are not reported on the income statement. Instead, they show up on the cash flow statement.

The cash-flow statement can be a valuable tool to determine how much cash is available now and how much will be available in the future and when. This activity, called cash flow management, requires careful planning. Although sales may be booming, if sufficient cash is not available to pay the expenses for the month, the business will be in an difficult position. This may result in a costly "emergency loan" or potentially a bankruptcy. Alternately, if excess cash balances are allowed to sit idle instead of being invested, a firm loses the potential opportunity for cash returns that it might have otherwise earned.

The cash flow statement has two primary purposes. First, it tracks the cash flowing into or out of the business over a period of time, usually a year or a 3-month quarter. Second, it reconciles the income statement and balance sheet. From the balance sheet, the cash flow statement shows the differences in the level of assets or liabilities from the previous period. From the income statement, it reconciles the accounting assumptions with the available cash "in the bank."

One major difference between the cash flow statement and the balance sheet and income statement is that there are no accounting assumptions or estimations on the cash flow statement. For example, the balance sheet estimates the worth of acquired businesses (goodwill) and intangibles, such as patents or brand names. Likewise, the income statement contains many accounting assumptions for things like depreciation and taxes. In contrast, the cash flow statement values are very real, representing the "exact" amount of cash coming in and going out of the business. Since creating cash from assets is the basic function of any business, investors consider the cash flow statement to be the most important of the three financial statements.

Cash flow statements are organized into three sections, cash from operations, cash from investing, and cash from financing activities.

- *Cash from operations* is the most important because it includes cash activities from day-to-day operations. Increases and decreases in receivables and payables are accounted for in this section of the cash flow statement along with other activities from operating your business and selling your products and services. Cash from operations reconciles reported net income from the income statement and adds back non-cash costs. It also accounts for the change in working assets, such as inventory.

An Introduction to Business

- *Cash from investing activities* include the purchase and sale of long-term fixed assets, such as property, plant and equipment. In addition, it may also include when the company lists out items like capital expenditures, acquired businesses, and purchase or sale of stock or bond holdings from other corporations.

- *Cash from financing activities* includes the borrowing and repayment of long-term liabilities. Cash from financing activities is where dividend payouts, stock repurchases, cash received from stock and bond issues, and debt repayments are recorded.

The Cash Flow Statement's unique purpose is to track the in-flow and out-flow of cash and track business activities from a cash perspective.

A Simple Cash Flow Statement

Cash Flows from Operating Activities	2012	2011
Net Income (Loss)	$2,382	$2,485
Adjustment for non-cash items		
Depreciation	$960	$960
Extraordinary gains/losses/write-offs	$22	$0
Change in Current Assets and Liabilities		
Accounts Payable	$339	$855
Inventory	$2,353	($2,000)
Accounts Receivable	($902)	$3,647
Net cash from operations	$5,154	$5,593
Cash Flows from Investing Activities		
Plant Improvements	$0	$0
Cash Flows from Financing Activities		
Dividends Paid	$0	($1,000)
Sales of Common Stock	$2,000	$0
Purchase of Common Stock	$0	$0
Cash from long-term debt	$0	$0
Retirement of long-term debt	($1,000)	$0
Change in current debt (net)	$0	$0
Net cash from financing activities	$1,000	($1,000)
Net Change in Cash Position	$6,154	$4,593
Closing Cash Position	$11,747	$5,240

Note: *Negative cash flows are denoted by numbers in parentheses in this example. Negative values may also be represented with a negative sign in front of the number and/or with the number shown in red.*

For example:

In the Cash Flow Statement on the previous page it shows a negative figure for "Inventory" in the year 2011. A negative figure in inventory represents the value of the cash required for that expense of ($2,000) to build inventory that was not sold. This represents a use of cash. When that inventory is sold, that will generate cash. In the 2012 column, a positive figure of $2,353 indicates the company sold "down" their inventory from the previous year's inventory level to generate cash for the company. In other words, the company had less inventory in the most recent period compared to the period before and the sale of that inventory generated cash. This represents a source of cash.

Other cash flow observations for 2012 from the cash flow statement on the previous page include:

- Accounts Receivable were ($902) less than the year before—decreasing cash flow

- Net Cash from operations increased by $5,154—indicating an increase in cash flow

- Stock was sold to bring in $2,000 of cash to use within the company—a source of cash

- A long-term debt, such as a bond, was paid off (retired) for $1,000—decreasing cash flow

- The combination of the cash from stock and retiring the bond ended up in a "Net cash from financing activities" of a positive $1,000—increasing cash flow

- The "Net change in the Cash Position" indicates a positive $6,154 on cash flow

- The year ended with a "Closing Cash Position" of $11,747 in available cash

The following table on the next page describes the cash flow activity and how each of these entries may result in a cash coming in to the business, or cash flowing out of the business.

Koss Corporation   *A business profile*

Michael Koss is president of Koss Corporation, a company that manufactures stereos headphones. He now knows the importance of cash flow management from experience. Koss expanded rapidly during the 1980's and it did not have sufficient cash flow. The corporation filed for reorganization under Chapter 11 and bankruptcy and emergency actions saved the business. Today, Koss manages with the determination never to repeat the same mistake. "I look at cash every single day" says Koss. "That is absolutely critical." [8]

Understanding the cash flow statement gives critical insight into the cash position of the company. All three of the key financial statements—the balance sheet, income statement, and cash flow statement—provide a unique view and each is critical to the overall health and wise management of a business.

---

[8] Karen M. Kroll, "Cash Wears the Crown," *Industry Week*, May 6, 1996. pp. 16-18.

Cash Flow Activity

Category	Cash Flow In *Positive Cash Flow:* *Bringing cash in*	Cash Flow Out *Negative Cash Flow:* *Taking cash out*
Cash Flow from Operating Activities		
Net Income (Loss)	Net income was higher than the previous period.	Net income was lower than the previous period
Depreciation	This captures the past investment in plant and equipment.	Depreciate will not cause a cash out-flow.
Account Payable	Account payable was greater compared to the previous period.	Account payable was less compared to the previous period.
Inventory	Inventory levels were less than the previous period.	Inventory levels were greater than before.
Accounts Receivable	Account receivable was less compared to the previous period.	Account receivable was greater compared to the previous period.
Cash Flows from Investing Activities		
Plant and Equipment	An investment in plant and equipment was sold.	An investment was made in plant and equipment.
Cash Flows from Financing Activities		
Dividends Paid	Does not apply.	Dividends were paid to stockholders.
Sale of Common Stock	Stock was sold (issued) to bring in cash.	Does not apply.
Purchase of Common Stock	Does not apply.	Stock was bought back (retired) by the company.
Retirement of Long-term Debt	Does not apply.	Long-term debt was paid (retired) by the company.
Change in Current Debt	Short term debt increased.	Short-term debt was paid.

Chapter Summary Questions

Be able to answer these types of questions in these areas:

Working Capital

1. Describe the difference between profit and cash.

2. Why is it important to understand working capital?

3. How is capital acquired through the finance department?

4. If you sell products on credit, how is that transaction recorded?

5. What might be the ramifications, financially and from a marketing perspective, of increasing the account receivable lag time?

6. How does working capital relate to the Cash Flow Statement?

Inventory Management

7. What is the Inventory Turnover Rate and how is it measured?

8. How can inventory costs be financed?

9. What is a line of credit?

Ratios

10. What does return on sales (ROS) measure and what relevance might that provide?

11. What insight might return on equity (ROE) provide?

12. What does leverage measure?

13. What might a radical change in leverage from year to year indicate?

14. What does earnings per share measure?

An Introduction to Business

Build Your Understanding
Foundation Exercise 9 - *Working and Investment Capital*

You know that you will need financial resources (capital) in order to operate your company effectively. You also know that over the next couple of years, you are going to also need large amounts of money to create the larger, more competitive company. There are only two sources of capital; you can borrow it or get additional investment from your owners. Both have advantages and disadvantages. Both have limits.

To build this understanding, your experts recommend a solid understanding of
- Team Member Guide – Operations: Finance
- Finance Demonstration (www.capsim.com >Help > Manager's Guide)
- Round 4: Rehearsal Simulation

Finance

You know that you can get money by borrowing funds or by seeking additional investments from your owners. What should you use? Under what conditions should you borrow and under what conditions should you seek owners' investments? You already know that there is no simple answer. Instead, you look to answer these two questions:
1. What limits the availability of funds?
2. How do my decisions affect my performance?

Debt

In your own life, you strive to eliminate debt. But you can't manage the company in that same way as you manage your personal finances. In your personal life, debt buys non-income producing assets. The interest payments on your loans consume your income and wealth. But, in business, you borrow money to acquire income producing assets. Without debt, your company's asset base (which defines your capacity to compete in the market) will not be as large as it would be if you used debt. When the cash from debt is used effectively within the company, it can be a valuable resource. Conceivably, a competitor could have identical levels of owners' investment and could have assets worth two to three times as much as yours.

If you can borrow money at 10% and make 20%, you should borrow all that you need. The relevant questions are:
- Can you find investments that generate a higher return than the cost of the borrowing?
- What is the risk that our investments will not produce the expected return?

However, you also know that the riskiness of your loans is a function of how much debt you have. The more debt you have; the higher the risk. The higher the risk, the higher the interest rate you have to pay. When you have a lot of debt, you are paying a high interest rate on a lot of money. The interest you pay is an expense that reduces your profit.

For bonds, you are limited because bondholders will lend you up to 80% of the current accounting value of your Plant and Equipment (80% of your Total Fixed Assets). Therefore, if the depreciated value of Plant and Equipment totaled $50M; you could issue no more than a total of $40M in bonds.

The Round 2 FastTrack reports that you have Total Fixed Assets worth $29,298 ($37,44 in Plant and Equipment that has been depreciated by $8,142). 80% of that value would be $23,438; the limit on your total amount of money you can borrow using bonds.

Long Term Debt

Retire Long Term Debt ($000)	$0
Issue Long Term Debt ($000)	$0
Long term interest rate	9.0%
Maximum issue this year	$16,105

You currently have outstanding bonds worth $7,333. If you subtract that from the limit, you get the maximum you can issue this year, $16,105. ($23,438 - $7,333 = $16,105). The Finance worksheet in the Foundation Spreadsheet calculates and reports this limit for you.

Equity

You can raise money by issuing shares of stock. Investors give you cash in exchange for ownership rights in the company. They freely enter into this exchange because they believe that you will make them better off. They are "better off" to the extent that the value of their shares of stock (the price at which it trades) increases over time. Stock price is the measure of how much wealth you have created for your owners.

> **Market Capitalization:** *Market Capitalization is the value that the stock market places on the firm—stock price times shares outstanding. One can argue that Market Capitalization is a better measure than stock price for evaluating the wealth created because if two firms have the same stock price but one firm has issued twice as many shares, then they would have created twice as much wealth.*

What drives stock price? Stock price is a function of three things:

1. **Book Value:** Book value is defined as total owner's equity divided by the number of shares outstanding. Owners' equity is the value of the owner's claim against the company's assets.

2. **Earnings Per Share (EPS):** EPS is a measure of how much profit is created for each share of stock. It is calculated by dividing profits by the number of shares outstanding.

3. **Dividends:** Dividends are a cash disbursement (payment) of profits to the owners. Declared on a "per share" basis ($2.00 per share), dividends set higher than EPS have no additional benefit to stock price.

Of course, stock prices are influenced by many other factors. Your goal is a simple understanding of stock price that gives you the ability to manage it.

Stock price is a measure of the market value of the company and that value is expressed on a per share basis. To understand what drives stock price, you want to think about what would influence the price you would be willing to pay to buy a business.

Perhaps the first thing would be the value of the assets the company owns. If you wanted to buy a restaurant that had land and building worth $450,000 and another $200,000 in equipment and fixtures, which information would influence how much you would be willing to pay?

Common Stock

Shares Outstanding (000)	2,475
Price Per Share 1/1/2012	$27.48
Earnings Per Share	$3.21
Max Stock Issue ($000)	$13,603
Issue Stock ($000)	$0
Max Stock Retire ($000)	$3,401
Retire Stock ($000)	$0
Dividend Per Share	$0.00

However, it is not the value of the assets (the building and equipment) but how much of those assets that the current owners own. So you would need to subtract how much they owe (Total Liabilities) from the value of the assets to get an accurate measure.

If the current owners owed $350,000, the value of the owner's claim against the restaurant would be $300,000 ($650,000 - $350,000).

Total Assets = Total Liabilities + Owners' Equity

The Owners' Equity is the value of the owners' claims against the assets of the company. If you divide that number by the number of "owners" you get the Book Value. In the case of a corporation, instead of dividing by the number of owners, you divide by the number of shares and get a "per share" measure of asset value owned free and clear.

The value of a business is much more than the value of its assets, it is in the new wealth (profit) that can be created employing those assets. How much profit did this company create last year? How much profit in the year before? More importantly, how much profit can the company create next year? In 5 years? In 10 years? You would be willing to pay a lot more for a company that generated $1,000,000 in profit every year than a company that generated $200,000. Earnings Per Share is the amount of profit generated expressed on a "per share" basis.

Dividends reflect your past performance. Your owners expect you to generate a profit every year. Within reason, they expect you to make more profit every year. What do they expect you to do with the profit? If your company is growing (bigger factories, new products, better machinery), the owners will let you use past profits to finance that growth. The owners let you do this with the expectation that you are developing an increased capacity to make them wealthier.

If the company has cash in excess of what it needs to operate and grow, the owners expect you to give them their money back. These are the profits you have earned in their name.

One of the reasons that dividend policy is going to be important to you is that your Board of Directors has limited your investment option. You have no freedom to invest outside the company. As you have more years of profitability, you have no investment options so you have to pursue an aggressive dividend policy. How do stockholders evaluate your dividend policy? First, dividends are averaged over the past two years. Second, dividend amounts above the current EPS (or above the two years average EPS if dividends are falling) are ignored. This makes sense to you. If you pay out more per share (dividend per share) than you earn per share (EPS), then the payment is not out of profits. You must be reducing your retained earnings; you must be reducing your book value. That is not a sustainable practice.

The best way to increase your stock price is to increase profits every year and give the profits to the owners if you don't have any other way to make them wealthier.

From the Finance section in the Foundation worksheet, you can set your dividend policy. If you enter $1.00 as the dividend per share, your cash position would decrease by $1.00 for each of the 2,475(000) shares, or $2,475,000. A dividend of $2.00 would reduce cash by $4,950,000 ($2 x 2,475).

You are limited as to how much new stock you can issue. Page 16 of the Team Member Guide states that new stock issues are limited to 20% of your company's outstanding shares. With 2,475(000) shares of stock outstanding, 20% of that is 495(000). That is the maximum number of new shares that could be offered (issued) in the coming year. Because your shares are currently trading for $27.48 each, if you issued 495(000) of them, you would raise $13,602,600. That is the amount of the stock limit reported.

Emergency Loans
If a normal business runs out of cash, it is in big trouble. It has to sell its assets, reducing its ability to compete. In the worst case, it goes bankrupt. You were really surprised and a little concerned when your Board informed you that if you have a shortage of cash, you will immediately get a loan from "Big Al" a legally suspect character. As this only will happen in emergencies, you start thinking about is as an emergency loan

The Foundation spreadsheet files provides you an accurate model of your company and the outcomes of your decisions. It uses "Your Sales Forecast" to determine *projected* outcomes. These projections establish the information in the Proforma statements. Whatever you enter, the program will show you how successful you will be in the market IF YOU WOULD SELL THAT NUMBER .

If your forecast is inaccurate — too high or too low — the information provided in the proforma statements may be meaningless or even deceptive.

As soon as you schedule production for a certain number of units, your inventory management targets (a least 1 but not more than 60 days of inventory) are established. If you were to enter the number of units from the top of that range, the profit and cash available at the end of the year reported in your FOUNDATION workbook is going to be the best possible outcome available to you.

You forecast sales and decide to make 1,800 units of Able available for sale at $35.00 each. You make your marketing decisions. You set your production schedule so that 1,800 are available. You make a $20,000 investment in increased capacity and automation. A total of 1,800 units is entered in the "your sales forecast" cell in the Marketing worksheet. You check and your Proforma Income Statement shows $9,765 profit. You started the year with $9,812 in cash and end with $1,206. You have financed a $20,000 investment out of operations; no loans, no increased owners' investments.

Your Sales Forecast	Cash Positions	
1,800	December 31, 2011	$9,812
	December 31, 2012	$1,206

But that is ONLY if you sell 1,800 units.

If you have 1,800 units available for sale, you want at least one unit but not more than 60 days of inventory in the warehouse at the end of the year. 60 days of inventory is 300 units. If you had 1,800 units available and had 300 left at the end of the year, you must have sold 1,500.

Your Sales Forecast	Cash Positions	
1,500	December 31, 2011	$9,812
	December 31, 2012	($6,878)

How good is your performance if you only sell 1,500 units? You enter 1,500 into the "your sales forecast" and check. You are still profitable but your profit has fallen to $6,184. You started the year with $9,812 in cash but end with a shortfall of $6,878 (because you still have the $20,000 investment in capacity).

You are definitely going to need to raise some additional capital. If you do not, you will run out of cash and have to take an emergency loan from "Big Al."

You decide on a rule for yourself. You will always make all of your operating and investment decisions first. You will calculate your inventory management range and enter the bottom of that range. This is your "worst case" into the sales forecast. Then, and only then, you will make your financing decisions.

Build Your Understanding
Foundation Exercise 9 Questions

Stock Table

Company	Close	Change	Shares	Market Cap ($M)	Book Value	EPS	Dividend	Yield	P/E
Andrews	$27.48	$10.28	2,474,994	$68	$12.96	$3.66	$0.00	0.0%	7.5
Baldwin	$19.98	$5.79	2,220,036	$44	$10.54	$2.38	$0.00	0.0%	8.4
Chester	$13.83	($0.26)	2,160,748	$30	$8.89	$0.88	$0.00	0.0%	15.6
Digby	$23.60	$7.31	2,137,845	$50	$11.49	$2.90	$0.00	0.0%	8.1
Erie	$12.43	($0.22)	2,226,367	$28	$8.52	$0.78	$0.00	0.0%	15.9
Ferris	$16.05	($0.44)	2,054,656	$33	$7.88	$1.01	$0.00	0.0%	15.8

1. Which company's owners had the greatest increase in wealth last year?

2. Which company has sold the most shares of stock?

3. How is market capitalization calculated?

4. Which company has created the most wealth for its owners?

5. How is book value calculated?

6. Looking only at the stock table, what is value of *Digby's* Total Owners' Equity (from the Balance Sheet)?

7. Who created the most profit per shareholder?

8. How is "EPS" of the stock table calculated?

9. Looking only at the stock table, how much profit did *Digby's* create last year?

10. If company *(select one)* had declared a dividend of $2 per share, how much would their cash position have decreased?

11. How is the "yield" of the stock table calculated?

12. How is "P/E" of the stock table calculated?

Bond Table

BOND MARKET SUMMARY					
Company	Series#	Face	Yield	Close	Rating
Andrews	12.0S2013	$1,733,333	11.4%	$105.28	AA
	13.0S2015	$2,600,000	11.5%	$112.96	AA
	9.0S2021	$3,000,000	9.0%	$100.00	AA
Baldwin	12.0S2013	$1,733,333	11.8%	$101.54	B
	13.0S2015	$2,600,000	12.3%	$105.88	B
	10.0S2020	$2,480,000	10.6%	$93.93	B
	11.0S2021	$5,044,916	11.1%	$99.41	B
Chester	12.0S2013	$1,733,333	11.9%	$101.02	B
	13.0S2015	$2,600,000	12.4%	$104.92	B
	10.0S2020	$2,366,478	10.8%	$92.37	B
	10.9S2021	$5,055,277	11.2%	$97.10	B
Digby	12.0S2013	$1,733,333	11.8%	$101.37	B
	13.0S2015	$2,600,000	12.3%	$105.56	B
	10.0S2020	$2,291,811	10.7%	$93.41	B
	10.9S2021	$4,863,235	11.1%	$98.25	B
Erie	12.0S2013	$1,733,333	11.9%	$101.19	B
	13.0S2015	$2,600,000	12.4%	$105.24	B
	10.0S2020	$2,366,478	10.8%	$92.89	B
	11.0S2021	$5,128,211	11.2%	$98.26	B
Ferris	12.0S2013	$1,733,333	11.9%	$100.68	CCC
	13.0S2015	$2,600,000	12.5%	$104.29	CCC
	10.0S2020	$425,144	10.9%	$91.34	CCC
	11.0S2021	$2,992,039	11.4%	$96.55	CCC

1. What is company *Digby's* long term debt?

2. Which company has the greatest long term debt?

3. What interest rate is company *Erie* paying on their bond that is due in 2021?

4. In 2015, how much will company *Chester* have to pay to retire their bonds that mature that year?

5. If I wanted to buy one of company *Baldwin's* series **13.0S2015** bonds (face value $1,000) on the secondary market, how much would I have to pay?

6. Who is the most risky company to loan money to?

7. How is yield calculated on the bond table?

Chapter 6

Business and Society: The Legal and Regulatory System

The private enterprise system requires laws to make corrections when markets do not produce the outcomes desirable for the people in a society.

Key terms to look for:

- Administrative law
- Agency
- Arbitration
- Civil law
- Contract elements
- Common law
- Contract law
- Criminal law
- Expressed warranty
- Fraud
- Limited warranty
- Mediation
- Statutory law
- Tort

Our society has agreed to live by a set of rules or laws that ensure that the conditions necessary for free private enterprise exist and are protected. These rules or laws are set by the customs of the society or through the action of the government, which acts as the agent for the society. While the law establishes the private enterprise system, it also corrects for the times when markets fail or when markets do not produce the outcomes most desired by the people in a society.

Chapter 1 discussed the four conditions required for the private enterprise system to work:

1. Right to private property
2. Right to keep profits
3. Freedom of Choice
4. Fair competition

These four conditions, necessary for the private enterprise system to function, are established in different bodies of law. When these conditions exist, competition for transactions in markets will create pressure for innovation and low prices and result in an efficient allocation of goods. As a society, we value these outcomes.

The right to *private property* and the right to *keep profits* are defined in a body of property law. **Property law** establishes the rights of a person to own, use, transfer, and captures the economic value of different kinds of property. It recognizes that property can be *tangible* (that is, has a physical existence, such as a car) and *intangible* (such as a trademark or stock in a corporation). Property law establishes:

- **Real property:** Real estate and everything attached to it

- **Personal property:** Property other than real property

- **Intellectual property:** Property generated by a person's creative activities. For example, patents give an inventor the exclusive right to exploit an invention for a period of time. A trademark provides legal protection to a created identity or brand based upon a name, a mark, or a symbol. Copyrights protect the "original works of authorship" and include categories such as literary works, musical works (including any accompanying lyrics and words), dramatic works (including any accompanying music, pantomimes and choreographic works), pictorial works, graphic works, sculptural works, motion pictures and other audiovisual works, sound recordings, and architectural works.

Fair competition is established in a wide variety of law and regulation. In general, fair competition is broadly established in laws that prevent businesses from:

- Restraining trade and monopolizing markets (Sherman Antitrust Act)

- Price discrimination, tying, and exclusive agreements that substantially lessen competition (Clayton Act).

All areas of law that influence business practice contribute to our shared definition of fairness. Examples are the laws and regulations that establish standards of conduct in negotiating contracts with a company's buyers or suppliers, providing information (advertising) to consumers, providing information to potential investors, and negotiating with employees or their representatives.

CONTRACT LAW

The heart of the private enterprise system is the transaction, or the mutual agreement of exchange. Virtually every transaction is carried out by means of a contract. A contract is a mutual agreement between two or more parties whose terms are enforceable in court. A contract does not have to be written. It is any agreement that meets three criteria, which are called ***contract elements*** include:

- ***Voluntary agreement:*** The offer and acceptance have to be freely and knowingly made; it is not a contract if any party uses fraud or force to come to agreement.

- ***Consideration:*** To be a contract, the agreement to exchange must involve something of economic value (money, goods, or services). Therefore, the word *consideration* is another term for *money*.

- ***Contractual capacity:*** To be a contract, both parties must have a legal ability to enter into the contract. Individuals who are minors (under the age of 18), mentally unstable, mentally incapable, insane, or intoxicated lack the capacity to enter into a legal contract.

The failure to live up to the terms agreed upon in a contract is called breach of contract. Unless mutually agreed to by all parties, a court can order the terms of the contract to be met and damages to be paid if the breach resulted in monetary damages.

Sources of Law

How did the "rules" of our society come into existence? There are three sources:

1. ***Statutory law:*** Written laws established by federal, state, county, or city governments

2. ***Common law:*** Unwritten laws that are established by judicial decisions; such law in the United States was inherited from English law

3. ***Administrative law:*** Regulations established by administrative agencies

Dispute Resolution

Whenever there are individuals acting in their own best interest, there will be conflict. As standards of behavior are established, there will be disputes over whether specific behaviors meet those standards. There are two kinds of disputes:

1. Disputes between an individual and the government

2. Disputes between two individuals. ("Individuals" can be any form of private party and can include different kinds of businesses).

A dispute between the government and an individual over whether behavior meets the set standards is a matter of ***criminal law***. Violation of criminal law is called a crime and may be punished by fines and/or imprisonment. A dispute between two individuals is considered a matter of ***civil law***. Violations of civil law may result in fines but not imprisonment.

Violations of criminal law are resolved through the court system. Each level of government (federal, state, and city levels, for example) has its own courts to resolve violations of the laws that they establish. **Trial courts** determine the facts of a case, the laws that pertain, and apply the law to resolve the dispute. If either party feels that the law was misinterpreted or misapplied, they can appeal the decision to an **appellate court**. Court judgments are binding and are enforced through the power of the government.

When two individuals have a dispute, it is called a civil dispute. Civil disputes are initiated and resolved through **lawsuits**. Lawsuits are the main remedy for business disputes. As with criminal law, they are resolved in trial and appellate courts.

Legal Options

The United States is a litigious society. This is a sophisticated way of saying we sue each other often. As a result of this demand and the consequent long delays in our court systems, alternative methods of dispute resolution are gaining popularity. These methods are typically faster and more cost effective than litigation through the traditional court system and include the following:

> **Arbitration** is a form of dispute resolution where the parties submit their case to a neutral third party called an arbitrator. The arbitrator decides how the dispute will be resolved and acts somewhat like a judge in the process. Although in most cases, arbitration is binding and requires the parties to accept the legally binding and enforceable solution, arbitration can be non-binding. Either party may appeal the arbitrator's decision to a court but the court will generally not change the arbitrator's findings but decide only whether the arbitrator acted properly.

> **Mediation** is a form of negotiated resolution using a third party mediator to help reach an agreement. A neutral negotiator helps the two parties negotiate a settlement. Typically the mediator meets with each side separately until both sides agree to a settlement. Mediation is nonbinding, and neither side has the power of the courts to enforce the settlement. The dissatisfied party can take this case to court. In other words, the mediator functions more like a counselor than a judge, and the parties do not have to accept the mediator's decision.

Agency

Agency law allows an individual to assign another person the power to act and to enter into agreements. The two parties (the principal and the agent) enter into an **agency agreement**. The **principal** is the person who wishes to have a specific task accomplished, and the **agent** is the one who acts on the principal's behalf. **Power of attorney** is a legal document that authorizes a person to act as another's agent. A **Partnership Agreement** establishes a business partnership (form of organization) and creates mutual agency for the partners on behalf of the company.

Bankruptcy

If an individual or business cannot meet its contractual obligations based on available assets, it can declare bankruptcy as an option of last resort. Bankruptcy, or legal insolvency, asks a court to declare an individual or company unable to meet its contractual obligations and to release them from those obligations. The assets of the person or company declared bankrupt are sold to meet as much of the contractual obligation as possible. There are different kinds of bankruptcy:

Chapter 7	Requires that the business be dissolved and assets liquidated
Chapter 11	Temporarily frees the business from its obligations while it reorganizes and works out a court-approved plan for meeting its obligations
Chapter 13	Similar to Chapter 11, except it is limited to individuals versus businesses

Uniform Commercial Code

The laws governing business practice can come from many sources. States (except Louisiana) have adopted a consistent set of statutory laws that simplify commerce called the Uniform Commercial Code (UCC). As an example, the UCC has a section covering sales agreements, which are of course contracts. The UCC addresses the rights of buyers and sellers, transfers of ownership, the legal assumption of risk, and warranties. A warranty defines the terms that the seller will honor.

All sales are covered by an ***implied warranty*** that allows the buyer to assume that:

- The seller has clear title to the product (that is, it has not been stolen)

- The product will perform the function for which it was produced and sold

- It will perform as advertised

An "***expressed warranty***" covers any additional terms the seller will honor. An automobile manufacturer, for example, might offer a 5-year, 50,000-mile warranty on a vehicle during which it will fix any defects in the car.

TORT

As a society, we expect that the conduct of business will not "wrong" or harm others. A ***tort*** is a civil wrong and includes all "wrongs" (other than breach of contract) in which one party through action or inaction causes harm to another. If a UPS driver, for example, loses control of a truck and causes injury to a person or their property, that person can sue the driver and the company for damages. The driver committed a tort.

Fraud is a form of a tort and specifically describes a criminal act in which one party in a transaction hurts another by purposefully deceiving or manipulating them. For example, a travel agency that sells you a vacation package but never intended to deliver the plane tickets is committing fraud. If a hospital bills your insurance company for services that it did not provide, that is fraud. A criminal act and fraud convictions can result in imprisonment and fines.

An important part of tort law is ***product liability***, which establishes a business's legal responsibility to be diligent (not negligent) in the design, production, sale, and consumption of products. Liability often relies on the concept of what a *reasonable person* might expect to happen when using a product. For example, a reasonable person would expect a kitchen knife to be sharp and could not sue if he or she were cut while using it. A reasonable person would not expect a kitchen knife to break or separate from its handle in normal use and could sue if this happened and an injury or damage resulted.

FEDERAL ADMINISTRATIVE AGENCIES

Governments can pass a law that sets up an administrative agency that establishes operating rules (regulations) to guide business practices. Many agencies also have the power to resolve disputes involving their regulations. In these disputes, an administrative law judge decides the issues at a "hearing" rather than at a trial. Most agencies are established to regulate the practices within a specific industry, but some have authority in multiple industries and are called "cross-industry."

Cross-industry Agencies:

- Federal Trade Commission (FTC): business practices; false and deceptive advertising, labeling, and pricing

- Consumer Product Safety Commission (CPSC): consumer safety

- Occupational Safety and Health Administration (OSHA): worker safety issues

- Equal Employment Opportunity Commission (EEOC): employment discrimination

- Environmental Protection Agency (EPA): pollution standards

Industry Specific Agencies

- Food and Drug Administration (FDA): foods, drugs, and medical devices

- Interstate Commerce Commission (ICC): railroads, trucks, buses, ships

- Federal Communications Commission (FCC) wire, radio, TV, satellite, and cable

- Federal Energy Regulatory Commission (FERC): electricity, gas

- Federal Aviation Administration (FAA): airline industry

- Federal Highway Administration (FHA): vehicle and transportation safety

- Securities and Exchange Commission (SEC): corporate securities trading

Chapter Summary Questions

Be able to answer these types of questions in these areas:

Contract Law and Dispute Resolution

1. What three sources have determined criminal and civil laws?

2. What are the requirements that a contract must meet to be enforceable by the courts?

3. What does the term "consideration" mean?

4. For what reasons may a person's contractual capacity be limited or nonexistent?

5. What alternative dispute resolution method(s) is a form of negotiation involving one or more third-parties, usually chosen by the disputing parties, to help reach a <u>binding</u> settlement?

6. What alternative dispute resolution method(s) is a form of negotiation involving one or more third-parties, usually chosen by the disputing parties, to help reach a <u>non-binding</u> settlement?

Bankruptcy

7. What is the primary purpose of the law of bankruptcy?

8. What "chapter" of bankruptcy temporarily frees the business from its obligations while it reorganizes and works out a court-approved plan for meeting paying its debts?

Uniform Commercial Code

9. What is the Uniform Commercial Code?

10. How does an expressed warranty differ from an implied warranty?

Torts and Fraud

11. What does the term "tort" mean?

12. What is fraud and how does that relate to tort?

13. Fraud is a civil wrong that may be intentional or result from negligence. True or False?

14. What are the requirements for the enforcement of a contract?

Federal Administrative Agencies

15. Although the FTC regulates a variety of business practices, it allocates a large portion of resources toward dealing with what?

16. Violations of the Clean Air Act are enforced by what federal agency?

17. The Equal Employment Opportunity Commission investigates and resolves discrimination in what type of practices?

Chapter 7

Business Ethics

Business ethics involve the moral and behavioral standards people apply as they make business decisions, solve business problems, and interact with stakeholders.

Key terms to look for:

- Code of conduct violation

- Conflict of interest

- Ethicism

- Ethics officers

- Externalities

- Falsification of records

- Sarbanes-Oxley Act of 2002

- Sarbox

- Social contracts theory

- Social responsibility

- Whistleblowers

The free enterprise system relies on people and companies making business decisions that are responsible. Business ethics involve the study of proper business policies and practices regarding controversial issues not address by laws and regulations that may result in a negative impact. They address behavior and decisions based on honesty, fair competition, and respect for the interests of the company, its owners, its employees and also the entire society. When Warren Buffet—the world's most successful business investor— was asked what he looked for in a new employee, he replied: "I look for three things. The first is personal integrity, the second is intelligence, and the third is high energy level. But it you don't have the first, the second two don't matter."[9]

Ethical organizations practice the following types of behaviors:
- Treating employees, customers, investors and the public "fairly"
- Making "fairness" a top priority
- Holding every member personally accountable for his or her actions
- Communicating core values and principles to all members
- Demanding and rewarding integrity from all members in all situations.[10]

What does "fair" mean? Business ethics attempt to answer this question.

Business ethics is the application of ethical behavior in a business context. Business ethics can be examined from various perspectives, including the perspective of the employee, the commercial enterprise, and society as a whole. In the course of business, situations arise in which there is conflict between one or more of these parties when satisfying the interest of one party is a detriment to the other. For example, a particular outcome might be good for the employee, whereas, it would be bad for the company. From this vantage point, ethicists see the principal role of ethics as the harmonization and reconciliation of these types of conflicting interests.

Ethical dilemmas may occur in the following situations:
- **_Code of conduct violation:_** Acting in a way that is inconsistent with the organization's ethical standards
- **_Conflict of interest:_** Choosing actions that promote your personal interest at the cost of others
- **_Falsification of records:_** Altering records to present inaccurate information to managers, owners and/or potential investors
- **_Whistleblower situations:_** Informing superiors or authorities of illegal or unethical organizational behavior.

Ethical Issues and Approaches

Philosophers and others disagree about the purpose of business in society. Some, including economist Milton Friedman, suggest that the principal role of business is to maximize returns to its owners. Under this view, only those activities that increase profitability and shareholder value should be encouraged. Therefore, companies that are likely to survive in a competitive marketplace are those that place profit maximization above everything else. However, others point out that self-interest would still require a business to obey the law and adhere to basic

---

[9] Quoted by Adrian Gostick and Dana Telford, The Integrity Advantage," Gibbs Smith, 2003, p. 3-4.
[10] Alan Axelrod, *My First Book of Business Ethics*, Quirk Books, 2007, p. 7.

moral rules. The consequences of failing to do so could prove to be very costly in terms of fines, loss of licensure, or the company's reputation.

Another perspective is that a business has moral duties that extend beyond serving the interests of its owners or stockholders. These duties consist of more than simply obeying the law. Those that support this view believe that a business has moral responsibilities towards the so-called *stakeholders*, the people who have an interest in the conduct of the business including employees, customers, vendors, the local community, or even society as a whole.

Baxter   *A business profile*

Harry M. Jansen Kraemer, Jr. is chairman and CEO of Baxter, a global medical equipment and supplies company. He was shocked when he discovered that several kidney dialysis patients in Spain mysteriously died and it was linked to their equipment. Several days later, additional deaths occurred in Croatia. A team of Baxter experts determined that a fluid manufactured by another company and used by Baxter's equipment was causing a pulmonary embolism. Kraemer and this management team had three choices: hide the findings, blame others, or take responsibility. The company publicly apologized, halted manufacturing the products, shut down the plants that made the filters, and made financial settlements with all of the families affected costing the company $189 million. Kraemer recommended to the board of directors that his bonus should be reduced by 40 percent and other executives' bonuses should be reduced by 20 percent. "We try to do the right thing," Kraemer says. "If we live the lives we profess, we'll add shareholder value."[11]

Social Contracts Theory

Theorists have adapted a social contract theory to business. In these situations, companies become quasi-democratic associations, and employees and other stakeholders are given voice over a company's operations. This approach has become especially popular through the revival of contract theory in political philosophy largely due to John Rawls' book *A Theory of Justice* and the advent of the consensus-oriented approach to solving business problems. This was an aspect of the "quality movement" that emerged in the 1980s.

Professors Thomas Donaldson and Thomas Dunfee proposed what they call ***Integrative Social Theory***, which is a version of the contract theory for business. Donaldson and Dunfee suggest that conflicting interests are best resolved by formulating a "fair agreement" between the parties by using a combination of:
1. Macro-principles that all rational people would agree upon as universal principles, and;
2. Micro-principles formulated by actual agreements among the interested parties.[12]

---

[11] Michael Sisk, "Do the Right Thing," Harvard Business School: Working Knowledge, September 29, 2003, http://hbsworkingknowledge.hbs.edu/item.jhtml?id_3689&tmoral_leadership.

[12] Thomas Donaldson and Thomas Dunfee, *Ties the Bind: A Social Contracts Approach to Business Ethics*, Harvard Business School Press, 1999, p. 5.

Critics state that the proponents of contract theories miss a central point, namely, that a business is someone's property and not a mini-state or a means of distributing social justice.

Ethical issues may take place when companies must comply with multiple and sometimes conflicting legal or cultural standards. This may occur when multinational companies operate in countries with varying practices. For example, should a company be obligated to obey the laws of its home country, or should it follow the less stringent laws of the developing country in which it does business? Although in some parts of the world, bribery is a customary and accepted way of doing business, U.S. law forbids companies from paying bribes domestically and overseas. Similar ethical issues occur with regard to child labor, employee safety, work hours, wages, discrimination, and environmental protection laws.

Concerns regarding the stockholder theory of business arise from the fear that those that survive in a competitive business environment are businesses that recognize that their only role is to maximize profits, not to behave ethically. This perspective suggests that the competitive system fosters a downward ethical spiral.

Consequences and Costs of Unethical Behavior

The costs of unethical behavior by organizations and individuals may include:

- Increasing unemployment, and therefore increases rates of poverty and crime
- Factors that endanger workers and their future health
- Increasing air, water, and soil pollution, and therefore increased rates of cancer, disease, and conflicts over water and food
- Factors that contribute to global warming
- Increasing obstacles to resolving long-term issues, such as reducing the use of fossil fuel with clean renewable energy options.

In addition to the potential costs to stakeholders, costs become "externalities." Externalities are those costs that are paid for by a third party, such as a government organization.

Tyco   *A business profile*

The former CEO of Tyco International Ltd., Dennis Kozlowski and its former chief of finance Mark Swartz were sentenced to up to 25 years in prison in a case that exposed the executives' extravagant personal lifestyles using company funds. They arranged for the corporation to pay for a toga birthday party on a Mediterranean island for Kozlowski's wife costing $2 million and for a Manhattan apartment worth $18 million that included a $6,000 shower curtain. Kozlowski and Swartz were also accused of giving themselves more than $150 million in illegal bonuses, forgiving loans to themselves, and manipulating the company's stock price. After a four-month trial, the jury deliberated for 11 days before returning 22 guilty verdicts on counts of grand larceny, falsifying business records, securities fraud, and conspiracy.[13]

---

[13] Grace Wong, "Kozlowski gets up to 25 years", *CNN/Money*, September 19, 2005, http://money.cnn.com/2005/09/19/news/newsmakers/kozlowski_sentence.

Corporate Ethics Policies

Many companies have formulated internal policies pertaining to the ethical conduct of employees as part of more comprehensive compliance and ethics programs. These policies can be simple exhortations in broad, highly-generalized language (typically called a corporate ethics statement), or they can be more detailed policies, containing specific behavioral requirements (typically called corporate ethics codes). These policies attempt to identify the company's expectations of workers and to offer guidance on handling some of the more common ethical problems. The objective of these policies is to create greater ethical awareness and a more consistent application to avoid ethical disasters. In some cases, businesses can also use ethical decision making to minimize the involvement of government agencies.

An increasing number of companies require employees to attend training sessions regarding business conduct. The content of these seminars often includes a discussion of the company's policies along with a discussion of specific case studies and legal requirements. For example, some companies require their employees to sign agreements stating that they will abide by the company's rules of conduct. Many organizations are currently assessing the environmental factors that can lead employees to engage in unethical conduct. Others have redefined their core values in the light of ethical considerations. For example, BP's "beyond petroleum" environmental spin draws attention from their original name, British Petroleum.

Inconsistent Views

Not everyone supports corporate policies that govern ethical conduct. Some claim that ethical problems are better dealt with by depending upon employees to use their own judgment. Others believe that corporate ethics policies are primarily rooted in utilitarian concerns and that they are mainly to limit the company's legal liability, or gain public favor by giving the appearance of being a good corporate citizen.

Ideally, the company can avoid a lawsuit because its employees will follow the rules. If a lawsuit occurs, the company can claim that the problems would not have arisen if the employee had only followed the code properly.

There may be a disconnection between the company's code of ethics and the company's actual practices. To be successful, most ethicists suggest that an ethics policy should be:

- Given the unequivocal support of top management, by both word and example.

- Explained in writing and orally, with periodic reinforcement.

- Made doable—something employees can both understand and perform.

- Monitored by top management, with routine inspections for compliance and improvement.

- Backed up by clearly stated consequences in the case of disobedience.

- Observed as neutral and free of biases.

Sarbanes-Oxley Act

The Sarbanes-Oxley Act of 2002 was signed into U.S. law on July 30, 2002 in response to a number of major corporate and accounting scandals. These scandals including Enron, Tyco International, Peregrine Systems and WorldCom, resulted in a decline of public trust in accounting and reporting practices. The legislation is wide-ranging and establishes new or enhanced standards for all U.S. public company boards, management, and public accounting firms. Supporters of these reforms believe that the legislation was necessary and useful while critics believe it does more economic damage than it prevents. The Sarbanes-Oxley Act is also known as the Public Company Accounting Reform and Investor Protection Act of 2002 and is commonly called *SOX* or *Sarbox*.

Whistleblowers

A *whistleblower* is a person who raises a concern about wrongdoing taking place in an organization and, in most cases, this person is from that organization. The identified misconduct may be classified in many ways such as a violation of a law, rule, regulation and/or a direct threat to public interest, such as fraud, health/safety violations, and corruption. Whistleblowers may make their allegations internally (to others within the accused organization) or externally (to regulators, law enforcement agencies, to the media or to groups concerned with the issues).

Whistleblowers frequently face reprisal from the organization or group which they have accused or from related organizations. In passing the 2002 Sarbanes-Oxley Act, the Senate Judiciary Committee found that whistleblower protections were dependent on the "patchwork and vagaries" of varying state statutes. Still, a wide variety of federal and state laws protect employees who call attention to violations, help with enforcement proceedings, or refuse to obey unlawful directions.

Ethics Officers

Ethics officers, sometimes called "compliance" or "business conduct officers," have been appointed formally by organizations since the mid-1980s. One of the catalysts for the creation of this new role was a series of fraud, corruption and abuse scandals that afflicted the U.S. defense industry at that time. In 1991, the Ethics & Compliance Officer Association (ECOA)—originally the Ethics Officer Association (EOA)—was founded at the Center for Business Ethics at Bentley College, Waltham, Massachusetts as a professional association for those responsible for managing the organizations' efforts to achieve ethical best practices.

Another critical factor in the decisions of companies to appoint ethics/compliance officers was the *Federal Sentencing Guidelines for Organizations Act* in 1991, which set standards for all organizations—large or small, commercial and non-commercial. Firms must follow these regulations to obtain a reduction in sentence if they should be convicted of a federal offense. Although intended to assist judges with sentencing, it is unclear if it has helped to establish best practices.

In the wake of numerous corporate scandals from 2001 to 2004, even small and medium-sized companies have begun to appoint ethics officers. Ethics officers are responsible for assessing the ethical implications of a company's activities, making recommendations regarding ' ethical policies, and disseminating information to employees.

Ethics officers often report to the Chief Executive Officer. They are particularly interested in uncovering or preventing unethical and illegal actions. This trend is partly due to the Sarbanes-Oxley Act in the United States, which was enacted in reaction to these scandals.

The effectiveness of the ethics officer position is unclear. If the appointment is made primarily as a reaction to legislative requirements, one might expect the impact to be minimal. Ethical business practices result from a corporate culture that consistently places value on ethical behavior starting from the very top of the organization. The mere establishment of a position to oversee ethics will most likely be insufficient. Instead, a more systematic program with consistent support from general management will be more necessary.

Professional Ethics

Professional ethics cover the myriad of practical ethical dilemmas that occur in specific functional areas of companies or in relation to recognized business professions.

Ethics of Accounting

Ethical issues regarding accounting practices address issues relating to financial reporting, trading, compensation, and payment policies and may include the following.

- "Creative" accounting, earnings management, and misleading financial analysis.

- Insider trading, securities fraud, and scams that concern criminal manipulation of the financial markets.

- Executive compensation: concerns excessive payments made to corporate CEO's.

- Bribery, kickbacks, and facilitation payments: while these may be in the (short-term) interests of the company and its shareholders, these practices may be anti-competitive or offensive to the values of society.

Ethics of Human Resource Management

The ethics of human resource management (HRM) covers those ethical issues arising around the employer-employee relationship. These involve the rights and duties owed between employer and employee and may include the following.

- Discrimination issues include discrimination on the basis of age, gender, race, religion, disabilities, weight, and attractiveness. Discrimination may also involve affirmative action and sexual harassment.

- Issues surrounding the representation of employees and the democratization of the workplace such as union busting and strike breaking.

- Issues affecting the privacy of the employee such as workplace surveillance and drug testing.

- Issues affecting the privacy of the employer, such as whistle-blowing.

- Issues relating to the fairness of the employment contract and the balance of power between employer and employee. This includes slavery, indentured servitude and other aspects of employment law.

- Occupational safety and health.

Ethics of Sales and Marketing

Marketing, which goes beyond the mere provision of information about (and access to) a product, may seek to manipulate values and behavior. To some extent, society regards this as acceptable, but where is the ethical line to be drawn? Marketing ethics overlap strongly with media ethics because marketing makes heavy use of media. However, media ethics is a much larger topic and extends outside business ethics. Ethics of sales and marketing may include the following.

- Pricing issues such as price fixing, price discrimination, and price skimming.

- Anti-competitive practices such as manipulation of loyalty and supply chains.

- Specific marketing strategies such as green washing, bait-and-switch, shill, viral marketing, spam , pyramid schemes, and planned obsolescence.

- Content of advertisements such as attack ads, subliminal messages, sex in advertising, and products regarded as immoral or harmful.

- Unethical marketing to children such as marketing in schools.

- Black market and grey market activities.

Ethics of Production

This area of business ethics deals with the duties of a company to ensure that products and production processes do not cause harm. Issues in this area can arise out of the fact that there is usually a degree of danger in any product or production process, and it is either difficult to define a degree of permissibility or the degree of permissibility may depend on the changing state of preventative technologies or changing social perceptions of acceptable risk. Ethical issues relating to production may include the following.

- Defective, addictive, and inherently dangerous products and services such as tobacco, alcohol, weapons, motor vehicles, chemical manufacturing, and bungee jumping.

- Ethical relations between the company and the environment such as pollution, environmental ethics, and carbon emissions trading.

- Ethical problems arising out of new technologies such as genetically modified food, mobile phone radiation, and health.

- Product testing ethics: animal rights and animal testing or use of economically disadvantaged groups (such as students) as test objects.

Ethics of Intellectual Property, Knowledge and Skills

Knowledge and skills are highly valuable to businesses but they are not tangible assets. It may not be obvious who has the greater rights to an idea: the company who trained the employee or the employee themselves? Does the country in which the plant grew, or the company that discovered and developed the plant's medicinal potential own the resource? As a result, attempts to assert ownership and ethical disputes over ownership arise. These ethical issues may include the following.

- Patent infringement, copyright infringement, and trademark infringement.

- Misuse of the intellectual property systems to stifle competition such as patent misuse, copyright misuse, patent troll, and submarine patent.

- Intellectual property itself has been criticized on ethical grounds.

- Employee raiding such as the practice of attracting key employees away from a competitor to take unfair advantage of the knowledge or skills they may possess.

- The practice of employing all of the most talented people in a specific field, regardless of need, in order to prevent any competitors from employing them.

- Biopiracy, which involves the appropriation of legal rights over indigenous biomedical knowledge without compensation to those who originally developed this knowledge

- Business intelligence and industrial espionage.

International Business Ethics

The issues here are grouped together because they involve a much wider, global view on business ethic matters. Looking back at the international developments of 1990s, international business ethics did not emerge until later in that decade. Many new practical issues arose out of the international context of business. Theoretical issues such as cultural relativity of ethical values receive more emphasis in this field. Other, older issues can be grouped here as well. Issues and subfields may include the following.

5. The search for universal values as a basis for international commercial behavior.

6. Comparison of business ethical traditions in different countries.

7. Comparison of business ethical traditions from various religious perspectives.

8. Ethical issues arising out of international business transactions such as bioprospecting and biopiracy in the pharmaceutical industry; the fair trade movement, and transfer pricing.

9. Issues such as globalization and cultural imperialism.

10. Varying global standards, such as the use of child labor.

11. The way in which multinationals take advantage of international differences, such as outsourcing production (clothing) and services (call centers) to low-wage countries.

12. The permissibility of international commerce with pariah states.

An Ethical Perspective

Business ethics is a form of the art of applied ethics that examines ethical rules and principles within a commercial context, the various moral or ethical problems that can arise in a business setting, and any special duties or obligations that apply to persons who are engaged in business activities. The foundation for ethical behavior goes well beyond corporate culture and the policies of any given company. It also depends greatly upon an individual's early moral training, the other institutions that affect an individual, the competitive business environment the company is in and, indeed, society as a whole.

The demand for more ethical business processes and actions—known as *ethicism*—is increasing. Simultaneously, pressure is applied on industry to improve business ethics through new public initiatives and laws. Although companies may set ethical standards and offer guidelines, the ultimate decision on whether to abide by ethical principles rests with the individual. Business ethics is a part of the pyramid of social responsibility.

Social Responsibility

Ethical behavior is a key component of social responsibility. *Social responsibility* is an ethical or ideological theory that an entity or individual has a responsibility to society at large. This responsibility can be "negative," meaning there is exemption from blame or liability, or it can be "positive," meaning there is a responsibility to act in a manner that benefits society as a whole.

In its most simplistic from, social responsibility involves these four steps that begin at the base on the pyramid below:

1. Be profitable *(required)*
2. Obey the law *(required)*
3. Be ethical *(expected)*
4. Be a good corporate citizen *(desired)*

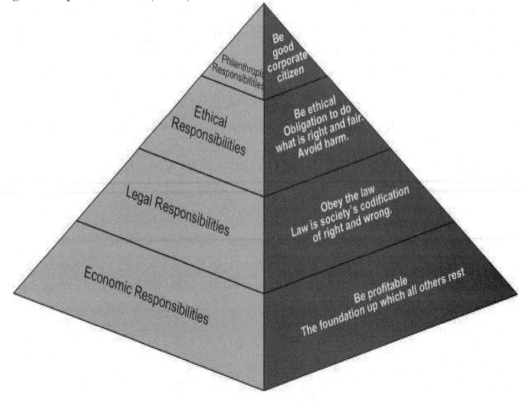

An Introduction to Business

Chapter Summary Questions

Be able to answer these types of questions in these areas:

Ethics in Business

1. What was Milton Friedman's view of the role of business in society?

2. What is a "social contract" and how might that impact the behavior of business?

3. Is it against the law for U.S. companies to offer bribes when doing business with other countries where bribery is acceptable? What are some potential ramifications to those businesses that follow the law?

4. Should corporate policies govern ethical conduct? What are some supporting and opposing views?

5. What are some attributes that "should" be incorporated into the ethics policy?

6. What did the Sarbanes-Oxley Act address and how has it changed business practices?

Ethics Officers

7. What is the role of an "Ethics Officer?"

8. Why is the effectiveness of ethics officers inconclusive?

Professional Ethics

9. What is an example of an ethics issue relating to the field of accounting?

10. What is an example of an ethics issue relating to the field of human resource management?

11. What is an example of an ethics issue relating to the field of sales and marketing?

12. What is an example of an ethics issue relating to the field of production?

13. What is an example of an ethics issue relating to the field of intellectual property rights?

14. What is an example of an ethics issue relating to the field of international business?

Chapter 8

Forms of Business Organization

Business owners choose the most attractive form of business ownership based on the number of owners, anticipated risk, expected profitability, and the potential future value of the firm.

Key terms to look for:

- Bylaws

- Common stock

- Corporation, or C Corporation

- Limited Liability Company

- Mutual agency

- Partnership

- Preferred stock

- S Corporation

- Sole proprietorship

When a business is established, the owners must decide on the form of ownership, a choice that affects both the owner and the business itself. This decision can be changed from one ownership form to another, but this may be complicated and potentially expensive with possible tax implications for owners. Therefore, this initial decision is an important one.[14]

There is no single "right" form of business organization, and the form of ownership that is best for one owner may not be suitable for another. Selecting the best form of ownership means that entrepreneurs must understand the characteristics of each form and how well those match the needs of their businesses. The most common considerations when evaluating the various forms of business ownership include:

Tax considerations: The amount of net income an entrepreneur expects the business to generate and the tax bill the owner must pay are important factors.

Liability exposure: Certain forms of ownership offer business owners greater protection from personal liability that might result from financial problems, faulty products, and other potential difficulties.

Start-up and future capital requirements: Forms of ownership differ in their ability to raise start-up and working capital.

Control: An owner automatically gives up some control over the company by choosing certain forms of ownership.

Managerial ability: The business owner may want to bring in other owners to provide a broader range of the necessary skills to successfully manage the venture.

Business goals: The projected size of the business is another factor, and businesses often may switch forms of ownership as they grow, although moving from some formats to others can be extremely complex and expensive.

Management succession plans: When choosing a form of ownership, business owners must look ahead to the day when they will pass their companies on to the next generation or to a buyer.

Cost of formation: Owners must weigh carefully the benefits versus the costs of the particular form they choose.[15]

The organizational forms most commonly used by businesses in the United States fall into these general categories:

- Sole Proprietorship
- Partnership
- Corporation, also known as a C Corporation
- S Corporation
- Limited Liability Company

---

[14] Scarborough, Norman M., Scarborough, Doug Wilson, Thomas W. Zimmerer, *Effective Small Business Management,* 9th edition. (Upper Saddle River, NJ: Pearson Education, 2008), page 75.
[15] Ibid.

To understand the differences between these forms and their advantages and disadvantages, you should know the answers to these questions:

- How are the profits and losses of the business taxed? *(taxes)*
- How is each type of legal organization set up? *(starting an organization)*
- Who owns the business? *(control)*
- Who is responsible if the business fails or has losses? *(liability)*
- How long does each type of organization last, and how does the owner sell the business? *(life of and sale of company)*

SOLE PROPRIETORSHIP

The sole proprietorship is the simplest and most common form of business organization. As its name implies, this business entity can have only one owner. This entity represents more than 70 percent of all businesses in the United States.[16] The primary advantages of the sole proprietorship are its:

- Ease of formation
- Least costly form of ownership to begin
- Total decision-making authority and control
- Minimal legal restrictions
- Ease of discontinuing

The most significant disadvantages of a sole proprietorship are its:

- Single owner status
- Unlimited liability
- The owner is individually responsible for all losses of the business
- Limited skills and capabilities
- Limited access to capital
- Challenges in transitioning the business to other owners

Starting a Sole Proprietorship

Starting a sole proprietorship is the easiest form of business to establish. First, select a business name, or a DBA which is the abbreviation for "doing business as." A sole proprietorship may be operated under the name of the individual owner or another name that has not already in use. You then register this name with your state of residence. Check with local government offices for information about licenses and permits. Examples of such include business licenses, zoning occupancy permits, and tax registrations. You are now ready to conduct your business! A part of this process is to set up a system to keep track of your business's finances and keep records of all revenues and expenses.

---

[16] Ibid, p. 163.

Management and Control

If you create a sole proprietorship, all the assets of the business are owned directly by you. A sole proprietorship may be owned by only one person. The owner controls the business. You may hire employees to help manage your business, but you will have legal responsibility for the decisions made by your employees.

Liability

In a sole proprietorship, the owner and the business are legally the same. As the owner, you will have unlimited personal responsibility for your business's liabilities. For example, if your business cannot pay its loans, the bank can take action against you individually, against both the business's assets and your personal assets, including your bank account, car, and house.

The Life and Sale of a Sole Proprietorship

A sole proprietorship exists as long as its owner is alive and wants to continue the business. When the owner dies, the assets and liabilities of the business become part of the owner's estate. A sole proprietor is free to sell all or any part of the assets of the business.

Taxes

Because there is no legal difference between the person and the business, the business's income (minus allowable expenses) are reported on the owner's individual tax return and taxed at individual tax rates. No separate federal income tax return is required of the sole proprietor.

Sole Proprietorship Advantages	Sole Proprietorship Disadvantages
Inexpensive to start	Unlimited personal liability
Simple to run and administer	Ownership is limited to one person
Ease of formation	Most limited access to capital
Single (simple) taxation on profits	Challenging transition to a new owner

When multiple owners are desirable, a partnership is one way to overcome the disadvantages of sole proprietorship.

TerraCycle   *A business profile*

A high school plant project and a subsequent business plan competition led Tom Szaky and some friends to create a totally organic fertilizer. The group continued their pursuit of the stalled plant project as they left for college—Tom to Princeton University and his friends to McGill University in Montreal. It was then that one of the friends learned about fertilizing the plants with worm waste. He created a compost heap in a box, placed red worms in it, and started feeding them table scraps. Tom discovered that his friend Jon Beyer's father was an ecotoxicologist—a person who studies the effects of pollution on ecosystems. They thought the worm waste product was an excellent solution and subsequently, a business venture and a partnership of complementary skills was born.[17]

---

[17] Bo Burlingham, "The Coolest Little Start-Up in America," *Inc. Magazine*, July 2006, page 78-83.

PARTNERSHIPS

In the most general form, a partnership is created when two or more individuals agree to create a business and jointly own the assets, be responsible for the liabilities, and to share both the profits and the losses. There are many different ways to structure a partnership, and you can limit a partner's "participation" (and their liability) in the partnership agreement.

The advantages of a partnership are:
- Acquisition of complementary skills and talents
- Flexibility of division of profits
- Larger pool of capital with the ability to attract more partners
- Minimal government regulation

The disadvantage is that the general partners have:
- Unlimited liability of at least one partner who is personally responsible for the losses and other obligations
- Challenges in accumulating additional capital
- Difficulty in changing partners
- Potential lack of continuity
- Potential for personality and authority conflicts
- Bound by the law of agency

Starting a Partnership

You can start a general partnership by agreeing with one or more individuals to jointly own and share the profits of a business. You can form a partnership with other individuals, other partnerships, or with corporations. You can have as many partners as you want.

A partnership agreement, also known as the articles of partnership, outlines the exact status and responsibility of each partner. This document states the terms under which the partners agree to operate the business and protects each partner's interest in the business. Every partnership should be based on a written agreement that acts as a guide for the partners when they face challenging business decisions, such as how to distribute profits or how to sell or liquidate the business.[18]

The standard partnership agreement will likely include the following:
- Name of the partnership
- Purpose of the business
- Domicile of the business
- Duration of the partnership
- Names of the partners and their legal addresses
- Contributions of each partner to the business, at the creation of the partnership and later
- Agreement on how the profits or losses will be distributed
- Agreement on salaries or drawing rights against profits for each partner
- Procedure of expansion through the addition of new partners

---

[18] Burlingham, p. 166.

- Sale of partnership interests
- Salaries, draws, and expense accounts for the partners
- Absence or disability of one of the partners
- Dissolution of the partnership and distribution of assets

The partnership agreement should specify who controls and manages the business. If there is a need to limit the participation and liability of a partner, those limits should be established in the partnership agreement. The law assumes "general" participation unless specific statutory requirements are met, so it is important to have a lawyer review the agreement. In the absence of a specific agreement, all general partners have equal control and equal management rights over the business. This means that all of the partners must consent and agree to partnership decisions. If the purpose of limiting the partnership is to limit the liability of a partner, then the limited partner must have limited managerial control as well. The premise of a partnership is that partners are responsible, and protection from responsibility cannot be given to active decision makers. This and other partner provisions must be specified in the partnership agreement.

A partnership may operate under the names of the partners. Some states require partnerships to file partnership certificates, often with the secretary of state's office. If the partners' names are not used, a "doing business as" form may need to be filed. The partnership should set up a system to keep track of the business's finances and keep records of all revenues and expenses so the partners know whether there are profits and how they accrue to the individual partner.

Frontera Foods   *A business profile*

The partners at Frontera Foods are in a perpetual creative struggle—with each other. "We are very different," concedes Rick Bayless as he thinks of his partner Manuel Valdes. Bayless's talents come out in the kitchen, Valdes has the business sense. The trio of successful companies the two co-founded and run—Frontera Foods, Frontera Media Productions, and Frontera Fresco–now exceed $15 million in annual sales. Over the past decade, the partners have butted heads and the creative tug-of-wars continue. "I'm ready to kill an idea," Says Valdes, "and he's ready to do it another way." Based on the performance of their businesses, they would not have it any other way.[19]

Management and Control

The partnership agreement defines the percentage of the business and profits each partner will own. The law may assume that each partner will have an equal claim on the assets of the business, its profits, and its liabilities. Most partnership agreements are negotiated on the principle of a proportional claim based on the cumulative investments of the partner.

---

[19] Emily Lambert, "The Odd Couple," *Forbes*, September 4, 2006, p. 73

Mutual Agency

Partnerships are based on the concept of mutual agency. The partnership is held responsible for the decisions and behavior of each partner (this is an example of "a chain is only as strong as its weakest link" principle). Any partner can bind the partnership to contracts or legal obligations without the approval of the other partners. Any partner can expose the partnership to criminal or civil actions.

Unlimited Liability of General Partners

A general partnership has some characteristics of a legal entity that is separate from its owners. For instance a partnership can own property and conduct business. However, the general partners have unlimited personal liability and are in an agency relationship with all other partners. All of the partners are liable together and each general partner is individually liable for any and all of the obligations of the partnership. This means, for example, that partner A could borrow money in the name of the partnership and the creditor could require other partners individually to pay back the money. If partner B cannot pay back the money partner A has borrowed, partner B's personal assets (home, car, etc.) might be used to meet this obligation.

Limited Liability of Limited Partners

Limited partners do not have personal liability for the business of the partnership. Limited partners risk only their investment in (or specified contributions to) the partnership.

The Life and Sale of a Partnership

A partnership lasts as long as the partners agree it will or as long as all of the general partners remain in the partnership. What happens when a partner dies or leaves the partnership should be specified in the partnership agreement. If the partnership dissolves, the assets of the partnership are sold, the liabilities are settled, and the remainder distributed to the partners. The partnership agreement should state whether a partner can sell his or her share, under what conditions, and how the share of the assets and profits of the partnership will be determined. For example, does it require unanimous consent of the partners and will those profits be divided equally?

Taxes

The partnership itself incurs no taxes although it files a partnership tax return for informational purposes. Each partner pays personal taxes on his or her share of the business income. A partner may be required to pay taxes on income without having received any cash disbursal from the partnership. Investing in the professional advice of a lawyer or accountant is worthwhile.

Partnership Advantages	Partnership Disadvantages
Access to capital of more than one person	Mutual agency
Avoids double taxation	Unlimited personal liability
Access to skills, talents, and energy of more than one person	Cannot sell without consent of partners
Few legal formalities	Dissolves at death of partner

CORPORATION

The most complex business entity is the corporation. It is a separate legal entity that exists independently of its owners, referred to as stockholders, and may engage in business, make contracts, sue and be sued, own property, and pay taxes. The U.S. Supreme Court defines the corporation as "an artificial being, invisible, intangible, and existing only in contemplation of the law."[20]

Starting a Corporation

A corporation is the most complex of all the business entities to create. Once the owners decide to form a corporation, they must choose a state in which to incorporate. A corporation (also known as a "C corporation") accepts the regulations and restrictions of the state in which it is founded and any other state in which it chooses to do business. Most states require the owners to file Articles of Incorporation or a Certificate of Incorporation with the appropriate state office, again most commonly the secretary of state's office.

In general, these articles include:

- The corporate name
- The number of shares of stock the corporation is authorized to issue
- The number of shares of stock each of the owners will buy
- Each owner's contribution to obtain these shares of stock
- The business of the corporation
- The management structure of the corporation (its directors and officers)

Although the assistance of an attorney may be valuable, most states allow businesses to incorporate without the assistance of an attorney, and some states even have "incorporation kits" to help in the process. There is a fee for filing the corporate documents and an annual fee for keeping the corporation in existence. States differ in the requirements they place on corporations. Delaware, for example, offers low incorporation fees, favorable laws, and minimal legal requirements, and many corporations are chartered there for these reasons.

After approval from the secretary of state, the corporation pays its fees, and the approved articles of incorporation become its charter. The corporation then holds a stockholders meeting where the members formally elect a board of directors who will appoint the corporate officers.

Structure and Management

The corporation also needs *bylaws*, the rules by which the corporation is run. Bylaws are general guidelines for managing a firm and specify such activities as annual stockholders meetings; meetings of the board of directors; and the number, titles, selection, and responsibilities of each officer. Because the corporate business entity is separate from its owners, it has to set up its own record-keeping system. The assets and liabilities, the profits and losses, are owned by the corporation and not by the shareholders.

---

[20] Chief Justice John Marshall, cited by Roger L. Miller and Gaylord A. Jentz in *Business Law Today* (St. Paul, MN: West Publishing, 1994), p. 632.

Corporations may operate in states and countries in addition to the state in which they have incorporated. Corporations fall into three categories:

Domestic Corporation: Operates in the state in which it was incorporated

Foreign Corporation: Incorporated in one state but has operations in another, and therefore the other state considers it a *foreign corporation*

Alien Corporation: Operates in a country in which it was not incorporated and so is considered an *alien corporation* in that country.

Management and Control

The owners, or the shareholders, of the corporation have to vote directly on certain major decisions, such as amendments to the articles of incorporation or dissolving the corporation. For most decision making that does not change the nature or characters of the organization, the owners elect a group of individuals to act as the board of directors. Usually, each share of stock gets one vote. Those who hold a majority of the shares have ultimate control over the corporation. Shareholders can elect themselves to the board of directors.

The board of directors is responsible for providing guidance to the executive management team of the corporation. Directors may be paid for their services, although it is not required. The board of directors determines who fills the role of the key officers within the corporation, who, in turn, are responsible for running the day-to-day business.

If you own stock in a corporation, you may be paid a dividend, or cash distribution on the stock you own. A dividend must be paid equally to all shares of common stock and is usually expressed as an amount per share, such as "$5 per share." The board of directors typically decides whether dividends shall be paid, how much, and when.

Liability

Because a corporation is a separate legal entity, creditors of the corporation only have a claim against the assets of the corporation for payment. Individual shareholders are not personally liable for the losses of the business beyond their initial investment. This limited liability makes investment in a corporation very attractive and is a major advantage of the corporation form.

The Life and Sale of a Corporation

The corporation, as a separate legal entity, lasts as long as its shareholders decide it should. For practical purposes, a corporation's life is considered perpetual. It can be stated within its articles that a corporation will continue in **perpetuity**. The sale of ownership rights in a corporation is through the sale of stock shares. Corporations can issue two types of stock: preferred and common.

1. **Preferred stock** conveys special ownership rights. The owners of this stock have a "preferred" claim on the profits of the company. This claim is in the form of a preferred dividend (if there is enough net income, the preferred stockholders are guaranteed a dividend). Preferred stockholders do not have a say in how the company is run and do not have voting rights in electing the board of directors.

2. **Common stock** conveys no special privileges with respect to the profits of the company but does convey voting rights in the corporation.

Shares of stock can be purchased from current owners (who wish to sell) or from the authorized and issued shares of the corporation. These transactions generally occur in the stock markets of the world.

Taxes and Double Taxation

As a separate legal entity, the corporation must file its own income tax returns and pay taxes on its profits. The corporation must report all income it has received from its business and may deduct certain IRS-approved expenses it has incurred while conducting its business. In addition to corporate income taxes, dividends paid to shareholders are regarded as personal income, and the shareholder must pay tax on that income. Therefore, corporations must pay these taxes at the *corporate* tax rate and then stockholders must pay taxes on the dividends they receive from these same profits at the *individual* tax rate. Thus, a corporation's profits are taxed twice. This double taxation is a distinct disadvantage of the corporate form of ownership. Legislation is now under review at the federal level that may change double taxation for corporations and not tax dividend earnings, therefore eliminating double taxation in the future.

C Corporation Advantages	C Corporation Disadvantages
Limited liability of owners	Costly to set up and maintain
Easy to transfer ownership to others	Double taxation
Easy to raise money and add additional owners	Legal and regulatory requirements
Ability to continue in perpetuity	Control of organization can be lost to larger shareholders

OTHER FORMS OF BUSINESS OWNERSHIP

With these three business entities in place—the sole proprietorship, partnership, and corporation—the Internal Revenue Service realized other forms of business were needed. Therefore, additional business entities have evolved over time and offer other entity options for business owners. Two of these options, the S Corporation and the Limited Liability Company, are presented here. You will notice that they combine select attributes of the partnership and the corporation business entities.

S Corporation

In 1954 the Internal Revenue Service Code created the "Sub-chapter Corporation" and subsequently shortened the title to "S Corporation" along with modifications in its qualifications. The "S" means small corporation. Although this is actually a special type of a partnership, an S Corporation is only a distinction for federal income tax purposes, and in terms of its legal characteristics, no different from any other corporation. If a corporation meets the S Corporation criteria, its shareholders must actually elect to be treated as one. All shareholders must consent to have the corporation treated as an S Corporation.[21]

---

[21] Zimmerer, Thomas W., and Norman M. Scarborough, *Essentials of Entrepreneurship and Small Business Management,* 5th ed. (Upper Saddle River, NJ: Pearson Education, 2008), p. 179.

An S Corporation structure places limits on the type and number of shareholders and must meet the following requirements:

- The corporation has no more than 100 shareholders
- The corporation has only one class of stock
- All of the shareholders are U.S. residents, either citizens or resident aliens
- All of the shareholders are individuals (i.e., no corporations or other entities own the stock)
- The corporation operates on a calendar-year financial basis.

If the business satisfies these criteria, then the S Corporation is not liable for "double taxation." That is, the S Corporation does not pay taxes on the income generated by the business. Instead, the income or losses are passed through to the individual shareholders and reported on their tax returns. The income or losses are divided among the shareholders based upon the percentage of stock of the corporation that they own.

S Corporation Advantages	S Corporation Disadvantages
Limited liability of owners	One hundred shareholder limit
Avoids double taxation	Some legal and regulatory requirements
Ability to continue in perpetuity	Shareholders can only be individuals
Easy to transfer ownership to others	Control of organization can be lost to larger shareholders

LIMITED LIABILITY COMPANY

The newest business entity recognized by the IRS is a Limited Liability Company, or LLC. This is another "hybrid" form of business and was introduced in part as a response to our litigious business climate. An LLC offers the simplicity of a partnership with the legal protection of a corporation.

Like S Corporations, LLCs offer their owners limited personal liability for the debts of the business and therefore provide a significant advantage over sole proprietorships and partnerships. LLCs, however, are not subject to many of the restrictions currently imposed on S Corporations and offer additional flexibility compared to S Corporations. An LLC is created according to the laws of the state where the business is located and in most states, an LLC can have multiple owners, with a few states requiring LLCs to have at least two owners.

LLC owners are referred to as "members" and may include non-U.S. citizens, partnerships, and corporations. An LLC does not restrict its members' ability to become involved in managing the company. These advantages make the LLC an attractive form of ownership for many companies, and due to these benefits LLCs have become a popular form of business ownership.[22]

---

[22] Zimmerer, Thomas W., and Norman M. Scarborough, *Essentials of Entrepreneurship and Small Business Management,* 5th ed. (Upper Saddle River, NJ: Pearson Education, 2008), p. 181.

An Introduction to Business

Starting a Limited Liability Company

Creating an LLC is similar to creating a corporation. It requires the owners to create two documents: the articles of organization (which must be filed with the secretary of state) and the operating agreement. The LLC's articles of organization establish its name, address, method of management (board-managed or member-managed), duration, and the names and addresses of each owner.

Unlike a corporation, an LLC does not have perpetual life and in most states, an LLC's charter may not exceed 30 years. The operating agreement, similar to a corporation's bylaws, outlines the provisions governing the way the LLC will conduct business, such as its members' capital contributions to the LLC, the admission or withdrawal of members, distributions from the business, and how the LLC will be managed.[23]

LLC Considerations

Despite their appeal, LLCs do have disadvantages. They can be expensive to create, they have limited life spans, are not suitable for companies whose owners plan to raise money through an initial public offering or who want to use stock options or an employee stock ownership plan as incentives for employees. Owners who want to provide attractive benefits to themselves and their employees will not find this form of ownership appealing because the cost of those benefits are not tax deductible in an LLC.

LLC Advantages	LLC Disadvantages
Limited personal liability	Cannot sell without consent of partners
Does not require strict government reporting	Control of organization can be lost to larger shareholders
Avoids double taxation	Limited life and dissolves at death of partner

Selecting the "Right" Form of Business

No single form of business ownership is ideal for all. When two or more owners are involved, a sole proprietorship is not a fit, and they need to look at other suitable options. If there are "risk" concerns regarding the nature of the business, then an LLC or corporation may be the best choices to consider. An attorney and a CPA are good advisors to consult with regarding selecting the best business entity.

---

[23] Ibid., p. 182.

Chapter Summary Questions

Be able to answer these types of questions in these areas:

Sole Proprietorship

1. What factors make the Sole Proprietorship attractive?

2. What are limitations of the Sole Proprietorship?

Partnership

3. What do the articles of partnership include?

4. What does the term "agency" mean to a partnership?

Corporation

5. What is the relationship between a common stockholder and the board of directors?

6. What are the major ownership advantages of a corporation?

7. What are the disadvantages of a corporation?

Limited Liability Company

8. What are the similarities and differences between an S Corporation and an LLC?

9. What are the benefits of an LLC versus a partnership or a corporation? Why would an organization choose one over the others?

The "Right" Choice

10. Which of the business organizations restricts the number of owners?

11. Which organization offers the optimal situation for raising capital?

12. What might be the best choice for a single business owner that is starting up a small "experimental" venture? Why might that choice be attractive?

An Introduction to Business

Appendix I: Foundation™ FastTrack Report

Foundation™
FastTrack Report

Round 2

Company: Andrews
Year: 2011

Foundation® FastTrack

Andrews	Bonus	Baldwin	Bonus	Chester	Bonus
Kate Ashworth	$0				

Digby	Bonus	Erie	Bonus	Ferris	Bonus

SELECTED FINANCIAL STATISTICS

	Andrews	Baldwin	Chester	Digby	Erie	Ferris
ROS	15.9%	7.7%	4.9%	8.6%	4.9%	4.8%
Turnover	1.30	1.51	1.00	1.50	0.93	1.26
ROA	20.7%	11.6%	4.9%	12.9%	4.6%	6.0%
Leverage	1.4	1.9	2.0	2.0	2.0	2.1
ROE	28.2%	22.6%	10.0%	25.3%	9.2%	12.9%
Emergency Loan	$0	$0	$0	$0	$0	$0
Sales	$57,063,443	$68,647,266	$39,173,800	$72,090,385	$35,191,293	$43,644,827
EBIT	$15,180,185	$10,228,715	$4,939,744	$11,801,971	$4,622,431	$4,947,195
Profits	$9,059,617	$5,281,293	$1,911,959	$6,209,542	$1,739,320	$2,081,537
Cumulative Profit	$15,717,302	$10,159,102	$6,738,550	$12,154,488	$5,826,499	$8,105,015
SG&A % Sales	10.3%	8.7%	10.3%	9.5%	11.3%	13.2%
Contrib. Margin %	40.7%	27.3%	28.4%	29.3%	30.3%	27.8%

Percent of Sales — Variable costs, Depreciation, SG&A, Other, Profit (Andrews, Baldwin, Chester, Digby, Erie, Ferris)

Market Share — Ferris 14%, Andrews 18%, Baldwin 23%, Chester 12%, Digby 23%

Page 1

STOCK MARKET SUMMARY

Company	Close	Change	Shares	Market Cap ($M)	Book Value	EPS	Dividend	Yield	P/E
Andrews	$27.48	$10.28	2,474,994	$68	$12.96	$3.66	$0.00	0.0%	7.5
Baldwin	$19.98	$5.79	2,220,036	$44	$10.54	$2.38	$0.00	0.0%	8.4
Chester	$13.83	($0.26)	2,160,748	$30	$8.89	$0.88	$0.00	0.0%	15.6
Digby	$23.60	$7.31	2,137,845	$50	$11.49	$2.90	$0.00	0.0%	8.1
Erie	$12.43	($0.22)	2,226,367	$28	$8.52	$0.78	$0.00	0.0%	15.9
Ferris	$16.05	($0.44)	2,054,656	$33	$7.88	$1.01	$0.00	0.0%	15.8

Closing Stock Price

BOND MARKET SUMMARY

Company	Series#	Face	Yield	Close	Rating
Andrews	12.0S2013	$1,733,333	11.4%	$105.28	AA
	13.0S2015	$2,600,000	11.5%	$112.96	AA
	9.0S2021	$3,000,000	9.0%	$100.00	AA
Baldwin	12.0S2013	$1,733,333	11.8%	$101.54	B
	13.0S2015	$2,600,000	12.3%	$105.88	B
	10.0S2020	$2,480,000	10.6%	$93.93	B
	11.0S2021	$5,044,916	11.1%	$99.41	B
Chester	12.0S2013	$1,733,333	11.9%	$101.02	B
	13.0S2015	$2,600,000	12.4%	$104.92	B
	10.0S2020	$2,366,478	10.8%	$92.37	B
	10.9S2021	$5,055,277	11.2%	$97.10	B
Digby	12.0S2013	$1,733,333	11.8%	$101.37	B
	13.0S2015	$2,600,000	12.3%	$105.56	B
	10.0S2020	$2,291,811	10.7%	$93.41	B
	10.9S2021	$4,863,235	11.1%	$98.25	B
Erie	12.0S2013	$1,733,333	11.9%	$101.19	B
	13.0S2015	$2,600,000	12.4%	$105.24	B
	10.0S2020	$2,366,478	10.8%	$92.89	B
	11.0S2021	$5,128,211	11.2%	$98.26	B
Ferris	12.0S2013	$1,733,333	11.9%	$100.68	CCC
	13.0S2015	$2,600,000	12.5%	$104.29	CCC
	10.0S2020	$425,144	10.9%	$91.34	CCC
	11.0S2021	$2,992,039	11.4%	$96.55	CCC

Page 2

Cash Flow Statement Survey	Andrews	Baldwin	Chester	Digby	Erie	Ferris
Cash flows from operating activities						
Net Income (Loss)	$9,060	$5,281	$1,912	$6,210	$1,739	$2,082
Adjustment for non-cash items						
Depreciation	$1,920	$2,171	$1,820	$2,201	$1,703	$1,267
Extraordinary gains/losses/writeoffs	$0	$0	$0	$0	$0	$0
Changes in current assets and liabilities						
Accounts payable	$79	$667	($548)	$920	($780)	($51)
Inventory	$3,140	$126	$862	($1,082)	$1,863	($2,881)
Accounts receivable	($1,092)	($1,405)	$376	($1,580)	$572	$215
Net cash from operations	$13,107	$6,840	$4,423	$6,669	$5,097	$631
Cash flows from investing activities						
Plant improvements (net)	($16,112)	($11,225)	($11,287)	($12,115)	($10,665)	($8,300)
Cash flows from financing activities						
Dividends paid	$0	$0	$0	$0	$0	$0
Sales of common stock	$2,000	$2,031	$1,535	$1,635	$2,208	$901
Purchase of common stock	$0	$0	$0	$0	$0	$0
Cash from long term debt issued	$3,000	$5,045	$5,055	$4,863	$5,128	$2,992
Early retirement of long term debt	$0	$0	$0	$0	$0	$0
Retirement of current debt	$0	($3,686)	($3,668)	($3,668)	($3,668)	($3,668)
Cash from current debt borrowing	$1,000	$5,268	$5,497	$7,013	$4,812	$7,069
Cash from emergency loan	$0	$0	$0	$0	$0	$0
Net cash from financing activities	$6,000	$8,658	$8,419	$9,843	$8,481	$7,294
Net change in cash position	$2,995	$4,273	$1,556	$4,397	$2,913	($375)

Balance Sheet Survey	Andrews	Baldwin	Chester	Digby	Erie	Ferris
Cash	$9,812	$12,070	$8,715	$13,236	$8,978	$7,313
Accounts Receivable	$4,690	$5,642	$3,220	$5,925	$2,892	$3,587
Inventory	$0	$3,216	$2,591	$4,016	$1,883	$5,639
Total Current Assets	$14,502	$20,928	$14,526	$23,177	$13,754	$16,540
Plant and equipment	$37,440	$32,569	$32,692	$33,015	$32,070	$25,300
Accumulated Depreciation	($8,142)	($8,036)	($8,047)	($8,021)	($7,930)	($7,200)
Total Fixed Assets	$29,298	$24,533	$24,645	$24,994	$24,140	$18,100
Total Assets	$43,800	$45,461	$39,171	$48,171	$37,894	$34,640
Accounts Payable	$2,523	$4,060	$1,841	$4,236	$1,415	$2,770
Current Debt	$1,867	$6,134	$6,364	$7,880	$5,679	$7,936
Long Term Debt	$7,333	$11,858	$11,755	$11,488	$11,828	$7,751
Total Liabilities	$11,723	$22,052	$19,960	$23,604	$18,922	$18,456
Common Stock	$8,323	$5,212	$4,436	$4,376	$5,109	$3,224
Retained Earnings	$23,754	$18,196	$14,775	$20,191	$13,863	$12,960
Total Equity	$32,077	$23,408	$19,211	$24,567	$18,972	$16,184
Total Liabilities & Owner's Equity	$43,800	$45,461	$39,171	$48,171	$37,894	$34,640

Income Statement Survey	Andrews	Baldwin	Chester	Digby	Erie	Ferris
Sales	$57,063	$68,647	$39,174	$72,090	$35,191	$43,645
Variable Costs (Labor, Material, Carry)	$33,831	$49,914	$28,052	$50,932	$24,537	$31,496
Depreciation	$1,920	$2,171	$1,820	$2,201	$1,703	$1,267
SG&A (R&D, Promo, Sales, Admin)	$5,882	$5,979	$4,032	$6,930	$3,962	$5,740
Other (Fees, Write Offs, TQM, Bonus)	$250	$354	$330	$325	$367	$195
EBIT	$15,180	$10,229	$4,940	$11,802	$4,622	$4,947
Interest (Short term, Long term)	$958	$1,938	$1,938	$2,054	$1,892	$1,679
Taxes	$4,978	$2,902	$1,051	$3,412	$956	$1,144
Profit Sharing	$185	$108	$39	$127	$35	$42
Net Profit	$9,060	$5,281	$1,912	$6,210	$1,739	$2,082

Page 3

For Industry F32795_001

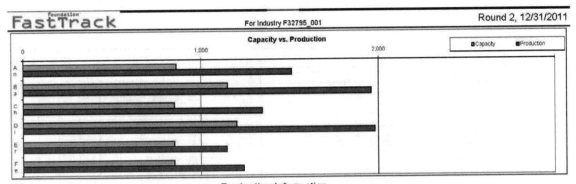

Capacity vs. Production

☐ Capacity ■ Production

Production Information

Name	Primary Segment	Units Sold	Units in Inventory	Revision Date	Age Dec.31	MTBF	Pfmn Coord	Size Coord	Price	Material Cost	Labor Cost	Contr Marg.	2nd Shift & Over-time	Auto-mation Next Round	Capac-ity Next Round	Plant Utiliz.
Able	Low	1,630	0	9-Nov-10	3.1	20000	5.3	14.7	$35.00	$10.93	$8.94	41%	77%	6.5	900	175%
Acex		0	0	17-Dec-12	0.0	0	0.0	0.0	$0.00	$0.00	$0.00	0%	0%	2.1	600	0%
Baker	Low	1,582	130	8-Mar-11	2.1	19800	6.5	14.1	$33.40	$12.84	$11.20	25%	88%	4.0	1,100	186%
Bold	High	373	0	13-May-11	0.6	22400	7.1	11.7	$42.35	$16.89	$10.90	34%	100%	3.5	448	125%
Cake	Low	1,353	126	19-Jan-11	3.3	17000	5.7	14.2	$28.95	$11.00	$8.53	28%	59%	5.7	948	158%
Cent		0	0	4-May-12	0.0	0	0.0	0.0	$0.00	$0.00	$0.00	0%	0%	4.0	245	0%
Daze	Low	1,500	146	20-Apr-11	2.1	19500	6.6	13.6	$35.00	$13.36	$11.41	27%	82%	3.7	1,096	181%
Dabble	High	436	11	9-May-11	0.6	22000	8.0	12.4	$45.00	$16.91	$11.34	36%	100%	3.2	596	127%
Eat	Low	1,201	93	15-Jan-11	3.3	16500	6.0	14.4	$29.30	$10.97	$8.14	30%	35%	5.6	899	135%
East		0	0	14-Mar-12	0.0	0	0.0	0.0	$0.00	$0.00	$0.00	0%	0%	4.0	297	0%
Fast	High	1,134	207	10-Oct-11	1.7	22000	8.5	11.6	$38.50	$18.29	$10.16	28%	47%	3.5	950	146%
Feast		0	0	20-May-12	0.0	0	0.0	0.0	$0.00	$0.00	$0.00	0%	0%	3.0	350	0%

For Industry F32795_001

Round 2, 12/31/2011

Low Tech

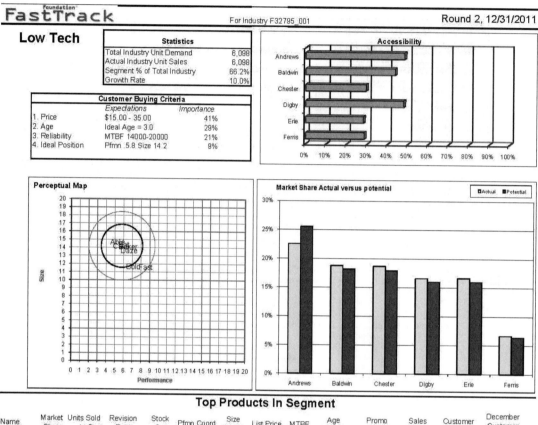

Statistics	
Total Industry Unit Demand	6,098
Actual Industry Unit Sales	6,098
Segment % of Total Industry	66.2%
Growth Rate	10.0%

Customer Buying Criteria		
	Expectations	Importance
1. Price	$15.00 - 35.00	41%
2. Age	Ideal Age = 3.0	29%
3. Reliability	MTBF 14000-20000	21%
4. Ideal Position	Pfmn .5.8 Size 14.2	9%

Top Products In Segment

Name	Market Share	Units Sold to Seg	Revision Date	Stock Out	Pfmn Coord	Size Coord	List Price	MTBF	Age Dec.31	Promo Budget	Sales Budget	Customer Awareness	December Customer Survey
Able	23%	1,375	9-Nov-10	YES	5.3	14.7	$35.00	20000	3.1	$2,000	$2,000	100%	28
Cake	19%	1,140	19-Jan-11		5.7	14.2	$28.95	17000	3.3	$925	$925	56%	20
Baker	18%	1,118	8-Mar-11		6.5	14.1	$33.40	19800	2.1	$1,350	$1,350	77%	23
Eat	17%	1,017	15-Jan-11		6.0	14.4	$29.30	16500	3.3	$875	$875	54%	18
Daze	17%	1,012	20-Apr-11		6.6	13.6	$35.00	19500	2.1	$1,450	$1,450	83%	20
Fast	7%	408	10-Oct-11		8.5	11.6	$38.50	22000	1.7	$1,500	$1,275	85%	1
Bold	0%	30	13-May-11	YES	7.1	11.7	$42.35	22400	0.6	$550	$550	33%	1

Page 5

High Tech

Statistics	
Total Industry Unit Demand	3,110
Actual Industry Unit Sales	3,110
Segment % of Total Industry	33.8%
Growth Rate	20.0%

Customer Buying Criteria		
	Expectations	Importance
1. Ideal Position	Pfmn 8.8 Size 11.2	33%
2. Age	Ideal Age = 0.0	29%
3. Price	$25.00 - 45.00	25%
4. Reliability	MTBF 17000-23000	13%

Accessibility

Perceptual Map

Market Share Actual versus potential

Top Products In Segment

Name	Market Share	Units Sold to Seg	Revision Date	Stock Out	Pfmn Coord	Size Coord	List Price	MTBF	Age Dec.31	Promo Budget	Sales Budget	Customer Awareness	December Customer Survey
Fast	23%	728	10-Oct-11		8.5	11.6	$38.50	22000	1.7	$1,500	$1,275	85%	30
Daze	16%	488	20-Apr-11		6.6	13.6	$35.00	19500	2.1	$1,450	$1,450	83%	12
Baker	15%	464	8-Mar-11		6.5	14.1	$33.40	19800	2.1	$1,350	$1,350	77%	11
Dabble	14%	436	9-May-11		8.0	12.4	$45.00	22000	0.6	$750	$750	39%	21
Bold	11%	344	13-May-11	YES	7.1	11.7	$42.35	22400	0.6	$550	$550	33%	20
Able	8%	256	9-Nov-10	YES	5.3	14.7	$35.00	20000	3.1	$2,000	$2,000	100%	5
Cake	7%	213	19-Jan-11		5.7	14.2	$28.95	17000	3.3	$925	$925	56%	5
Eat	6%	184	15-Jan-11		6.0	14.4	$29.30	16500	3.3	$875	$875	54%	4

Industry Unit Sales vs demand

Market segment shares

Actual Market Share in Units

	Low	High	Total
Industry Unit Sales	6,098	3,110	9,209
% of Market	66.2%	33.8%	100.0%
Able	22.5%	8.2%	17.7%
Total	22.5%	8.2%	17.7%
Baker	18.3%	14.9%	17.2%
Bold	0.5%	11.1%	4.1%
Total	18.8%	26.0%	21.2%
Cake	18.7%	6.8%	14.7%
Total	18.7%	6.8%	14.7%
Daze	16.6%	15.7%	16.3%
Dabble	0.0%	14.0%	4.7%
Total	16.6%	29.7%	21.0%
Eat	16.7%	5.9%	13.0%
Total	16.7%	5.9%	13.0%
Fast	6.7%	23.3%	12.3%
Total	6.7%	23.3%	12.3%

Potential Market Share in Units

	Low	High	Total
Units Demanded	6,098	3,110	9,209
% of Market	66.2%	33.8%	100.0%
Able	25.5%	9.1%	20.0%
Total	25.5%	9.1%	20.0%
Baker	17.6%	14.3%	16.5%
Bold	0.6%	12.9%	4.7%
Total	18.2%	27.2%	21.2%
Cake	17.9%	6.6%	14.1%
Total	17.9%	6.6%	14.1%
Daze	16.0%	15.0%	15.6%
Dabble	0.0%	14.1%	4.7%
Total	16.0%	29.0%	20.4%
Eat	16.0%	5.7%	12.5%
Total	16.0%	5.7%	12.5%
Fast	6.4%	22.4%	11.8%
Total	6.4%	22.4%	11.8%

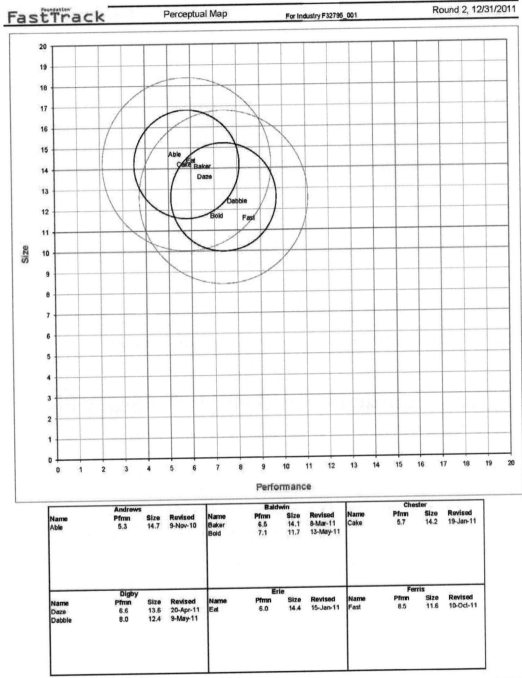

	Andrews				Baldwin				Chester		
Name	Pfmn	Size	Revised	Name	Pfmn	Size	Revised	Name	Pfmn	Size	Revised
Able	5.3	14.7	9-Nov-10	Baker	6.5	14.1	8-Mar-11	Cake	5.7	14.2	19-Jan-11
				Bold	7.1	11.7	13-May-11				

	Digby				Erie				Ferris		
Name	Pfmn	Size	Revised	Name	Pfmn	Size	Revised	Name	Pfmn	Size	Revised
Daze	6.6	13.6	20-Apr-11	Eat	6.0	14.4	15-Jan-11	Fast	8.5	11.6	10-Oct-11
Dabble	8.0	12.4	9-May-11								

An Introduction to Business   189

Appendix II: Customer Attractiveness Scores

Foundation™
Customer Attractiveness Scores
for the
Low Tech and High Tech Market Segments

Estimating a Monthly Customer Survey Score... Low Tech

MTBF: 14,000 – 20,000

	14,000	15,000	16,000	17,000	18,000	19,000	20,000
CSS points	1	17	33	50	67	83	100

Price: $15.00 - $35.00

Low Tech	$15	$20	$25	$30	$35
CSS points	100	70	40	20	1

Age: 3.0 is ideal

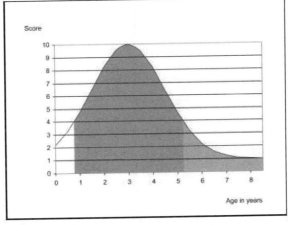

Position: Ideal is center of segment

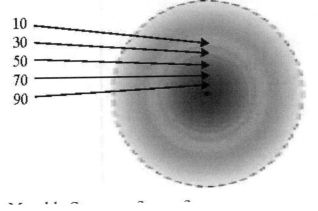

10
30
50
70
90

Estimating a Monthly Customer Survey Score: High Tech

MTBF: 17,000 – 23,000

High Tech	17,000	18,000	19,000	20,000	21,000	22,000	23,000
CSS points	1	17	33	50	67	83	100

Price: $25.00 - $45.00

High Tech	$25	$30	$35	$40	$45
CSS points	100	70	40	20	1

Age: "Ideal" = 0 years

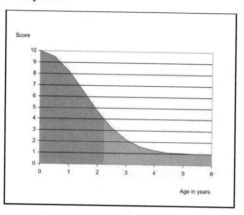

Position: "Ideal" = 1.4 units smaller and 1.4 units faster than segment center

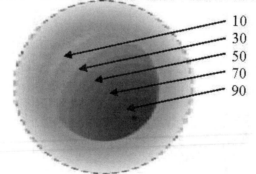

Glossary

A comprehensive online business glossary that you may find useful is:
http://www.nytimes.com/library/financial/glossary/bfglosa.htm

A

Accessibility
The availability of the product for the customer to gain access to. The higher the accessibility, the more easily a customer may purchase a particular team's product. Investments in the distribution network improve a product's accessibility.

Accounting
A summary and analysis of the firm's financial position.

Accounts Payable
Amount owed to suppliers for raw materials delivered. This value is affected by the number of days taken to pay suppliers (Accounts Payable expressed in days) which may be adjusted on the marketing screen.

Accounts Receivable
The amount of money owed to the company by its debtors. This value is affected by both sales volume and credit policy (accounts receivable lag, expressed in days).

Accumulated Depreciation
Cumulative total of each year's depreciation charge for plant and equipment.

Actual Industry Unit Sales
Units actually sold into the segment from all products represented. If this value is lower than Available Unit Sales then insufficient units were produced for sale into the segment.

Adjustment for Non-cash Items
Adjustments for income statement transactions, where no cash actually changed hands.

Administration
Cost of general administration such as legal services, accounting, and human resources.

Age
The preferred perceived age customers would like a product to possess. Perceived age is affected by redesigning the product (changing the performance attribute, size attribute, or both).

Assets
Anything owned by a firm—the organization's "stuff."

Asset Turnover
Sales, generated in a particular year, divided by the value of total assets for the same period.

Automation
The automation the company will enjoy on each of its production lines during the coming round.

B

Balance Sheet Reports the book value of all assets, liabilities, and owner's equity of the firm at a point in time.

Benchmarking A method of evaluating the performance of a business by comparison to some other specified level of accomplishment, typically a level achieved by another company.

Benefits The annual cost of the benefits package for each employee.

Board of Directors A set of executives who are responsible for monitoring the activities of the firm's president and other high-level managers, also referred to as the executive management team.

Book Value The amount an asset is valued at in business records; not necessarily the same amount as what the asset is worth on the open market.

Bonds Long-term debt securities purchased by investors.

Business Plan A detailed description of a proposed or existing business including the product or services offered, the types of customers it would attract, the competition, and the facilities needed for production.

C

Capacity The straight-time capacity the company will enjoy, on each of its production lines, during the coming round.

Cash The amount of money available in the bank.

Cash flow Statement This statement is published in conformity with the Finance and Accounting Standards Board's (FASB) most recent statements and opinions on the format for a cash flow analysis.

Cash from Long-Term Debt
Cash received for issuing new, ten-year bonds is an example of cash generated from long-term debt.

Change in Current Assets and Liabilities
Items in this category are assets and liabilities that have either increased or decreased since last year's balance sheet. These line items either expel (spend) or draw in (generate) cash.

Change in Current Debt
This is the net value of any current debt owed (and therefore had to be paid) last year and any additional current debt acquired.

Close The price being paid for the bond in the third-party market at the end of the last period. This price is a function of the interest rate and the risk inherent in the security as expressed by its credit rating.

Closing Cash Position Value in the cash account at the end of this year, also shown on the Balance Sheet.

Common Stock   Value of monies received for the issuing of stock since the company's inception (the value of additional paid-in capital is included here).

Contribution Margin   Sales revenue less all of the variable costs (does not include depreciation).

Cumulative Profits   Cumulative total of all profits (losses) generated since the game's inception.

Current Debt   The value of debt owed and payable on January 1st of the year for which decisions are currently being made.

Customer Awareness   That portion of the total segment that was aware of a particular product.

Customer Survey   This is an assessment of the desirability of a particular product.

D

Depreciation   An accounting for the portion of the equipment that was effectively "used up" in the period. The government recognizes this wear and tear and allows it to be deducted before declaring a profit. It is added back to get a true picture of the cash account. Although depreciation is expensed on the income statement, no company check was actually written. Unlike a check for the rent, the cash account never saw a check for depreciation.

Direct Labor   Cost of all labor associated with manufacturing the product. This value may be impacted by increasing or lowering the amount of automation (a capital cost) present on a particular line.

Direct Material   Cost of all raw materials necessary to manufacture a product.

Dividends   The income the firm provides to its owners, or shareholders, based on profits.

Dividends Paid   Value of cash expended on paying dividends. Dividend payment is made on the finance screen and each year defaults to zero unless another value is entered.

E

Earnings Before Interest and Taxes (EBIT)
                          Net margin less fees, write-offs, and bonus income; this information appears on the income statement.

Earnings per Share (EPS)
                          EPS is calculated by dividing net profit into the number of shares outstanding.

Economies of Scale   The process where the cost of each good produced decreases as the volume produced increases. This reduction in cost per unit occurs when the initial investment of capital is shared with an increasing number of units of output, and therefore, the cost of producing a good or service decreases as production increases.

Emergency Loan   Amount of cash injected during the year when the company is completely devoid of cash. This is usually a result of inventories building at unexpected levels thus drying up all liquidity. Loans made on an emergency basis have a punitive interest rate (5% above current rate) attached to them.

F

Face Value
    The face value of the entire bond issue. This value is also what would be paid back to the bondholders at the maturity of the debt. However, if bonds are retired (called in) early the amount paid may be higher or lower than this.

Fees and Write-offs
    This is a compilation of charges that may be incurred during any given period.

G

Gain/Loss on Equipment Sales
    If machinery is sold at a value that is higher than the net or depreciated value of the machinery, then this shows up as a profit on the income statement. Such gains and losses must be reported on the income statement. However they do not represent a true movement of cash. The cash flow is the total amount received for selling off the line, this amount is shown (net of any purchases) in the cash flows from the investing section of the cash flow statement.

Gross Margin
    Revenue left after deducting direct labor, raw materials, and depreciation expressed as a percentage of sales.

Growth Rate
    Annual compound rate at which unit demand will grow.

I

Income Statement
    The income statement, also known as a profit-and-loss statement, shows the entire value that an account has accumulated over the previous period (in this case twelve months).

Industry Sales
    Dollar sales into each segment.

Industry Unit Sales
    Total units sold by all companies into each segment.

Industry Unit Sales vs. Unit Demand
    The number of units sold, by all companies, in each segment of the market, versus the number of units demanded. In cases where the units demanded is larger than the units sold, there was an inadequate supply of minimally acceptable product available and thus some demand was unfulfilled.

Inventory Carrying Costs
    The cost of having inventory in stock.

Inventory Turnover
    The relationship between the cost of goods sold and inventory calculated by cost of goods sold/inventory.

Inventory Value
    The value of inventory on hand valued using "average cost accounting." This will rise and fall based on the production scheduled (on the production screen) versus units sold.

L

Labor Cost The per-unit cost of labor in the year just ended.

Leverage Total assets at the end of the period under review divided by owners' equity for the same period. The smaller the number, the lower the dependence on debt and the higher the amount of owners' equity. Therefore, a smaller number is more attractive.

List Price Price charged for the product in the round just ended.

Long-Term Debt The value of all outstanding bonds (ten-year) that will become due at some future date.

Long-Term Interest Interest paid on outstanding bonds.

M

Market Share Overall percentage share, of the dollar volume, gained each year.

Market Share Actual Market share actually achieved by each product in each segment of the market. The market shares based on units are shown in the left-hand group of columns and the market shares based on dollars are shown in the right-hand group of columns.

Market Share Actual vs. Potential
Compares what was sold by a team into a segment with what the team would have sold if they had produced sufficient inventory.

Market Share by Segment
Dollar market share of each segment enjoyed by each team.

Market Share Potential
This shows the respective market shares each product should have earned if all products had been manufactured in sufficient quantity. In cases where actual share is larger than potential share, then other teams ran out of product and "chased" demand to a team with an inferior product. In cases where potential share is larger than actual, then the team stocked out and chased demand to other teams.

Material Cost The per-unit cost of direct materials in the year just ended.

Mean Time Between Failure
Also referred to as MTBF, this measures the reliability of product expressed in a standard unit of measure, such as in thousands of hours. It is the average time between expected product failures. The longer the duration, or MTBF, the better the product performs.

N

Net Cash from Operations

The subtotal of all activities on the cash flow statement to this point. Conceptually it is the actual cash either generated (if positive) or used up (if negative) by the core activities of the business. The remainder of the cash flow statement summarizes activities involved in either capital budgeting or tax and treasury activities.

Net Change in Cash Position

The difference between the balance in the cash account at the end of last year and the value of the cash account at the end of this year. The entire cash flow statement is designed to reconcile to this value.

Net Income

Value of profits as calculated on the income statement.

Net Margin

Value of total sales less variable and period costs.

Net Profit

Earnings left after all expenses are paid. Net profit can only be allocated to one of two directions: It is either paid out to the owners of the business in the form of dividends, or it is retained in the business to grow the company and is thus added to the Retained Earnings of the business.

O

Overtime

Typically paid at 1.5 times the expected wage, this can also be expressed as the percentage of the production that was undertaken using overtime.

P

Percent of Market

Share of total units sold, represented by each segment of the market.

Perceptual Map

A graph showing marketing information, such as a particular segment of the market and identifies all products that sold 1% or more into that segment.

Period Costs

Costs that generally tend not to move in proportion to sales volume.

Plant Utilization

Volume actually produced during the previous round compared to the actual capacity for that round. For example, levels in excess of 100% indicate overtime was utilized.

Plant and Equipment

Gross value of capacity and automation available (or purchased) for each production line.

Plant Improvements

Net value, after deducting any equipment sold for scrap, of cash invested in automation and capacity.

Positioning

Proximity of product to the "sweet spot" within the segment.

Price

Price charged for a product this year.

Price/Earnings Ratio

The closing stock price divided by the earnings per share or EPS. The P/E is sometimes referred to as the earnings multiple, or simply, the multiple.

Primary Segment	The segment into which the largest proportion of this product was sold.

Production vs. Capacity

Number of units actually built versus the straight-time capacity of the entire plant for the year just ended. When production is larger than capacity, overtime must have been scheduled in order to achieve the production level.

Profits	This shows the dollar profit earned each year since the game's inception.
Profit Sharing	That share or percentage of the profits paid to technicians and assemblers as per the union agreement.
Promotions Budget	Value of monies expended on media advertising, as set on the Marketing screen.

Q

Quality	Desired performance standard of a product or service. This may be measured by MTBF of the product.

R

R&D Costs	Annual costs associated with redesigning an existing, or designing an entirely new, product. If an R&D project is more than a year in duration, then the cost will be charged out over the full life of the project, with a maximum of 1 million dollars being charged on a single project in any given year. For example, if a project is estimated to cost $1.5 million then $1 million will be charged against this year's income statement and $.5 million will be charged against the next year's.
Retained Earnings	Total of all company profits and losses of the life of the company, less any dividends paid out. This *does not* represent a pile of cash. The monies are captured in the assets of the company. This may be cash, but it may just as easily be in the form of plant/equipment or even accounts receivable.

Retirement of Long-Term Debt

Cash consumed in the early retirement of bonds that are outstanding. These bonds are retired at the value at which they were trading in the third party market at the end of the previous year.

Revision Date	The last time product came out of a redesign cycle, in R&D, or the next time it will come out of the redesign cycle if it is currently being redesigned.
ROA	Return on Assets; net profit divided by the value of total assets for the same period.
ROE	Return on Equity; net profit divided by the value of owners' equity for that year.
ROS	Return on sales; net profit divided by total sales for the same period.

S

S&P
The Standard and Poor's credit rating for additional underwriting of debt for the company; it ranges from AAA to D.

Sales
The value of products sold over the previous twelve months, broken out by product line.

Sales Budget
Monies expended for paying sales personnel and expanding the distribution network. This value is an input on the Marketing screen.

Sales of Common Stock
Value of cash received from the issuing of additional stock. Maximum issue in any year is 20% of the total currently outstanding stock. Stock is issued at its spot prices as of December 31st of the year just ended.

Series Number
The first half of a bond issue's series number refers to the interest or coupon rate paid on the bonds, which are issued in $1000 denominations. The second half of the series number (after the letter "S" which is placed there by convention) refers to the date of maturity, for example a "10" after the "S" would indicate the bond is to mature in the year 2010.

SG&A % Sales
Total of selling general and administrative expenses as a percentage of total sales for that period.

Shares
Number of shares currently outstanding. At the beginning of the game each company has 2 million shares outstanding.

Short-Term Interest
Interest paid on current debt, including interest on emergency loans.

Stock Out
A situation where all products are sold out and it has had a negative effect on sales performance. Thus, it is likely a higher sales level would have been experienced had more units been manufactured and available.

T

Taxes
Taxes paid on income, using a 35% taxation rate.

Total Assets
Total of all current and fixed assets.

Total Equity
Also known as shareholder equity, owners' equity, or net worth. This represents the net value of the company after liabilities are deducted from the value of total assets. The value is calculated by adding, in this case, common stock and retained earnings. This highlights the inherent relationship of the balance sheet. This relationship being owners' equity equals total assets less total liabilities.

Total Fixed Assets
The value of plant and equipment less total accumulated depreciation.

Total Liabilities
Sum total of accounts payable, current debt, and long-term debt.

Total Period Costs
Accumulation of all period costs described above.

Total Units Demanded
Total units that could have been sold into each segment had sufficient, appropriate product been made available.

U

Units in Inventory Number of units of the product left in inventory as of December 31st (in thousands of units).

Unit Sales vs. Unit Demand

Number of units our company sold, in each segment of the market, versus the number of units that segment wished to purchase from our company. In cases where the units demanded is greater than units sold, we did not build sufficient product and thus stocked out. In cases where units demanded are less than units sold, other teams stocked out and pushed demand to us that our product did not "deserve." However, as our product was minimally acceptable, it was begrudgingly purchased by the market.

Units' Sold The total number of this product sold into all market segments.

V

Variable Costs Costs that vary in direct proportion to the number of units sold.

W

Wage Escalator Annual cost of living adjustment applied to assemblers and technicians' hourly wages.

Y

Yield Dividend payment as a percentage value of the closing stock price, or the interest paid on the bond divided by the actual trading price of the bond.

Index

A

Accessibility......................17, 49
Account receivable 117, 118
Accounting 8
Accounts payable 68, 71, 121, 122, 125, 139
Accounts payable lag 117, 125
Accounts receivable 68
Accounts receivable lag 117
Accrual accounting 116
Administrative law 152
Agency 153, 155
Agency agreement 153
Agent 151, 153
Alien corporation 176
Appellate court 153
Arbitration 152, 153
Articles of incorporation 175
Articles of partnership 172
Asset turnover 134
Assets 67
Attractiveness score 34

B

Balance sheet .. 67, 69, 76, 78, 80, 132
Bankruptcy 78, 137, 138, 140, 154
Benchmarking 97
Binding 153
Bond issue 126, 127, 130
Bond rating 127, 128, 129
Bonds 126, 129, 149
Book value 73, 132, 144, 145, 194
Breach of contract 152, 154
Bribery 160
Budgeting 65
Business conduct 161, 162
Business entity 175
Bylaws 175

C

Capacity 93
Carrying costs 94, 120
Cash accounting 116
Cash flow 73, 78, 116
Cash flow management 138
Cash flow statement 78, 138, 139
Certificate of incorporation 175
Certificates of deposit 118
Civil law 152
Closing price 130, 133
Code of conduct violation 158
Commercial paper 118
Common law 152
Common stock ...68, 72, 130, 139, 176

Conflict of interest 158
Consideration 152
Contract elements 171
Contractual capacity 152
Contribution margin 11, 47, 74, 75, 46, 82, 83, 107, 110, 195
Corporate ethics policies 161
Corporation 177
Cost analysis 65
Cost of goods sold 74, 75, 83, 107
Cost of labor 83
Cost of materials 83
Credit policy 119
Criminal law 152, 153
Current assets 68, 69, 71, 72, 116
Current debt 71
Current liabilities 71, 72
Customer survey score 34, 36, 43

D

Debt-to-assets ratio ..72, 124, 125, 137
Decision making 6
Demand 5
Demographic segmentation 24
Depreciation 70, 74, 76, 84
Diminishing return 25
Discrimination 163
Dividends..72, 130, 131, 132, 133, 144, 145, 176, 177
Domestic corporation 176
Double taxation 177

E

Earnings per share 77, 133, 137, 144, 145
EBIT 74, 77
Economic cost 7
Economics 4
Economies of scale 93
Emergency loan 125, 138
Ethical conduct 161
Ethicism 166
Ethics & Compliance Officer Association 162
Ethics officers 162
Expenses 73
Expressed warranty 154
Externalities 160

F

Face value 118, 128, 129
Falsification of records 158
FastTrack Report 29, 30, 34, 49, 75, 102, 181, 190

Federal Sentencing Guidelines for Organizations Act 162
Finance 8
Financial accounting 62
Fine cut 88
Fixed assets 70
Fixed costs 93
Foreign corporation 176
Fraud 154

G

GAAP 63
Generally Accepted Accounting Principles 63
Geographic segmentation 24
Gross margin 76

H

Human resources 93

I

Ideal position 37
Ideal spot 32
Implied warranty 154
Income statement 73- 76, 78, 107, 116, 125
Indenture 126
Initial public offering 130
Innovation 9
Insolvency 78
Integrative social contracts theory...... 159
Interest 74, 77
Interest payments 85
Interest rate 77, 120, 124, 125, 126, 128, 130
Internal Revenue Service 63, 177
Inventory 68, 70, 74, 119
Inventory carrying costs 120
Inventory control 94
Inventory turnover 119
Inventory turnover rate 120
Investment bank 127, 131
Investor Protection Act 162
IPO 130
IRS 63

J

JIT 94
Just-in-time 16, 94

An Introduction to Business